Heinz-Dietrich Fischer

Eugene O'Neill as Nobel Laureate and Four-Time Pulitzer Prize Winner

Pulitzer Prize Panorama

edited by

Prof. Dr. Heinz-Dietrich Fischer
(Bochum)

Volume 51

LIT

Heinz-Dietrich Fischer

Eugene O'Neill as Nobel Laureate and Four-Time Pulitzer Prize Winner

Life, Works and Honors of the Unique American Dramatist

LIT

Front Cover shows Playwright Eugene O'Neill, photographed 1938, and his signature.

Back cover shows the one dollar stamp, issued by the U.S. Postal Service on October 16, 1967, by honor Eugene O'Neill.

Gefördert durch Mittel der Pressestiftung RWV gemeinnützige GmbH Essen

This book is printed on acid-free paper.

Bibliographic information published by the Deutsche Nationalbibliothek
The Deutsche Nationalbibliothek lists this publication in the Deutsche Nationalbibliografie; detailed bibliographic data are available on the Internet at https://dnb.dnb.de.

ISBN 978-3-643-91870-3 (pb)
ISBN 978-3-643-96870-8 (PDF)

Contact:
Fresnostr. 2 D-48159 Münster
Tel. +49 (0) 2 51-62 03 20 Fax +49 (0) 2 51-23 19 72
e-Mail: lit@lit-verlag.de https://www.lit-verlag.de
Distribution:
In the UK: Global Book Marketing, e-mail: mo@centralbooks.com

Preface

Many prominent literary figures and theatre professionals have acknowledged the importance of Eugene O'Neill's work, citing him as an innovator and key figure in American drama. Numerous critics and scholars have recognized his lasting influence on American literature and theater, noting his use of expressionism, inner monologue, and his exploration of complex themes. O'Neill's innovative techniques and exploration of serious themes have been influential on subsequent generations of playwrights aud directors, making him a significant figure in the history of American theater.

But 0'Neill had a bizarre personal life, reflected in the dark mirror of his plays. Everything in his life became significant because everything affected his plays. He was a highly personal writer who proceeded through a succession of obsessions. It became obvious that the philosophical life of the dramatist developed out of the experiences and temperaments of his mother and father: His real sources were his emotional and spiritual heritage. The father and mother lived in a spacious theatre that their son helped to destroy.

Although O'Neill had a charming personality, former *New York Times* star theatre critic Brooks Atkinson once stated,.“he was an extremely complex man. Brooding, restless, distrustful, dramatic, he rejected everything in life that did not bear directly on his writing. Except for his passion for writing, he would probably have drunk himself to an early death, like his hopeless brother. If the term 'beatnik' had existed in his youth, he would have been recognized as a perfect example of the rootless, rebellious, dissipated, egoistical, self-pitying renegade. His passion for writing saved him by imposing on him a certain discipline... His life was a long day's journey into night.“

Thc book at hand does not intend to paint a new picture of this very outstanding dramatist and his work. Instead, it concentrates on the aspects of O'Neill's successes in America and abroad, demonstrated in his Nobel Literature Prize and his four Pulitzer awards. Emphasis is given to the decision-making processes in the Swedish Academy as well as within the Pulitzer Prize committees. Thanks to Columbia University I had access to the confidential jury reports containing details about O'Neill's Pulitzer decorations.

So my sincere thanks first go to Marjorie Miller and Edward M. Kliment, the administrators of the annual Pulitzer Prizes, located in the Graduate School of Journalism at Columbia University in New York City. At Yale University in New Haven, Connecticut, Michelle Light, Moira Fitzgerald and Mary Ellen Budney of the Beinecke Rare Book and Manuscript Library were extremely helpful and provided printouts of O'Neill's main personal documents like his

Nobel Prize Diploma, all of his four Pulitzer Prize Certificates and his Yale Honorary Doctorate document. For the very first time anywhere the complete set is reproduced in this book!

Ruhr University
of Bochum, Germany
July 4, 2025

H.-D. Fischer

CONTENTS

O'NEILL's BIOGRAPHICAL PHASES

The Life and Works 1888 - 1953

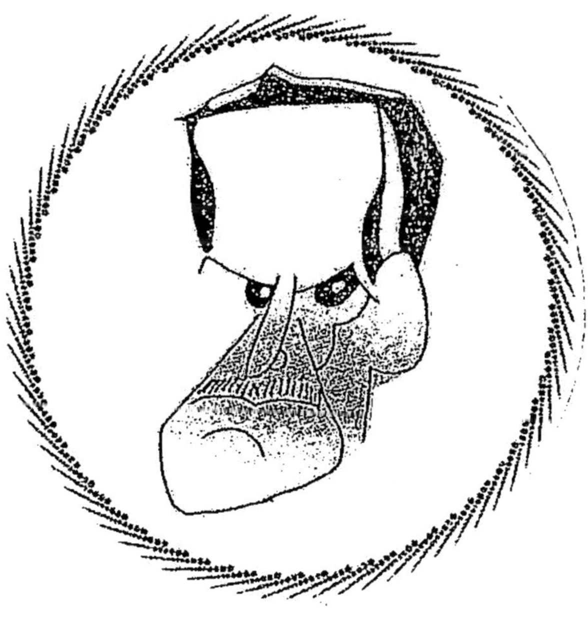

Plaque at Times Square

The plaque honoring O'Neill was dedicated on October 16, 1957, the anniversary of the writer's birth, at the northeast corner of the 43rd Street and Brodway in New York City. It was fixed to a pillar in front of a store building on the side. The plaque was then lost in 1961 during the building's renovation. A new plaque was introduced on November 27, 1973. Nearly forty years after it disappeared, the original 1957 plaque was found and rededicated on October 16, 2000.

Eugene Gladstone O'Neill (October 16, 1888 – November 27, 1953) was an outstanding American playwright. His poetically titled plays were among the first to introduce into the U.S. the drama techniques of realism, earlier associated with Chekhov, Ibsen, and Strindberg. The tragedy Long Day's Journey into Night is often included on lists of the finest U.S. plays in the 20th century, alongside Tennessee Williams's A Streetcar Named Desire and Arthur Miller's Death of a Salesman. He was awarded the 1936 Nobel Prize in Literature. O'Neill is also the only playwright to win four Pulitzer Prizes for Drama.

O'Neill's plays were among the first to include speeches in American English vernacular and involve characters on the fringes of society. They struggle to maintain their hopes and aspirations, ultimately sliding into disillusion and despair. Of his very few comedies, only one is well-known (Ah, Wilderness!). Nearly all of his other plays involve some degree of tragedy and personal pessimism.

His Early Life

O'Neill was born on October 16, 1888, in a hotel, the Barrett House, on what was then Longacre Square (now Times Square) in New York City. A commemorative plaque was first dedicated there in 1957.[4][5] The site is now occupied by 1500 Broadway, which houses offices, shops and the ABC Studios.

He was the son of Irish immigrant actor James O'Neill and Mary Ellen Quinlan, who was also of Irish descent. His father suffered from alcoholism; his mother from an addiction to morphine, prescribed to relieve the pains of the difficult birth of Eugene, who was her third son. Because his father was often on tour with a theatrical company, accompanied by Eugene's mother, in 1895 O'Neill was sent to St. Aloysius Academy for Boys, a Catholic boarding school in the Riverdale section of the Bronx. In 1900, he became a day student at the De La Salle Institute on 59th Street in Manhattan.

The O'Neill family reunited for summers at the Monte Cristo Cottage in New London, Connecticut. He also briefly attended Betts Academy in Stamford. He attended Princeton University for one year. Accounts vary as to why he left. He may have been dropped for attending too few classes, been suspended for "conduct code violations", or "for breaking a window", or according to a more concrete but possibly apocryphal account, because he threw "a beer bottle into the window of Professor Woodrow Wilson", the future president of the United States.

O'Neill spent several years at sea, during which he suffered from depression, alcoholism and despair. Despite this, he had a deep love for the

O'Neill in the Mid-1930s

sea and it became a prominent theme in many of his plays, several of which are set on board ships like those on which he worked. O'Neill joined the Marine Transport Workers Union of the Industrial Workers of the World (IWW), which was fighting for improved living conditions for the working class using quick 'on the job' direct action. O'Neill's parents and elder brother Jamie (who drank himself to death at the age of 45) died within three years of one another, not long after he had begun to make his mark in the theater.

His Career Steps

After his experience in 1912–13 at a sanatorium where he was recovering from tuberculosis, he decided to devote himself full-time to writing plays (the events immediately prior to going to the sanatorium are dramatized in his masterpiece, Long Day's Journey into Night). O'Neill had previously been employed by the New London Telegraph, writing poetry as well as reporting. In the fall of 1914, he entered Harvard University to attend a course in dramatic technique given by George Piece Baker, but left after one year.

During the 1910s O'Neill was a regular on the Greenwich Village literary scene, where he also befriended many radicals, most notably Communist Labor Party of America founder John Reed. O'Neill also had a brief romantic relationship with Reed's wife, writer Louise Bryant. O'Neill was portrayed by Jack Nicholson in the 1981 film Reds, about the life of John Reed; Louise Bryant was portrayed by Diane Keaton. His involvement with the Provincetown Players began in mid-1916. Terry Carlin reported that O'Neill arrived for the summer in Provincetown with "a trunk full of plays", but this was an exaggeration. Susan Glaspell describes a reading of Bound East for Cardiff that took place in the living room of Glaspell and her husband George Cram Cook's home on Commercial Street, adjacent to the wharf (pictured) that was used by the Players for their theater: "So Gene took Bound East for Cardiff out of his trunk, and Freddie Burt read it to us, Gene staying out in the dining-room while reading went on. He was not left alone in the dining-room when the reading had finished." The Provincetown Players performed many of O'Neill's early works in their theaters both in Provincetown and on MacDougal Street in Greenwich Village. Some of these early plays, such as The Emperor Jones, began downtown and then moved to Broadway.

In an early one-act play, The Web, written in 1913, O'Neill first explored the darker themes that he later thrived on. Here he focused on the brothel world and the lives of prostitutes, which also play a role in some fourteen of his later plays. In particular, he memorably included the birth of an infant into the world of prostitution. At the time, such themes constituted a huge innovation, as these sides of life had never before been presented with such success.

O'Neill's first published play, Beyond the Horizon, opened on Broadway in 1920 to great acclaim, and was awarded the Pulitzer Prize for Drama. His first major hit was The Emperor Jones, which ran on Broadway in 1920 and obliquely commented on the U.S. occupation of Haiti that was a topic of debate in that year's presidential election.[His best-known plays include Anna Christie (Pulitzer Prize 1922), Desire Under the Elms (1924), Strange Interlude (Pulitzer Prize 1928), Mourning Becomes Electra (1931), and his only well-known comedy, Ah, Wilderness!, a wistful re-imagining of his youth as he wished it had been.

O'Neill was elected to the American Philosophical Society in 1935. In 1936, O'Neill received the Nobel Prize in Literature after he had been nominated that year by Henrik Schück, member of the Swedish Academy. O'Neill was profoundly influenced by the work of Swedish writer August Strindberg,[23] and upon receiving the Nobel Prize, dedicated much of his acceptance speech to describing Strindberg's influence on his work.[24] In conversation with Russel Crouse, O'Neill said that "the Strindberg part of the speech is no 'telling tale' to please the Swedes with a polite gesture. It is absolutely sincere. [...] And it's absolutely true that I am proud of the opportunity to acknowledge my debt to Strindberg thus publicly to his people". Before the speech was sent to Stockholm, O'Neill read it to his friend Sophus Keith Winther. As he was reading, he suddenly interrupted himself with the comment: "I wish immortality were a fact, for then some day I would meet Strindberg". When Winther objected that "that would scarcely be enough to justify immortality", O'Neill answered quickly and firmly: "It would be enough for me".

After a ten-year pause, O'Neill's now-renowned play The Iceman Cometh was produced in 1946. The following year's A Moon for the Misbegotten failed, and it was decades before coming to be considered as among his best works. He was also part of the modern movement to partially revive the classical heroic mask from ancient Greek theatre and Japanese Noh theatre in some of his plays, such as The Great God Brown and Lazarus Laughed.

His Family Life

O'Neill was married to Kathleen Jenkins from October 2, 1909, to 1912, during which time they had one son, Eugene O'Neill, Jr. (1910–1950). In 1917, O'Neill met Agnes Boulton, a successful writer of commercial fiction, and they married on April 12, 1918. They lived in a home owned by her parents in Point Pleasant, New Jersey, after their marriage. The years of their marriage—during which the couple lived in Connecticut and Bermuda and had two children, Shane and Oona—are described vividly in her 1958 memoir

TIME Magazine Cover of March 17, 1924

Part of a Long Story. They divorced on July 2, 1929, after O'Neill abandoned Boulton and the children, for the actress Carlotta Monterey. O'Neill and Carlotta married less than a month after he officially divorced his previous wife.

In 1929, O'Neill and Monterey moved to the Loire Valley in central France, where they lived in the Château du Plessis in Saint-Antoine-du-Rocher, Indre-et-Loire. During the early 1930s they returned to the United States and lived in Sea Island, Georgia, at a house called Casa Genotta. He moved to Danville, California, in 1937 and lived there until 1944. His house there, Tao House, is today the Eugene O'Neill National Historic Site.

In their first years together, Monterey organized O'Neill's life, enabling him to devote himself to writing. She later became addicted to potassium bromide, and the marriage deteriorated, resulting in a number of separations, although they never divorced.

In 1943, O'Neill disowned his daughter Oona for marrying the English actor, director, and producer Charlie Chaplin when she was 18 and Chaplin was 54. He never saw Oona again.

He also had distant relationships with his sons. Eugene O'Neill Jr., a Yale classicist, suffered from alcoholism and committed suicide in 1950 at the age of 40. Shane O'Neill became a heroin addict and moved into the family home in Bermuda, Spithead, with his new wife, where he supported himself by selling off the furnishings. He was disowned by his father before also committing suicide (by jumping out of a window) a number of years later. Oona ultimately inherited Spithead and the connected estate (subsequently known as the Chaplin Estate).In 1950 O'Neill joined The Lambs, the famed theater club.

His Illness and Death

After suffering from multiple health problems (including depression and alcoholism) over many years, O'Neill ultimately faced a severe Parkinson's-like tremor in his hands that made it impossible for him to write during the last 10 years of his life; he tried dictation but found himself unable to compose that way. While at Tao House, O'Neill had intended to write a collection of works he called "the Cycle" chronicling American life spanning from 1755 to 1932. Only two of the eleven plays O'Neill proposed, A Touch of the Poet and More Stately Mansions, were completed. As his health worsened, O'Neill lost inspiration for the project and wrote three largely autobiographical plays, The Iceman Cometh, Long Day's Journey into Night, and A Moon for the Misbegotten, which he completed in 1943, just before leaving Tao House and losing his ability to write. The book "Love and Admiration and Respect":

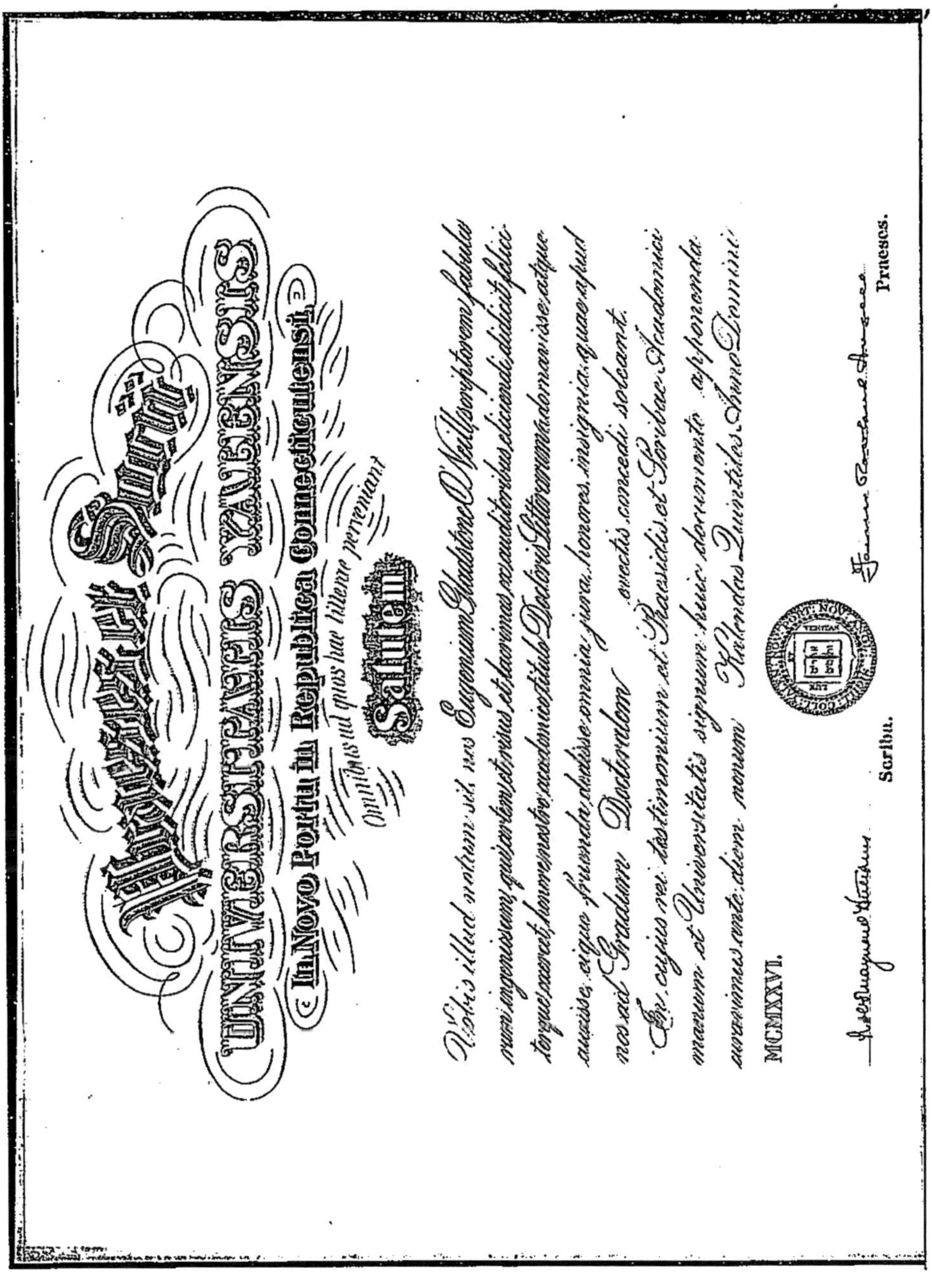

Praeses et Socii
Universitatis Yalensis
In Novo Portu in Republica Connecticutensi,
Omnibus ad quos hae litterae pervenient
Salutem

Vobis illud notum sit nos Eugenium Gladstone O'Neill scriptorem fabularum ingeniosum, qui artem et risus et lacrimas ex auditoribus eliciendi didicit feliciterque exercet, honore nostro academico titulo Doctoris Litterarum adornavisse atque auxisse, eique fruenda dedisse omnia jura, honores, insignia quae apud nos ad Gradum Doctoralem evectis concedi soleant.

In cujus rei testimonium et Praesidis et Scribae Academici manum et Universitatis signum huic documento apponenda curavimus ante diem nonum Kalendas Quintiles Anno Domini MCMXXVI.

Scriba. Praeses.

1926 Yale University Honorary Doctorate for O'Neill, written in Latin

The O'Neill-Commins Correspondence" includes an extended account written by Saxe Commins, O'Neill's publisher, in which he talks of "snatches of dialogue" between Carlotta and O'Neill over the disappearance of a group of manuscripts that O'Neill had brought with him from San Francisco. "When the table was cleared I learned the cause of the tension; the manuscripts were lost. They had disappeared mysteriously during the day and there was no clue to their whereabouts."

O'Neill died at the Sheraton Hotel (now Boston University's Kilachand Hall) on Bay State Road in Boston, on November 27, 1953, at age 65. As he was dying, he whispered: "I knew it. I knew it. Born in a hotel room and died in a hotel room." He is interred in the Forest Hills Cemetery in Boston's Jamaica Plain neighborhood.

In 1956, Carlotta arranged for his autobiographical play Long Day's Journey into Night to be published, although his written instructions had stipulated that it not be made public until 25 years after his death. It was produced on stage to tremendous critical acclaim and won the Pulitzer Prize in 1957. It is widely considered his finest play. Other posthumously published works include A Touch of the Poet (1958) and More Stately Mansions (1967).

In 1967, the United States Postal Service honored O'Neill with a Prominent Americans series (1965–1978) $1 postage stamp. In 2000, a team of researchers studying O'Neill's autopsy report concluded that he died of cerebellar cortical atrophy, a rare form of brain deterioration unrelated to either alcohol use or Parkinson's disease.

His Impressive Legacy

In Warren Beatty's 1981 film Reds, O'Neill is portrayed by Jack Nicholson, who was nominated for the Academy Award for Best Supporting Actor for his performance. George C. White founded the Eugene O'Neill Theatre Center in Waterford, Connecticut in 1964. Eugene O'Neill is a member of the American Theater Hall of Fame.

O'Neill is referenced by Upton Sinclair in The Cup of Fury (1956), Dianne Wiest's character in Bullets Over Broadway (1994), by J.K. Simmons' character in Whiplash (2014), by Tony Stark in Avengers: Age of Ultron (2015), specifically Long Day's Journey into Night, and Long Day's Journey into Night is also referenced by Patrick Wilson's character in Purple Violets (2007). O'Neill is referred to in Moss Hart's 1959 book Act One, later a Broadway play.

O'Neill's home in New London, Monte Cristo Cottage, was made a National Historic Landmark in 1971. His home in Danville, California, near San Francisco, was preserved as the Eugene O'Neill National Historic Site in 1976.

Connecticut College maintains the Louis Sheaffer Collection, consisting of material collected by the O'Neill biographer. The principal collection of O'Neill papers is at Yale University. The Eugene O'Neill Theater Center in Waterford, Connecticut, fosters the development of new plays under his name.

There is also a theatre in New York City named after him located at 230 West 49th Street in midtown-Manhattan. The Eugene O'Neill Theatre has housed musicals and plays such as Yentl, Annie, Grease, M. Butterfly, Spring Awakening, and The Book of Mormon.

His Published Works

This Chronological Table contains all of Eugene O'Neill's published plays and the first theatre productions in New York or several other cities.

TITLE	Year written	Date and Place of first New York Production
A Wife for a Life Thirst	1913-1914	Unproduced
Thirst	1913-1914	(Wharf Theatre, Province-town, summer, 1916)
The Web	1913-1914	Unproduced
Warnings	1913-1914	Unproduced
Fog	1913-1914	The Playwrights Theatre, Jan. 5, 1917
Recklessness	1913-1914	Unproduced
Round East for Catrdiff	1913-1914	The Playwrights Theatre, Nov. 3, 1916
Servitude	1913-11014	Unproduced
Abortion	1913-1014	Unproduced
The Sniper	1915	The Playrights Theatre, Feb.16, 19 17

Before Breakfast	1916-1917	The Playwrights Theatre, Dez.1, 1916
The Movie Man	1916-1917	Unproduced
Tie	1916-1917	The Playwrights Theatre, Nov. 30, 1917
In the Zone	1916-1917	Comedy Theatre, Oct. 31, 1917
The Long Voyage Home	1916-1917	The Playwrights Theatre, Nov.2, 1917
The Moon of the Caribbees	1916-1917	The Playwrights Theatre, Dec. 20, 1918
The Rope	1918	The Playwrights Theatre, Nov.22, 1918
The Dreamy Kid	1918	The Playwrights Theatre, April 28, 1918
Beyond the Horizon	1918	The Playwrights Theatre, Oct. 31, 1918
Where the Cross is Made	1918	Morosco Theatre, Feb. 2, 1920
Chris Christopherson	1918	(Atlantic City, March 8, 1920)
The Straw	1918-1919	Greenwich Village Theatre, Nov. 10, 1921
Gold	1920	Frazee Theatre, June 1, 1921
Anna Christie	1920	Vanderbuilt Theatre, Nov. 10, 1921

The Emperor Jones	1920	The Playwrights Theatre, Nov. 3, 19120
Diff'rent	1920	The Playwrights Theatre, Dec. 27, 1919
The First Man	1921	Neighborhood Playhouse, March 4, 1922
The Hairy Ape	1921	The Plaxwrights Theatre, Marc 9, 1922
The Fountain	1921-1922	Greenwich Village Theatre, Dec. 10, 1925
Welded	1922-1923	39th Street Theatre, March 17, 1924
All Good's Chilliun Got Wings	1923	Provincetown Playhouse, May 15, 1924
Desire Under the Elms	1924	Greenwich Village Theatre, Nov., n, 1925
Marco Millions	1923-1925	Gild Theatre, Jan. 9, 1928
The Great God Brown	1925	Greenwich Village Theatre, Jan. 23, 191
Lazarus Laughed	1925-1926	Pasadena Cal., April 9, 1928
Strange Interlude	1926-1927	Joh Golden Theatre, Jan. 30, 1928
Dynamo	1928	Martin Beck Theatre, Feb.11, 1929
Mourning Becomes Electra	1929-1931	Guild Theatre, Oct. 26, 1931
Ah, Wilderness1	1932	Guild Theatre, Oct. 2, 1933

The Iceman Cometh	1939	Martin Beck Theatre, Sept. 2, 1946
Long Day's Journey Into Night	1939-1941	Helen Hayes Theatre, Nov.7, 1956
Hughie	1941-1942	Royale Theatre, Dec. 22, 1964
A Moon for the Misbegotten	1943	Bijou Theatre, May 2, 1957
More Stately Mansions	Unfinished	Broadhurst Theatre, Oct. 31, 1967

O'NEILL's CONTEMPORARY COMPETITORS

Notable Award Winners 1918 - 1958

Multiple Pulitzer Drama Winners

Eugene O'Neill
1888 - 1953
Four-time Laureate

Edward Albee
1928 - 2016
Three-time Laureate

Robert E. Sherwood
1896 - 1955
Three-time Laureate

Tennessee Williams
1911 - 1983
Two-time Laureate

THE PULITZER PRIZE

OVER 40 YEARS

Among the prizes that Joseph Pulitzer (1847–1911) defined in detail in his last will, which he formulated in 1903, there was also one for outstanding achievements in the theater. The original description for this award read: "For the original American play, performed in New York, which shall best represent the educational value and power of the stage in raising the standard of good morals, good taste, and good manners."[1] Entrusted with the annual presentation of the prize, Pulitzer bestowed upon the Advisory Board in his will not just the "power in its discretion to suspend or to change any subject or subjects," but furthermore also the authority that "if all prize nominees fell below the 'standard of excellence fixed by the Board' in any subject in any given year, then the Board could withhold an award or awards." Although, as John Hohenberg continues, "the American theater was stagnant at the time the first Pulitzer Prizes in Drama were awarded... there was a lot of excitement on Broadway, particularly about the *Ziegfeld Follies* and George M. Cohan's brassy musical shows." But, he adds, "much of the standard fare was both trivial and banal. In the hinterlands, there were a few struggling stock companies and occasional road shows. What it all added up to... was distressingly little."[2] Therefore, in the beginning, it was rather difficult for the jurors to reach decisions that met with general acceptance, so that the results in some years understandably became "a source of irritation and resentment."[3]

In view of this constellation it is hardly surprising that the first Pulitzer Prize Drama Jury (Richard Burton, Hamlin Garland and Augustus Thomas), that had to judge in the spring of 1917 on the Broadway production of the previous year, had considerable problems to extract an outstanding performance. "Considering the conditions of the Pulitzer award for drama, its aims

1 Quoted from DeForest O'Dell, The History of Journalism Education in the United States, New York 1935, p. 109.

2 John Hohenberg, The Pulitzer Prizes. A History of the Awards in Books, Drama, Music, and Journalism, New York - London 1974, pp. 18 f., 43.

3 John L. Toohey, A History of the Pulitzer Prize Plays, New York 1967, p. VII.

and requirements," the jurors wrote in the end in their report to the Advisory Board, "your committee is not agreed upon a recommendation."[4] The Board consented to this vote, thus deciding on "no award" right away in the very first year of the drama category.[5] Similarly unanimous were the three jurors in 1918 (Richard Burton, Hamlin Garland and Augustus Thomas), when the chairman of the jury stated in his report: "My vote emphatically is for Williams' Comedy *Why Marry?*"[6] And another member of the jury expressed among other things the following opinion: "I have seen *Why Marry?* by Jesse Lynch Williams and find it an admirable piece of comedy... There are some things in the piece which I do not like but on the whole it is the best piece of drama I have seen this year."[7] The third juror also voted "in favor of *Why Marry?...* for the award to the play produced in 1917."[8] Faced with such extreme concordance in the jurors' judgment the Advisory Board endorsed this evaluation and gave the Pulitzer Prize for drama to Jesse Lynch Williams for the performance of his play *Why Marry?*[9]

Right at the beginning of their report the jury for the award of 1919 (Richard Burton, Hamlin Garland and Clayton Hamilton) came to the crucial point by explaining to the Advisory Board: "In the judgement of your committee no play produced in New York City within the calendar year 1918 is entirely worthy the prize of the Pulitzer Bequest. Whether by reason of the turmoil of war or from some change in the temper of managers and audiences, most of the plays of the year in question are either very light entertainment or so crudely melodramatic as to be of little literary value. No play by a native author stands out commandingly and as your committee can not wholeheartedly commend any candidate, we advise that the award go over to another year."[10] The Advisory Board accepted the vote of the jury and likewise decided on "no award."[11] In their report the jurors recommended furthermore "that as the period of play production is during the winter months, the theatrical and not the calendar year be taken as the limit in which the competing plays shall be staged. Confusion results from splitting the theatrical

4 Richard Burton/Hamlin Garland/Augustus Thomas, Report of the Pulitzer Prize Drama Jury, New York, May 1, 1917, p. 1.

5 Columbia University (Ed.), The Pulitzer Prizes 1917-1991, New York 1991, p. 54.

6 Richard Burton, Letter to Frank D. Fackenthal, Columbia University, New York, March 6, 1918, p. 1.

7 Hamlin Garland, Letter to Frank D. Fackenthal, Columbia University, New York, March 25, 1918, p. 1.

8 Augustus Thomas, Letter to Frank D. Fackenthal, Columbia University, New York, March 29, 1918, p. 1.

9 Columbia University (Ed.), The Pulitzer Prizes, *op. cit.*, p. 54.

10 Richard Burton/Hamlin Garland/Clayton Hamilton, Report of the Pulitzer Prize Drama Jury, New York, March 22, 1919, p. 1.

11 Columbia University (Ed.), The Pulitzer Prizes, *op. cit.*, p. 54.

THE MEAT AND POTATOES CO.
PRESENTS

Jesse Lynch Williams'

WHY MARRY?

A Feminist Comedy &
the first play to win
The Pulitzer Prize!

Directed by Neal Weaver

Oct. 11 - Nov. 11

$8 or TDF plus $3.50

Thurs.–Sat. at 8 P.M.
Sundays at 3 P.M.
Reservations (212) 564-3293

Lighting Design by David L. Arrow
Production Stage Manager – Tom Farrell

Equity Approved
Funded Non-Profit
Theatre Code Production

This production was made possible, in part, by a grant from The New York State Council On The Arts.

WITH
JAYNE CHAMBERLIN*
TOM FARRELL
KENNETH GRAY
JOHN HEPPENSTALL
ELLIOTT LANDEN*
JILL LARNETT
TERRENCE McDONNELL
RICHARD McWILLIAMS*
LAURA NEAL*
DONALD PACE
KAREN RIZZO
RONALD WILLOUGHBY*

* Member Actors' Equity Association

ASTOR THEATRE

ASTOR

Broadway and 45th Street

New York City

season in half. Furthermore the author is less likely to be shut out of the year to which he naturally belongs if he has the entire theatrical year in which to bring his play to a New York stage."[12] This suggestion also was taken up by the Advisory Board and so henceforth "the theatrical season, and not the calendar year" became "the period of judgment for the Pulitzer Prize."[13]

In spite of certain disagreements among the jurors of 1920 (Richard Burton, Walter P. Eaton and Hamlin Garland) about who was to be the potential prize-winner, in the end it said in the report of the jury chairman: "Up to the present moment *Beyond the Horizon* by Eugene O'Neill has no competitor as 'the outstanding play of the season.' It is not an 'uplifting play' in the terms of the Pulitzer Bequest but it is highly significant and I will join the other members in commending it for the prize although I am still in doubt about the author's motive. It certainly is not a mere 'show' and could not have been composed with any commercial success in mind. It is well written and presents some of the literary characteristics which have made the short stories of Mary Willins Freeman so honorably representative of village New England."[14] And another member of the jury added: "The committee is almost a unit in favor of *Beyond the Horizon*, Eugene O'Neill's play... So far as my own judgment is concerned I can not bring myself to vote for a prize to a mere entertainment such as most of the successful plays are, and yet I can not regard O'Neill's play as 'Noble' or 'Uplifting' which are... the expressed terms of the bequest. Nevertheless as it is the outstanding play of the season, thus far, I will join in the award."[15] As the verdict of the jury was not unanimous this resulted in extensive discussions within the Advisory Board, but in the end "the Board agreed with the Drama Jury and recommended *Beyond the Horizon*" for the award, and the Columbia University Trustees also "voted to give O'Neill his first Pulitzer Prize."[16]

Varying views also surfaced when the members of the jury of 1921 (Richard Burton, Hamlin Garland and William L. Phelps) met and put *The First Year* by Frank Craven on their short-list, *Nemesis* by Augustus Thomas and *Miss Lulu Bett* by Zona Gale. Although one of the jurors was "disposed to vote 'No Prize,'"[17] finally several compromises were reached, and soon it

---

12 Richard Burton/Hamlin Garland/Clayton Hamilton, Report..., *op. cit.*, p. 1.

13 John Hohenberg, The Pulitzer Prizes, *op. cit.*, p. 44.

14 Richard Burton/Walter P. Eaton/Hamlin Garland, Report of the Pulitzer Prize Drama Jury, New York, April 30, 1920, p. 1.

15 Hamlin Garland, Letter to Nicholas M. Butler, President of Columbia University, New York, May 11, 1920, p. 1.

16 John Hohenberg, The Pulitzer Prizes, *op. cit.*, p. 48.

17 Hamlin Garland, Letter to Frank D. Fackenthal, Columbia University, New York, May 11, 1921, p. 1.

Theatre Of The Evening Light
Presents
EUGENE O'NEILL'S
PULITZER PRIZE WINNING
Beyond The Horizon
Directed By
Shan Covey
THE LITTLE THEATRE
West Side YMCA
5 W. 63rd. St.

became evident that *Miss Lulu Bett* still had the best chances to win a majority: That very juror, who at first had pleaded for 'no award', gave in and indicated that he would join the vote of the two other members of the jury in favor of "*Lulu Bett* if that will solve the difficulty. Zona Gale is the kind of writer to encourage by official recognition... It would be a handsome thing to recognize a woman."[18] The chairman of the jury then declared in his final vote on behalf of the whole jury: "*Lulu Bett* is not a great play but it is original and interesting, and Miss Gale is a woman to whom such an honor can go with justice... As the award has not gone to a woman before perhaps it would be a graceful concession to give her this year's prize... Personally," the chairman of the jury remarked in adding to the report from his own point of view, "I do not feel deep enthusiasm for any of the plays... of the year. Not one has in it the element of greatness. Not one really stands out in a commanding position."[19] Despite these concerns the Advisory Board decided to bestow the Pulitzer Prize on Zona Gale for her play *Miss Lulu Bett*.[20]

As Hohenberg writes, in 1922, "Eugene O'Neill once again became an active contender for the Pulitzer Prize... with a more conventional play, *Anna Christie*, which did not please the critics as much as his earlier work."[21] Therefore, it came as no surprise that the jurors (Hamlin Garland, William L. Phelps and Jesse L. Williams) partly also had differing opinions as is evident from their report, where it says in the words of William L. Phelps among other things: "Mr. Jesse Lynch Williams and I vote for *Anna Christie* by Eugene O'Neill. In our opinion this deserves the prize for the best play of the year, and we have no second choice; in fact we are quite strongly of the opinion that the prize should not be given to any other play. Mr. Hamlin Garland has not seen *Anna Christie* but feels sure that he would not like it and will not vote for it. He has no other play to suggest and in his opinion the prize should not be given at all; he thinks that it would be better for the interests of the drama that no prize should be given this year. Mr. Williams and I feel, on the contrary, first, that it is exceedingly important that the prize should be given, and second, that it should be given to *Anna Christie*."[22] Hohenberg reports that "Garland lost the decision, however.

18 Richard Burton/Hamlin Garland/William L. Phelps, Letter to Frank D. Fackenthal, Columbia University, New York, May 20, 1921, p. 1.

19 Richard Burton/Hamlin Garland/William L. Phelps, Report of the Pulitzer Prize Drama Jury, New York, May 22, 1921, p. 1.

20 Columbia University (Ed.), The Pulitzer Prizes, *op. cit.*, p. 54.

21 John Hohenberg, The Pulitzer Prizes, *op. cit.*, p. 51.

22 Hamlin Garland/William L. Phelps/Jesse L. Williams, Report of the Pulitzer Prize Drama Jury, New York, May 1, 1922, p. 1.

Phelp's championship of O'Neill was upheld by both the Advisory Board and the Trustees... When the prize for *Anna Christie* was announced... – O'Neill's second in the first five years of the awards – it received nothing but applause and a gratifying amount of publicity."[23]

There also was to be no unanimous vote of the jury (Clayton Hamilton, Owen Johnson and William L. Phelps) in 1923, either, as can be inferred from the report to the Advisory Board: "By a two to one vote, your Committee vote to give the Pulitzer Prize to *Icebound* by Owen Davis."[24] As Hohenberg found out, "Elmer Rice's remarkable play... *The Adding Machine*" was also under consideration,[25] but the Advisory Board decided in favor of *Icebound* by Owen Davis.[26] In the following year the recommendation of the jurors (Clayton Hamilton, Owen Johnson and William L. Phelps) was brief and concise as well with the report stating: "The Committee have decided that the Pulitzer Prize for the best current American play should go to *The Show-Off* by George Kelly. We think this is an extremely good and original American play."[27] But before the Advisory Board could discuss the suggestion of the jury, a docent of Columbia University, although neither a member of the jury nor member of the Advisory Board, intervened and spoke out against its verdict. "Professor Brander Matthews, who had taught dramatic literature at Columbia University for thirty-three years," Hohenberg discovered, "wrote privately to (University) President Butler... to protest the Drama Jury's selection of George Kelly's satirical comedy... Instead... (he) called for a prize for *Hell-Bent Fer Heaven*, a hillbilly drama set in the Kentucky mountains, by a fellow member of the Columbia faculty, Hatcher Hughes... The Board knew it would have to account for the intervention of a Columbia professor for a faculty colleague through the president of the university. Nevertheless, it voted for *Hell-Bent Fer Heaven*,"[28] and so Hatcher Hughes won the Pulitzer Prize for best drama.

Because of the course the events had taken the previous year, the jury that went to work in 1925 (Hamlin Garland, Clayton Hamilton and Jesse L. Williams) had two new members. This new jury, however, did not stay complete up until the final decision was reached, as is pointed out at the beginning of its report: "The resignation of Mr. Hamlin Garland... has reduced the Drama

23 John Hohenberg, The Pulitzer Prizes, *op. cit.*, p. 54.
24 Clayton Hamilton/Owen Johnson/William L. Phelps, Report of the Pulitzer Prize Drama Jury, New Haven, Ct., March 31, 1923, p. 1.
25 John Hohenberg, The Pulitzer Prizes, *op. cit.*, pp. 94 f.
26 Columbia University (Ed.), The Pulitzer Prizes, *op. cit.*, p. 54.
27 Clayton Hamilton/Owen Johnson/William L. Phelps, Report of the Pulitzer Prize Drama Jury, New Haven, Ct., April 3, 1924, p. 1.
28 John Hohenberg, The Pulitzer Prizes, *op. cit.*, pp. 94 f.

The VANDERBILT Theatre
ANNA CHRISTIE
—with—
PAULINE LORD
GEORGE MARION and FRANK SHANNON
A Play in Four Acts
By Eugene O'Neill

Jury to two members," and the remaining two thirds of the jury had to work out an acceptable candidate on their own. Their discussion resulted in the following proposal: "We recommend for the Pulitzer Prize (season of 1924-25) the play called *They Knew What They Wanted* by Sidney Howard. In our opinion, this play stands head and shoulders above all the other American plays of the season, with only one exception (*What Price Glory?* by Maxwell Anderson and Laurence Stallings)... We have chosen it positively, because we believe that it would stand out in any season, as one of the best plays ever written by an American author. *They Knew What They Wanted* treats a difficult and delicate theme with rare human insight and even rarer philosophical profundity... A minor point, not necessarily important, is that *They Knew What They Wanted* has been praised without reservations by all of the professional reviewers and that it has been exceedingly successful with the public. In this instance the broadest popular opinion is in agreement with the verdict of the Drama jurors."[29] Faced with this praise the Advisory Board agreed with the vote of the jury and announced that Sidney Howard was winner of the Pulitzer Prize for his Broadway play *They Knew What They Wanted.*[30]

When the prize was to be decided upon in 1926 a completely new jury (Owen Davis, Walter P. Eaton and Albert E. Thomas) was put together, writing in its report to the Advisory Board that it was "unanimously of the opinion that the prize should go to *Craig's Wife* by George Kelly... The Jury has seen all the plays of American authorship eligible for the award. Several of them seemed meritorious to the Jury. It may not seem invidious to mention as among them: *In a Garden* by Philip Barry, *A Man's Man* by Patrick Karney, and *The Wisdom Tooth* by Marc Connelly. Neither of the Eugene O'Neill plays, *The Fountain* and *The Great God Brown* seemed to the Committee to be among the author's best works. *Craig's Wife* has been selected by the Jury on account of the dignity of its theme, the soundness of its construction, the excellence of its dialogue and its effectiveness in the theatre. Without sacrificing any of these essentials of a good play, it possesses in addition considerable literary quality – a thing none too common on the stage of today."[31] The play *Craig's Wife* "about a domineering woman who wrecked her marriage by alienating her husband from his friends" had, as

29 Clayton Hamilton/Jesse L. Williams, Report of the Pulitzer Prize Drama Jury, New York, March 15, 1925, pp. 1 f.

30 Columbia University (Ed.), The Pulitzer Prizes, *op. cit.*, p. 54.

31 Owen Davis/Walter P. Eaton/Albert E. Thomas, Report of the Pulitzer Prize Drama Jury, New York, March 25, 1926, p. 1.

Hohenberg puts it, "no rivals for the award,"[32] and so the Advisory Board also reached the decision to give the Pulitzer Prize for drama to the theatrical play *Craig's Wife*, thus honoring its author, George Kelly.[33]

The jurors of 1927 (Walter P. Eaton, Clayton Hamilton and Albert E. Thomas) discussed plays such as *Saturday's Children* by Maxwell Anderson, *The Silver Cord* by Sidney Howard, *Broadway* by Philip Dunning and George Abbott and several others, but soon had a clear favorite for the prize. "It is the unanimous opinion of the Drama Jury," it says at the beginning of the report, "that the Pulitzer Prize for the current theatre-season should be awarded to Paul Green for his play entitled *In Abraham's Bosom*... The play does not sentimentalize on the tragic situation of the negro. It is scrupulously fair to the white race. But it brings us face to face with one of the most serious of the social problems of this country, and forces us to view this problem in the light of tragic pity. The piece is loosely constructed... But this loose construction is almost necessitated by the nature of the material. The characterization is magnificently true, and the writing of the dialogue reveals a mastery of racial and local dialect... *In Abraham's Bosom* is not without its faults, most of which are merely technical; but the jurors feel that it is an admirable example of precisely the sort of composition which Mr. Pulitzer most desired to encourage when he established the Pulitzer Prize for Drama."[34] As "both the Advisory Board and the University Trustees agreed" and declared *In Abraham's Bosom* to be an outstanding achievement, Paul Green, as Hohenberg puts it, "a stranger to the alluring qualities of Broadway and the very antithesis of the box-office type of playwright, won the Pulitzer Prize for 1927."[35]

Looking for an outstanding dramatist, the jury of 1928 (Walter P. Eaton, Clayton Hamilton and Albert E. Thomas) put no fewer than eight plays on its short-list, namely *The Royal Family* by Edna Ferber and George S. Kaufman, *The Racket* by Bartlett Cormack, *Behold the Bridegroom* by George Kelly, *The Trial of Mary Dugan* by Bayard Veiller, *Paris Bound* by Philip Barry, *Coquette* by Ann P. Bridgers and George Abbott, *Four Walls* by Dana Burnett and George Abbott as well as *Strange Interlude* by Eugene O'Neill. Whereas the production of *Four Walls* was second choice on the jurors' list of priorities, O'Neill's *Strange Interlude* was regarded as the absolute favorite. "This play, by a man who has twice won the prize," it says

32 John Hohenberg, The Pulitzer Prizes, *op. cit.*, p. 100.
33 Columbia University (Ed.), The Pulitzer Prizes, *op. cit.*, p. 54.
34 Walter P. Eaton/Clayton Hamilton/Albert E. Thomas, Report of the Pulitzer Prize Drama Jury, New York, March 15, 1927, pp. 1 ff.
35 John Hohenberg, The Pulitzer Prizes, *op. cit.*, p. 101.

in the jury-report, "repeats nothing of his former work. It develops a new technique to make possible a play of Freudian interpretations... This drama of the subconscious and of frustration is sound and thoughtful in its development; but it also has great intensity of feeling, moments of beauty, and above all it shows dramatically that the conscious emotions, which give us dignity in our own eyes as individuals, cannot be ignored... *Strange Interlude* gets its fingers deeply tangled in the web of human life, it has depth and intellectual power above any and all of its rivals. It is... the logical recipient of the Pulitzer Prize for 1927-1928."[36] This vote was brought forward so convincingly that the Advisory Board joined in, awarding Eugene O'Neill his third Pulitzer Prize for *Strange Interlude*.[37]

The jurors that had to decide upon a potential Pulitzer Prize winner in 1929 (Walter P. Eaton, Clayton Hamilton and Albert E. Thomas) presented in their report no finalists, but concentrated on only one favorite instead. This favorite, however, was controversely discussed. "Unfortunately," they wrote to the Advisory Board, "the Committee is devided in its opinion. The majority... are completely persuaded that the play *Street Scene* by Elmer Rice is not only the best American play of the year, coming under the terms of the Pulitzer award, but also that it is the only play of the year, deserving of the prize... The majority... consider *Street Scene* as a technical achievement in American drama of rather high order, inasmuch as it dramatizes the melting pot in a New York tenement... Incidentally, the play is, no doubt for that very reason, extremely popular, its truthful qualities of observation being amply recognized."[38] Although one member of the jury did not agree with this praise and even made the suggestion to give no award at all,[39] the Advisory Board bestowed the award on *Street Scene* and thus on its author, Elmer L. Rice.[40] "*Street Scene* might not have had much of a chance," Hohenberg explains, "if the terms of the drama award had remained" in the original version, but "the 1929 revisions of the Plan of Award" made it possible that the former wordings of "good morals, good taste, and good manners" were dropped and, therefore,[41] it became easier for pieces like *Street Scene* to take part in the Pulitzer competition.

36 Walter P. Eaton/Clayton Hamilton/Albert E. Thomas, Report of the Pulitzer Prize Drama Jury, New York, March 17, 1928, pp. 1 f.
37 Columbia University (Ed.), The Pulitzer Prizes, *op. cit.*, p. 54.
38 Walter P. Eaton/Clayton Hamilton/Albert E. Thomas, Report of the Pulitzer Prize Drama Jury, New York, April 1, 1929, p. 1.
39 *Ibid.*
40 Columbia University (Ed.), The Pulitzer Prizes, *op. cit.*, p. 54.
41 John Hohenberg, The Pulitzer Prizes, *op. cit.*, p. 102.

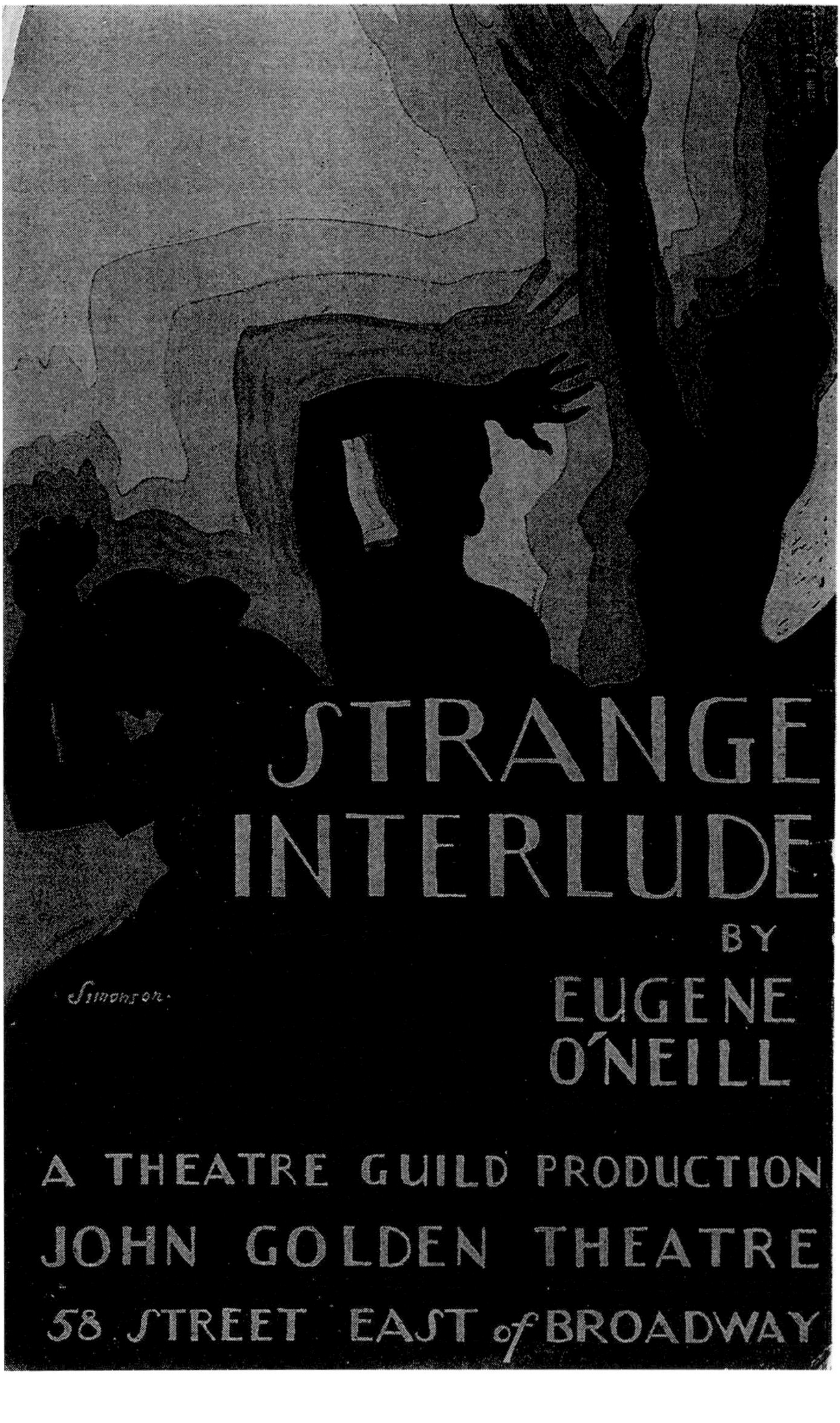
STRANGE
INTERLUDE
BY
EUGENE
O'NEILL
Simonson
A THEATRE GUILD PRODUCTION
JOHN GOLDEN THEATRE
58 STREET EAST of BROADWAY

In 1930, the jury (Walter P. Eaton, Clayton Hamilton and Austin Strong) was partly reconstituted, and after its members "had visited all the American plays of the New York season which showed any pretension to serious consideration," it arrived at the following vote: "One play – *The Green Pastures* by Marc Connelly – towers so far above the other American plays of the season and comes so near to setting a new standard of excellence for the American drama of all time that the jurors desire, with unusual enthusiasm, to recommend it for the Pulitzer Prize. It is a work of astonishing originality; and it is rich in all those qualities which Mr. Pulitzer – in the opinion of the jurors – desired most to foster and encourage. It is simple, gentle, kindly, tender, humorous, compassionate, wise, beautiful, exalted, and exulting. It interprets the religion of thousands of Negroes in the deep South with the simple sincerity of the very best of the Mediaeval Mystery Plays. A delicate task has been accomplished with faultless taste; and the piece deserves to be cherished as a Devine Comedy of a living religion interpreted consistently in the terms of its believers. On this occasion, the jurors state emphatically that they have no second choice."[42] Yet this play was based on sketches by Roark Bradford, published under the title *Ol' Man Adam an' His Chillun*, and so the question arose whether it was indeed "an original American play" in accordance with the Plan of Award. But because both the jury and the Advisory Board affirmed this classification,[43] the Pulitzer Prize for drama was given to *The Green Pastures* by Marc Connelly.[44]

In 1931, the decision-making process turned out to be more complicated as the jurors (Walter P. Eaton, Clayton Hamilton and Austin Strong) did not reach an unanimous vote, even though the jury-report at first glance might give a different impression, stating among other things: "The jury... consider *Alison's House* by Susan Glaspell... as the best candidate. The reason for this choice to a considerable extent is found in the fine sincerity of the dramatist, her choice of a theme which is fresh, taken out of American life, and worthy of serious attention, and her evident interest in what she had to say, quite apart from any considerations of temporal styles or box office appeal. Technically the play is by no means perfect, less nearly so than some others of the season, but it excels all of them in the freshness of its theme and the honesty of its treatment."[45] The majority of the jurors put *Five Star Final* by Louis Weitzenkorn under second place on their lists of finalists, while *As*

42 Walter P. Eaton/Clayton Hamilton/Austin Strong, Report of the Pulitzer Prize Drama Jury, New York, undated (spring 1930), p. 1.
43 Cf. John Hohenberg, The Pulitzer Prizes, *op. cit.*, p. 103.
44 Columbia University (Ed.), The Pulitzer Prizes, *op. cit.*, p. 54.
45 Walter P. Eaton, Report of the Pulitzer Prize Drama Jury, New York, March 21, 1931, p. 1.

Husbands Go by Rachel Crothers ranked third.[46] One member of the jury, however, regretted that he could not endorse the "enthusiasm for *Alison's House*. But... I do not want to stand in the way of this play receiving the prize, as it is sincerely written and without thought of commercial success. For myself I would like to suggest... that it might be a wise decision to give no prize this season."[47] Yet the Advisory Board did not follow this recommendation, but supported the majority vote of the jury instead, and therefore declared *Alison's House* by Susan Glaspell to be the best play of 1931.[48]

The year 1932 was to bring a special surprise as the jurors (Walter P. Eaton, Clayton Hamilton and Austin Strong) had the courage to give preference to a genre hitherto neglected in the tradition of the Pulitzer Prize. "The jury for drama recommends," it can be read in the report, "that the award... be given to George S. Kaufman and Morrie Ryskind for the play, or 'book', of the musical comedy *Of Thee I Sing*. This may seem unusual, but the play is unusual. Not only is it coherent and well knit enough to class as a play, aside from the music, but it is a biting and true satire on American politics and the public attitude toward them... It may well be that this play, *Of Thee I Sing*, will influence our stage (as) much as *The Beggar's Opera* influenced the 18th century stage, and Gilbert and Sullivan that of our fathers... The play is genuine, and we feel the prize could not serve a better purpose than to recognize such work. Few other plays," the jury-report continues, "this past season deserve much consideration. Those which have been seriously considered are, in order of merit: *Mourning Becomes Electra* by Eugene O'Neill, *The Animal Kingdom* by Philip Barry, and *The House of Connelly* by Paul Green, with *The Left Bank* by Elmer Rice a possibility."[49] The Advisory Board publicly announced *Of Thee I Sing*, George S. Kaufman and Morrie Ryskind as winners of the Pulitzer Prize, also including Ira Gershwin, the lyricist, among the honorees.[50] But the Board as well as the jurors did not mention at all George Gershwin, the composer!

Those plays taken into consideration by the jury of 1933 (Walter P. Eaton, Clayton Hamilton and Austin Strong) belonged once again to more traditional genres. The jury-report gave the following comments on the resultant short list: "The Play Jury recommend that the Pulitzer Prize for

46 Clayton Hamilton, Letter to Frank D. Fackenthal, Columbia University, New York, March 23, 1931, p. 3.

47 Austin Strong, Letter to the Committee of Award for the Pulitzer Prize, New York, March 21, 1931, p. 1.

48 Columbia University (Ed.), The Pulitzer Prizes, *op. cit.*, p. 54.

49 Walter P. Eaton/Clayton Hamilton/Austin Strong, Report of the Pulitzer Prize Drama Jury, New York, March 16, 1932, pp. 1 f.

50 Columbia University (Ed.), The Pulitzer Prizes, *op. cit.*, p. 54.

SAM H. HARRIS
PRESENTS
THE MUSICAL COMEDY SENSATION
"OF THEE I SING"
Lyrics by IRA GERSHWIN
Music by GEORGE GERSHWIN
PULITZER PRIZE WINNER
1931-32
ERGREEN FOR PRESIDENT
THROTTL BOTTO
FOR VICE PRESID
ZIEGFELD THEATRE
54th STREET & 6th AVENUE

Drama... be awarded to Maxwell Anderson for his play *Both Your Houses...* The spirit of the play is idealistic, it breathes a fine indignation, but it is so conducted that legitimate entertainment values are not lost, and the characters speak and act with convincing naturalness... Incidentally, this play would fulfill Mr. Pulitzer's ideal of a prize winner, and its presentation through the country would be of public service. The play considered next in value by the jury is *Another Language* (by Rose Franken)... It was a truthful and interesting picture of domestic life in a family which tried to put the same stamp on all its members. Miss Rachel Crothers' *When Ladies Meet* was probably third choice, a comedy of manners not so spontaneous in development as *Another Language*. *Alien Corn* by Sidney Howard seemed not so good as the play with which he had already won a prize, and so was not seriously considered. Two other candidates, not quite up to the prize standard, were *Pigeons and People* by George M. Cohan, and *Biography* by Samuel N. Behrman."[51] The Advisory Board decided as the jury had suggested, thus granting, as Hohenberg formulates, "Maxwell Anderson his long deferred award."[52]

In 1934, the search for an outstanding dramatist led to a resounding row, after the members of the jury (Walter P. Eaton, Clayton Hamilton and Austin Strong) gave notice in their report that they had "voted unanimously in favor of *Mary of Scotland* by Maxwell Anderson, an historical play of fine dramatic and literary accomplishment... The merits of this piece have been so generally recognized that a detailed criticism is not deemed necessary in this report. The jurors," they added, "have not endeavored to agree upon a second choice."[53] Despite this definite recommendation the Advisory Board turned down the proposal of the jury and did not give the award to *Mary of Scotland* but declared *Men in White* by Sidney Kingsley as best play of the theatrical season.[54] Although the winning play had been among the six titles compiled by the jurors as being worthy of further discussion, it had not reached the jury's short list.[55] Hohenberg stresses that "none of the jurors questioned the right of the Board to reverse them," but the snub did annoy them all the same.[56] Walter P. Eaton, long-standing member of the drama jury, commented on the conduct of the Advisory Board as follows: "They

51 Walter P. Eaton/Clayton Hamilton/Austin Strong, Report of the Pulitzer Prize Drama Jury, New York, March 23, 1933, p. 1.

52 John Hohenberg, The Pulitzer Prizes, *op. cit.*, p. 107.

53 Walter P. Eaton/Clayton Hamilton/Austin Strong, Report of the Pulitzer Prize Drama Jury, New York, March 22, 1934, p. 1.

54 Columbia University (Ed.), The Pulitzer Prizes, *op. cit.*, p. 54.

55 Walter P. Eaton/Clayton Hamilton/Austin Strong, Report..., *op. cit.*, p. 1.

56 John Hohenberg, The Pulitzer Prizes, *op. cit.*, p. 148.

don't want dramatic experts any more. They want office boys. No self-respecting, intelligent critic would serve on such a jury." Although Nicholas M. Butler, President of Columbia, asked the jurors to return as members of the Pulitzer Prize jury in the following year, all three declined.[57]

Consequently, in 1935, three new jurors (John Erskine, William L. Phelps and Stark Young) selected the prize-worthy plays and, according to a modification of the instructions as to how to draw up jury-reports, worked out a list of "four plays in the order of preference: 1. *The Old Maid* (by Zoe Akins), 2. *Personal Appearance* (by Lawrence Riley), 3. *Merrily We Roll Along* (by George S. Kaufman), 4. *Valley Forge* (by Maxwell Anderson)."[58] Once again there were lots of rumours and speculations about the way this list materialized all the while until finally the winner was announced, but the Advisory Board as well as the University Trustees decided in favor of *The Old Maid*, and so the Pulitzer Prize for drama went to Zoe Akins.[59] In 1936, when the jury consisted of only two persons (Mary M. Colum and William L. Phelps), the following constellation arose: "1. We are absolutely in complete agreement in recommending... *Idiot's Delight* by Robert E. Sherwood," it says in the report. "It is a first-rate play, full of dramatic invention, and one or two of the comedy scenes have a Molièrian richness... 2. ... *End of Summer* by Samuel N. Behrman. This is a sophisticated society comedy with possibly smarter and more finished dialogue... 3. *Murder in the Cathedral* by Thomas S. Eliot. This within limits is a very fine poetic drama, but its appeal is that of a pageant rather than of a play... We may add," the two members of the drama jury stated at the end of their report, "that... we... have no hesitation in recommending *Idiot's Delight*."[60] The Advisory Board accepted the verdict of the jury, and so Robert E. Sherwood received his first Pulitzer Prize.[61] Hohenberg adds that the jurors "overlooked that year one of the greatest contributions to the American theatre, George Gershwin's *Porgy and Bess*."[62]

The jury of 1937 was this time once again made up of three members (Mary M. Colum, William L. Phelps and Arthur H. Quinn), who, after watching and judging all of the eligible plays, however, found themselves, as is obvious in their report, "unable to agree after a number of extremely

57 *Ibid.*, pp. 148 f.
58 John Erskine/William L. Phelps/Stark Young, Report of the Pulitzer Prize Drama Jury, New York, March 14, 1935, p. 1.
59 John Hohenberg, The Pulitzer Prizes, *op. cit.*, pp. 149 f.
60 Mary M. Colum/William L. Phelps, Report of the Pulitzer Prize Drama Jury, New York, April 3, 1936, pp. 1 f.
61 Columbia University (Ed.), The Pulitzer Prizes, *op. cit.*, p. 54.
62 John Hohenberg, The Pulitzer Prizes, *op. cit.*, p. 152.

IDIOT'S
DELIGHT
A Play by Robert E. Sherwood
with
ALFRED
LUNT
AND
LYNN
FONTANNE
SHUBERT THEATRE
44th ST., W.
OF B'WAY

interesting and wholly amicable discussions... Since no agreement was reached, each member of the Committee is presenting an individual, signed statement," although all of these statements contained evaluations of the following four plays: *You Can't Take It With You* by Moss Hart and George S. Kaufman, *High Tor* by Maxwell Anderson, *Marching Song* by John Howard Lawson, and *Tide Rising* by George Brewer Jr.[63] Whereas Arthur H. Quinn explained that his "preference among the plays of Mr. Anderson is for *High Tor*," followed by other plays by the same author,[64] Mary Colum criticized that so much attention was being paid to the work of this one dramatist, even to the point of interceding that no award should be given that year. She indicated, however, that she was "willing to agree that *You Can't Take It With You* is the most lively and entertaining dramatic offering of the year."[65] The third juror, William L. Phelps, was of the opinion, "that *You Can't Take It With You* is far and away the best play of the season... because it is first-rate theatre and keeps the audience in a state of continued excitement and delight; secondly, because it is wholly original in plot, dialogue and treatment; third, because the philosophy, as expressed by the chief character, contains valuable ideas."[66] So the Advisory Board had altogether favorable assessments of this play by two jurors, and therefore it decided to honor *You Can't Take It With You*, thus giving the Pulitzer Prize to the team of Moss Hart and George S. Kaufman.[67]

The jurors of 1938 (Mary M. Colum, William L. Phelps and Schuyler Watts) had only one clear favorite. In their report they informed the Advisory Boars that the "Drama Jury are enthusiastically and unanimously agreed in nominating and recommending... for the award... *Our Town* by Thornton Wilder. We are not only agreed on this, but we are also agreed that there is really no good second choice."[68] When afterwards one of the heads of Columbia University "asked for an additional report, evidently because he felt the Advisory Board might need some convincing before going out on another limb,"[69] this was what the jurors added about the selection of *Our Town*: "Our reasons for this (suggestion) are that both from the standpoint of dramatic ability and of the theatre the play seems to us the most original, the

63 Mary M. Colum/William L. Phelps/Arthur H. Quinn, Report of the Pulitzer Prize Drama Jury, New Haven, Ct., undated (April 1937), p. 1.
64 Arthur H. Quinn, Report, Philadelphia, Pa., April 7, 1937, p. 1.
65 Mary M. Colum, Report, New York, April 7, 1937, p. 1.
66 William L. Phelps, Report, New Haven, Ct., undated (April 1937), p. 1.
67 Columbia University (Ed.), The Pulitzer Prizes, *op. cit.*, p. 54.
68 Mary M. Colum/William L. Phelps/Schuyler Watts, Report of the Pulitzer Prize Drama Jury, New Haven, Ct., March 15, 1938, p. 1.
69 John Hohenberg, The Pulitzer Prizes, *op. cit.*, p. 154.

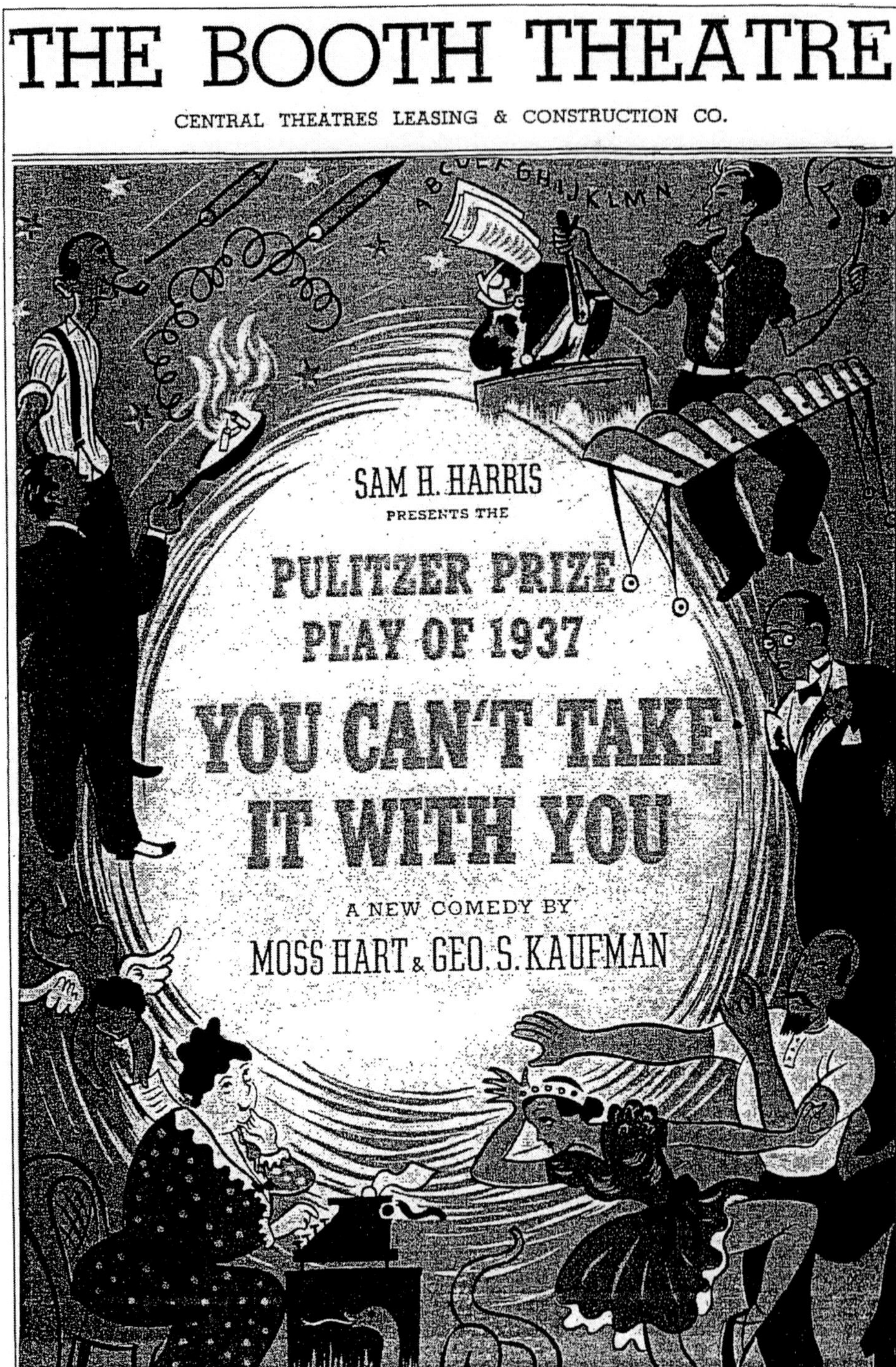
THE BOOTH THEATRE
CENTRAL THEATRES LEASING & CONSTRUCTION CO.
ABCDEFGHIJKLMN
SAM H. HARRIS
PRESENTS THE
PULITZER PRIZE
PLAY OF 1937
YOU CAN'T TAKE
IT WITH YOU
A NEW COMEDY BY
MOSS HART & GEO. S. KAUFMAN

most beautiful, and the most impressive of the season. Furthermore, it is wholly American, confined entirely to an American scene and American characters. The structure of the play is original, the dialogue is written by a master of English, and there is a dignity and a nobility about the whole play and its performance worthy of the highest praise. We wish it distinctly understood that in our judgment there is, strictly speaking, no second place because we think that all the other plays, good as they may be, are inferior to our first

Playwrights George S. Kaufman and Moss Hart
completing their comedy *You Can't Take It With You*

choice."[70] In an additional paragraph the jurors simply stated that they had also discussed in detail the plays *Susan and God* by Rachel Crothers, *The Star-Wagon* by Maxwell Anderson as well as *On Borrowed Time* by Paul Osborn.[71] Faced with this explicit praise for *Our Town* the Advisory Board gave the award to Thornton Wilder.[72]

Referring to the unanimity of the jurors in the preceding year, the chairman of the jury of 1939 (Mary M. Colum, William L. Phelps and Schuyler Watts) wrote to the Advisory Board: "I am sorry that I can't report an agreement in the three members of the committee. But one reason for this, in my own judgment, is that there is no absolutely first-class outstanding play as there was last year... It is only fair to say that Mr. Watts fully believes that *Family Portrait* (by Leonore Coffee and William J. Cowen) is an outstanding play of this season and fully deserves the prize. Mrs. Colum has a much lower opinion of it... I am equally devided in my own mind for first place between *Abe Lincoln in Illinois* (by Robert E. Sherwood) and *Family Portrait*."[73] Mary M. Colum spoke out in favor of *Abe Lincoln in Illinois*, because "first of all, it is an American chronicle-play, and, as such, of importance in American theatrical history; secondly, it is a competent play by an experienced dramatist, with the chief figure movingly presented, with the minor characters done adequately and adroitly."[74] After William L. Phelps and Mary M. Colum finally supported the idea of ranking *Abe Lincoln in Illinois* first on their short-list, the third juror, Schuyler Watts, stated with vehemence that he himself did not endorse this vote, as he still considered *Family Portrait* to be the best theatrical play.[75] So *Abe Lincoln in Illinois* ranked first with two jurors, while the third juror held the play in lower regard,[76] yet the majority vote was accepted by the Advisory Board. Therefore, the Pulitzer Prize for drama was given to Robert E. Sherwood,[77] receiving the prestigious award for the second time.

In 1940, the three members of the jury (Mary M. Colum, William L. Phelps and Schuyler Watts) reached a certain consensus of opinion, making

---

70 Mary M. Colum/William L. Phelps/Schuyler Watts, General Report of the Pulitzer Prize Drama Jury, New York, March 18, 1938, p. 1.
71 *Ibid.*
72 Columbia University (Ed.), The Pulitzer Prizes, *op. cit.*, p. 54.
73 William L. Phelps, Letter to Frank D. Fackenthal, Columbia University, New York, April 3, 1939, p. 1.
74 Mary M. Colum, Report on Plays 1938-1939, New York, April 2, 1939, p. 1.
75 William L. Phelps, Letter to Frank D. Fackenthal, Columbia University, New York, April 23, 1939, p. 1.
76 Mary M. Colum/William L. Phelps/Schuyler Watts, Report of the Pulitzer Prize Drama Jury, New Haven, Ct., April 26, 1939, p. 1.
77 Columbia University (Ed.), The Pulitzer Prizes, *op. cit.*, p. 54.

MOROSCO THEATRE

JED HARRIS
presents

OUR TOWN

A PLAY BY
THORNTON WILDER
with
FRANK CRAVEN

clear at the beginning of their report: "Our Pulitzer Prize drama committee agrees on the following: first, the theatre season in New York has been the poorest in years; second, it is much better to award the prize than to withhold it; third, we agree unanimously on recommending to the Board that the prize be awarded to *The Time of Your Life* by William Saroyan. This play is wholly original, not taken from any novel, is wholly American in theme and treatment, and contains more *promise* for the future than any other play of the past season. It shows a knowledge of human nature and a sympathy with various obscure specimens of mankind, without any propaganda."[78] Furthermore, the jurors had long discussions on the following plays, even though their individual evaluations and rankings differed: *Life With Father* by Russel Crouse and Howard Lindsay, *Key Largo* by Maxwell Anderson, *The Male Animal* by James Thurber and

Shown at rehearsal of *There Shall Be No Night*: Playwright Robert E. Sherwood, Richard Whorf, Lynn Fontanne, Alfred Lunt, Sydney Greenstreet

78 Mary M. Colum/William L. Phelps/Schuyler Watts, Report of the Pulitzer Prize Drama Jury, New Haven, Ct., April 2, 1940, p. 1.

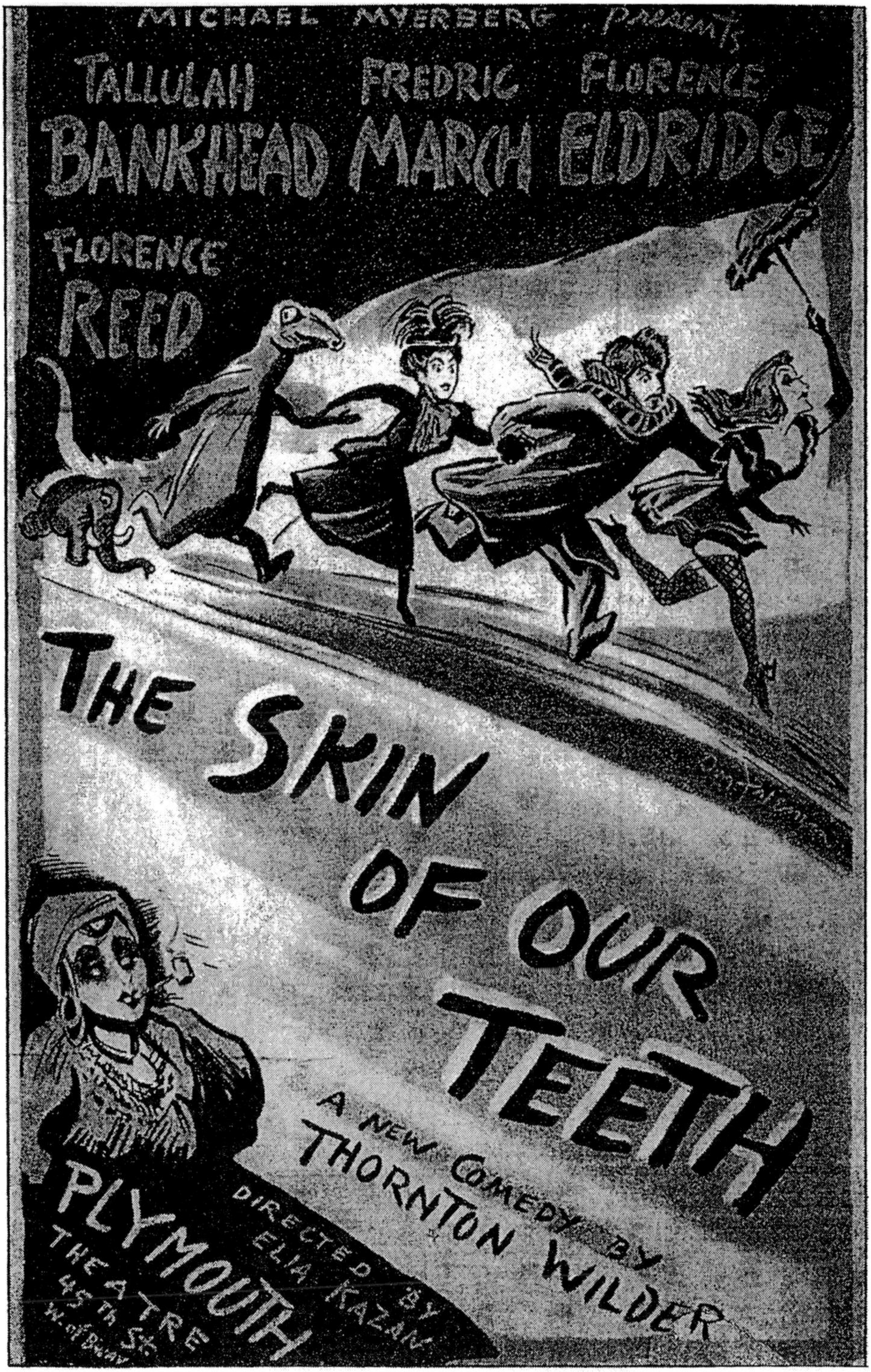
MICHAEL MYERBERG presents
TALLULAH BANKHEAD
FREDRIC MARCH
FLORENCE ELDRIDGE
FLORENCE REED
THE SKIN OF OUR TEETH
A NEW COMEDY BY THORNTON WILDER
DIRECTED BY ELIA KAZAN
PLYMOUTH THEATRE 45th St.

Elliott Nugent, *The Man Who Came to Dinner* by George S. Kaufman and Moss Hart, *Two on an Island* by Elmer Rice as well as *Night Music* by Clifford Odets.[79] The Advisory Board gave the prize to *The Time of Your Life*, and thus William Saroyan received the award.[80] But the author, as Hohenberg found out, "rejected the $ 1,000 prize immediately after the announcement because he said it would compromise his art to accept it... The check, when it was returned, went back into the Pulitzer Fund,"[81] however William Saroyan did not reject the honor itself.

The selection process caused comparatively few problems in 1941, although one of the three jurors (Mary M. Colum, William L. Phelps and Schuyler Watts) temporarily did not wholeheartedly support the one favorite for the award who arose out of the discussions, even suggesting to consider "no award." Nevertheless, there was far-reaching agreement that *There Shall Be No Night* by Robert E. Sherwood should be regarded as best theatrical production. "This play is very far ahead of all possible competitors during the season," it says in the report, "and this not because of its opportuneness but because of its immense dramatic value, its profound sincerity, and its splendid artistic dealing with great issues; and furthermore its deeply spiritual quality which is felt by every spectator and yet always leaves the play as a work of art and never vulgarizes it into a sermon."[82] In the evaluation of two jurors *Claudia* by Rose Franken ranked next on the list of recommendations, because it was "a good American play dealing in an unusual but wholly honest and sincere manner with marriage." *The Talley Method* by Samuel N. Behrman also was put on the list of finalists, as were *Johnny Belinda* by Elmer Harris and *Arsenic and Old Lace* by Joseph Kesselring. "We were especially fortunate in having such a magnificent drama as *There Shall Be No Night*,"[83] the jury-report concluded. Hohenberg explains that "all the leading plays had war themes,"[84] and the favorite for the award was no exception, its main theme being the invasion of Finland. The Advisory Board approved the vote of the jury and declared *There Shall Be No Night* best play of the season, thereby bestowing upon Robert E. Sherwood his third Pulitzer Prize.[85]

79 Schuyler Watts, Report on the Theatrical Season 1939-40, New York, April 2, 1940, pp. 1 f.
80 Columbia University (Ed.), The Pulitzer Prizes, *op. cit.*, p. 54.
81 John Hohenberg, The Pulitzer Prizes, *op. cit.*, p. 155.
82 Mary M. Colum/William L. Phelps/Schuyler Watts, Report of the Pulitzer Prize Drama Jury, New York, undated (April 1941), p. 1.
83 *Ibid.*
84 John Hohenberg, The Pulitzer Prizes, *op. cit.*, p. 155.
85 Columbia University (Ed.), The Pulitzer Prizes, *op. cit.*, p. 55.

In 1942, when an author of international reputation was one of the jurors (Mary M. Colum, W. Somerset Maugham and William L. Phelps), the jury discussed among other plays the drama *The Moon Is Down* by John Steinbeck as well as *Cafe Crown* by Hyman S. Kraft, Hyman S.. But in the end it reached the following verdict: "Reviewing the whole season, we are... positively and unanimously agreed that it is better not to give the Pulitzer Prize this season."[86] The Advisory Board considered the reasons for this vote, given in detail in the jury-report, and then accepted it, deciding on "no award."[87] The same three jurors (Mary M. Colum, W. Somerset Maugham and William L. Phelps) selected the prize-worthy production in 1943, and once again their judgment was unanimous. This time, however, all three were unanimously supporting one particular play. Aside from *Harriet* by Florence Ryerson and Colin Clements, *The Patriots* by Sidney Kingsley or *The Eve of St. Mark* by Maxwell Anderson, there was above all one outstanding achievement: *The Skin of Our Teeth* by Thornton Wilder. "I am of the opinion that this play shows more imagination, more fresh theatrical invention, more of an innovating spirit than any other play of the season," one juror commented, stressing: "It is far from being successfully projected, it is even in parts confused and confusing, but it represents the highest imaginative and intellectual reach of any of the Broadway plays."[88] And another juror added: "This has vitality, a gay and fantastic invention, and is almost consistently entertaining."[89] In view of this unanimity the Advisory Board raised no objections and gave the award to *The Skin of Our Teeth*. Thus Thornton Wilder received his second Pulitzer Prize.[90]

The jury of 1944 (Mary M. Colum, W. Somerset Maugham and Glenway Wescott) was partly reconstituted and dealt in particular with the production of *The Voice of the Turtle* by John Van Druten and *Winged Victory* by Moss Hart. Although two jurors deemed Van Druten's play to be prize-worthy, the author's nationality – he was no American citizen – proved to be an obstacle.[91] "What the Board did," Hohenberg writes, "was to pass the prize, but at the same time it took the unprecedented step of announcing a special award for *Oklahoma!* by Richard Rodgers and Oscar Hammerstein II. This was

86 Mary M. Colum/W. Somerset Maugham/William L. Phelps, Report of the Pulitzer Prize Drama Jury, New York, April 12, 1942, p. 2.
87 Columbia University (Ed.), The Pulitzer Prizes, *op. cit.*, p. 55.
88 Mary M. Colum/W. Somerset Maugham/William L. Phelps, Report of the Pulitzer Prize Drama Jury, New York, March 25, 1943, p. 1.
89 *Ibid.*, p. 7.
90 Columbia University (Ed.), The Pulitzer Prizes, *op. cit.*, p. 55.
91 Mary M. Colum/W. Somerset Maugham/Glenway Wescott, Report of the Pulitzer Prize Drama Jury, New York, March 29, 1944, p. 1.

OKLAHOMA!
ST. JAMES THEATRE
44th ST. W. of BROADWAY
MATINEES THURS. & SAT.

evidently done on the Board's own initiative for there was no mention of *Oklahoma!* in the jury report."[92] In 1945, the members of the jury (Oscar J. Campbell, Mary M. Colum and Joseph W. Krutch), however, had hardly any problems at all in agreeing on a favorite: After conducting exhaustive discussions on *Dark of the Moon* by Howard Richardson and William Berney as well as *The Hasty Heart* by John Patrick they decided on *Harvey* by Mary Chase. They held this comedy in high regard "on account of its richness of content and the fresh imaginative field it has taken over; in plot and character it marks a departure from the usual Broadway play." Only one of the jurors even mentions *The Glass Menagerie* by Tennessee Williams, writing in his report: "I have not seen *The Glass Menagerie* but I am seeing it tonight and if, as seems unlikely, I should wish to put it first, I shall send... a supplementary report."[93] Yet, as Hohenberg found out, "there was no supplementary report," and so the Advisory Board "without dissent voted the... award to *Harvey*,"[94] thus making Mary Chase a Pulitzer Prize-winner.[95]

Passing judgment on the theatrical achievements of 1946, the drama jury (Oscar J. Campbell, Mary M. Colum and Joseph W. Krutch) recommended to give the award to *State of the Union* by Russel Crouse and Howard Lindsay.[96] The Advisory Board did not object and announced this team of authors to be joint-winners of the Pulitzer Prize.[97] In 1947, the work of the jurors (Oscar J. Campbell, Mary M. Colum and Joseph W. Krutch) was characterized by fairly differing opinions concerning a potential prize-winner. Whereas one member of the jury regarded the New York production of *Christopher Blake* by Moss Hart as well as *The Iceman Cometh* by Eugene O'Neill as outstanding, a second juror also mentioned *Christopher Blake*, but then introduced *All My Sons* by Arthur Miller and *The Fatal Weakness* by George Kelly as ranking next on his list. The third member of the jury offered the following ranking: *All My Sons*, *The Fatal Weakness* and *The Iceman Cometh*. He remarked additionally that he did "not really believe the prize should go again to Mr. O'Neill, who has had it on two previous occasions and for better plays."[98] Referring to O'Neill one juror made the comment that his "play is too long and is somewhat dated; ... but at the

92 John Hohenberg, The Pulitzer Prizes, *op. cit.*, p. 206.
93 Oscar J. Campbell/Mary M. Colum/Joseph W. Krutch, Report of the Pulitzer Prize Drama Jury, New York, April 3, 1945, pp. 2, 5.
94 John Hohenberg, The Pulitzer Prizes, *op. cit.*, pp. 207 f.
95 Columbia University (Ed.), The Pulitzer Prizes, *op. cit.*, p. 55.
96 John Hohenberg, The Pulitzer Prizes, *op. cit.*, p. 208.
97 Columbia University (Ed.), The Pulitzer Prizes, *op. cit.*, p. 55.
98 Oscar J. Campbell/Mary M. Colum/Joseph W. Krutch, Report of the Pulitzer Prize Drama Jury, New York, March 31, 1947, p. 1.

same time it has qualities rare on Broadway – emotional power, strong communication with life, fine character creation, and a superb theatrical sense. O'Neill simply knows more about people than any other Broadway dramatist, but he is long winded which defect may come from a lack of control of his material... I do not see how this jury could pass over O'Neill's excellencies in favor of other plays that are swifter in movement, more modern in technique."[99] Despite this fairly positive evaluation of *The Iceman Cometh* the Advisory Board decided to give "no award."[100]

Playwrights Howard Lindsay and Russel Crouse at work for *State of the Union*

99 *Ibid.*, p. 3.
100 Columbia University (Ed.), The Pulitzer Prizes, *op. cit.*, p. 55.

The jurors of 1948 (Oscar J. Campbell, Joseph W. Krutch and Maurice J. Valency) took into consideration several Broadway production of the preceding season, among them *Command Decision* by William W. Haines and *Mr. Roberts* by Thomas Heggen and Joshua Logan, but all attention focused on *A Streetcar Named Desire* by Tennessee Williams. "It is a superb drama – full of originality and power both in conception and in execution," the jury-report underlines. It then continues its eulogy: "It tells with sincerity and compassion the poignant story of a woman's inevitable degradation. Though on the surface the author treats his theme with savage realism, yet it is in essence a story of intangibles, revealing perceptions and understandings of human nature that are deep and subtle. His prose is instinct with the feeling and nuance of poetry. The play is expertly composed, beginning in a low key and moving relentlessly to a catastrophe which awakens the mixture of pity and terror that all authentic tragedy should. The production and acting of this play are also of superlative quality ... There is... no... doubt... that it is not only incomparably the best American play of the year but also both the best in several years and even, by absolute standards, a remarkable work... To fail to give it the prize would be absurd and, from a perfectly practical standpoint, would seriously damage the prestige of the prize."[101] The Advisory Board completely agreed and awarded Tennessee Williams the Pulitzer Prize for his play *A Streetcar Named Desire*.[102]

The jurors of 1949 (Oscar J. Campbell, Joseph W. Krutch and Maurice J. Valency) could not reach complete concordance, because one of them voted in favor of *Summer and Smoke* by Tennessee Williams, whereas the other two preferred Arthur Miller's *Death of a Salesman*.[103] "I strongly recommend that the prize be given to *Death of a Salesman*," one member of the drama jury wrote in his report, adding: "This tragedy is by all odds the most notable American play of the season. Indeed, I am inclined to regard it as the best modern American tragedy of the last decade. In a sense, it is the tragedy of every one who plays an important part in our acquisitive civilization... The Pulitzer award would add to its already great prestige by crowning so distinguished a work by a young American playwright."[104] Another juror, also inclined to give the prize to *Death of a Salesman*, called it "the year's outstanding play" although he did not think it a "great" one. "It is," he wrote, "open to very grave objections from the point of view of intellectual

101 Oscar J. Campbell/Joseph W. Krutch/Maurice J. Valency, Report of the Pulitzer Prize Drama Jury, New York, undated (April 1948), pp. 1 f.
102 Columbia University (Ed.), The Pulitzer Prizes, *op. cit.*, p. 55.
103 John Hohenberg, The Pulitzer Prizes, *op. cit.*, p. 210.
104 Quoted *ibid.*

Morosco Theatre

Operated by City Playhouses Inc. | Louis A. Lotito, President

KERMIT BLOOMGARDEN and WALTER FRIED
present

LEE J. COBB

in

ELIA KAZAN'S Production of

death of a Salesman

A New Play by ARTHUR MILLER
Directed by ELIA KAZAN

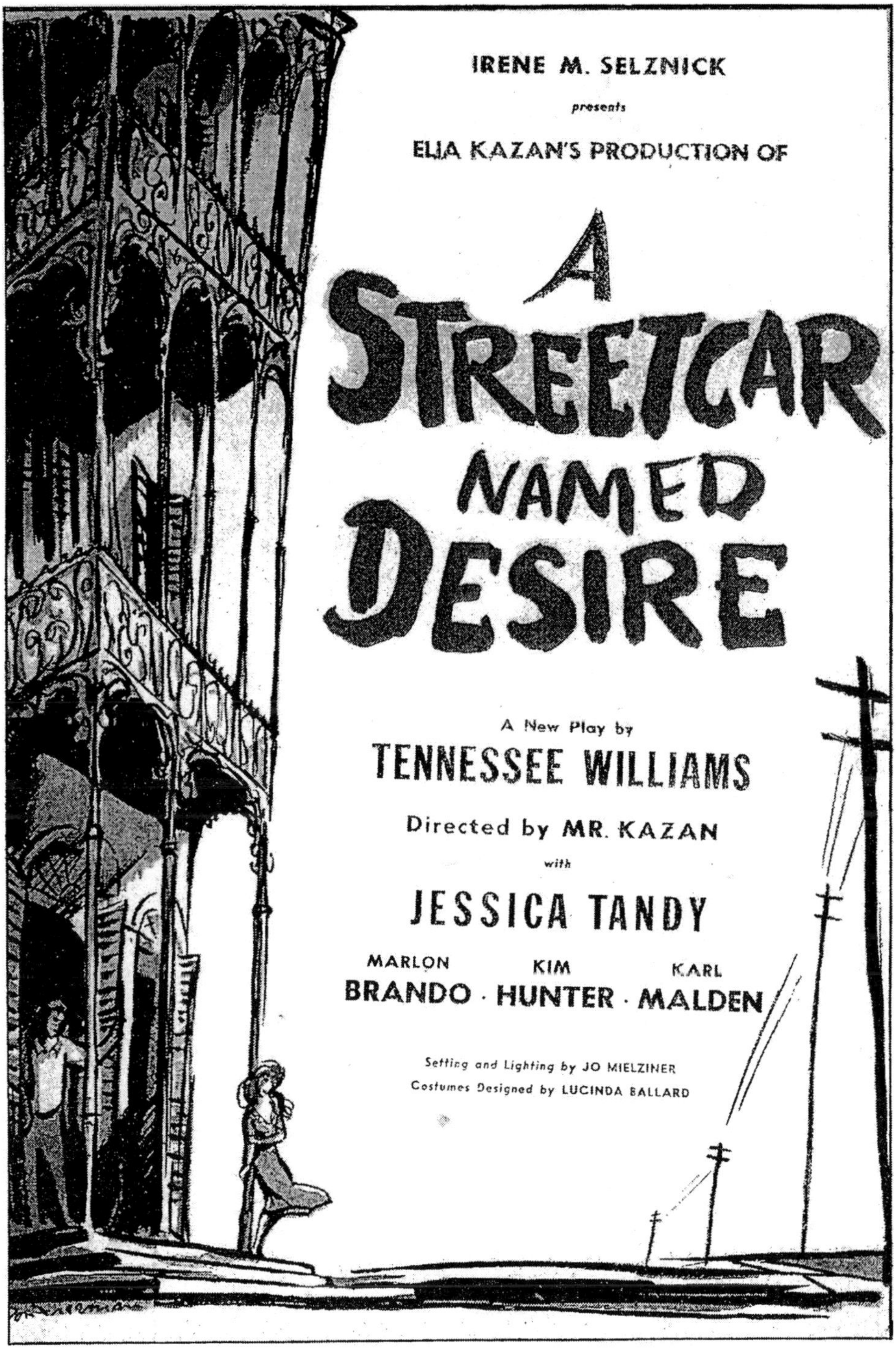
IRENE M. SELZNICK
presents
ELIA KAZAN'S PRODUCTION OF
A STREETCAR NAMED DESIRE
A New Play by
TENNESSEE WILLIAMS
Directed by MR. KAZAN
with
JESSICA TANDY
MARLON BRANDO · KIM HUNTER · KARL MALDEN
Setting and Lighting by JO MIELZINER
Costumes Designed by LUCINDA BALLARD

content, style, and construction. Nevertheless, it is an extremely powerful play and I believe it will have consequences in the development of the sphere of drama which has not previously been practiced with conspicuous success in this country."[105] The very high esteem for Arthur Miller's drama on the part of the jurors was also shared by the Advisory Board, and so the playwright won the Pulitzer Prize for his work *Death of a Salesman.*[106]

In 1950, the jurors (Oscar J. Campbell, Joseph W. Krutch and Maurice J. Valency), as Hohenberg puts it, "ran into trouble because they recommended Gian-Carlo Menotti's *The Consul*, which was, as it turned out, also the first choice in the Music Jury and the eventual winner of the Pulitzer Prize in Music that year. The Advisory Board, in a thoroughly musical mood, decided on its own that the Pulitzer Prize in Drama for that year should go to *South Pacific*,"[107] and so the honor went to Richard Rodgers, Oscar Hammerstein II

Director Joshua Logan, composer Richard Rodgers, librettist Oscar Hammerstein II, Mary Martin, author James A. Michener at rehearsal of *South Pacific*

105 Quoted *ibid.*
106 Columbia University (Ed.), The Pulitzer Prizes, *op. cit.*, p. 55.
107 John Hohenberg, The Pulitzer Prizes, *op. cit.*, p. 211.

and Joshua Logan for their musical.[108] The jury of 1951 was made up of only two persons (Oscar J. Campbell and Maurice J. Valency) and "recommended a dramatization of Herman Melville's novel *Billy Budd* by Louis O'Coxe and Robert Chapman, but the Advisory Board refused to accept it for undetermined reasons"[109] and opted for "no award" instead.[110] The same two jurors in 1952 judged 19 Broadway productions before finally coming up with a list of three suggestions consisting of *Point of No Return* by Paul Osborn, *One Bright Day* by Sigmund Miller as well as *The Shrike* by Joseph Kramm. Kramm's play ranked first with the jury for the following reasons: "It is an expertly constructed play on a subject of great importance, extremely well produced and acted. We both feel that it would best serve the interest of the American theatre if this play were awarded the Pulitzer Prize."[111] The Advi-

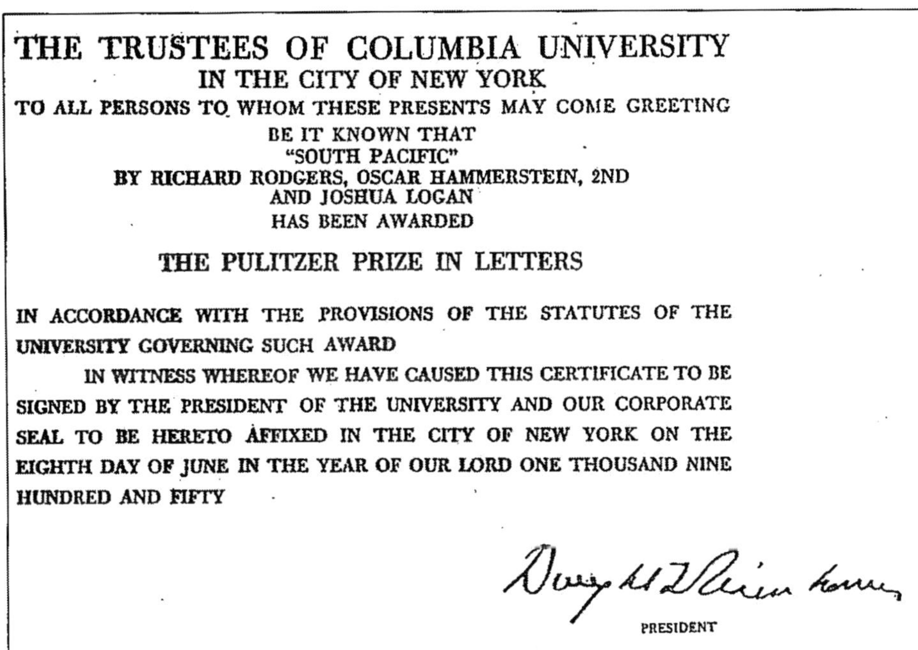

THE TRUSTEES OF COLUMBIA UNIVERSITY
IN THE CITY OF NEW YORK
TO ALL PERSONS TO WHOM THESE PRESENTS MAY COME GREETING
BE IT KNOWN THAT
"SOUTH PACIFIC"
BY RICHARD RODGERS, OSCAR HAMMERSTEIN, 2ND
AND JOSHUA LOGAN
HAS BEEN AWARDED

THE PULITZER PRIZE IN LETTERS

IN ACCORDANCE WITH THE PROVISIONS OF THE STATUTES OF THE UNIVERSITY GOVERNING SUCH AWARD

IN WITNESS WHEREOF WE HAVE CAUSED THIS CERTIFICATE TO BE SIGNED BY THE PRESIDENT OF THE UNIVERSITY AND OUR CORPORATE SEAL TO BE HERETO AFFIXED IN THE CITY OF NEW YORK ON THE EIGHTH DAY OF JUNE IN THE YEAR OF OUR LORD ONE THOUSAND NINE HUNDRED AND FIFTY

Dwight D. Eisenhower
PRESIDENT

Courtesy: The Library of Congress, Washington, D.C.

Pulitzer Prize Certificate for the Drama Winners of 1950,
signed by Dwight D. Eisenhower,
President of Columbia University from 1948–1953

108 Columbia University (Ed.), The Pulitzer Prizes, *op. cit.*, p. 55.
109 John Hohenberg, The Pulitzer Prizes, *op. cit.*, p. 211.
110 Columbia University (Ed.), The Pulitzer Prizes, *op. cit.*, p. 55.
111 Oscar J. Campbell/Maurice J. Valency, Report of the Pulitzer Prize Drama Jury, New York, April 2, 1952, pp. 1 f.

South Pacific
with
MARY MARTIN
EZIO PINZA
Music by RICHARD RODGERS
Lyrics by OSCAR HAMMERSTEIN 2nd
Book by OSCAR HAMMERSTEIN 2nd & JOSHUA LOGAN
Adapted from JAMES A. MICHENER'S Pulitzer Prize Winning "TALES OF THE SOUTH PACIFIC"
Directed by JOSHUA LOGAN
DREAM GIRL
Majestic Theatre

sory Board endorsed this opinion by awarding Joseph Kramm the Pulitzer Prize for his play *The Shrike*.[112]

When the jury (Oscar J. Campbell and Maurice J. Valency) had to select the best play of 1953 it judged 18 theatrical productions and wrote in the report that followed: "The most successfully original stage entertainment of the season was without doubt *John Brown's Body* (by Charles Laughton). It also brought to a triumph a new sort of play which may properly be called 'poetic platform drama' and set the standard for a new form. Since it cannot be regarded as a new play and the poem (by Stephen Vincent Benét) from which Charles Laughton has made the platform drama has already received a Pulitzer Prize,[113] we assume that *John Brown's Body* does not fulfill the conditions which a Prize play must meet... Apart from *John Brown's Body* we believe that *Picnic* by William Inge is most deserving of the award. This is a notable play about a group of people in a small Kansas town on a hot Labor Day... It is an expertly composed piece, beautifully written and American to the core. Joshua Logan has staged a fine performance and the acting is superb. Mr. Inge's first play, *Come Back Little Sheba*, showed great promise which *Picnic* has splendidly fulfilled."[114] Although *The Crucible* by Arthur Miller and *The Time of the Cuckoo* by Arthur Laurents also were mentioned on the list of the jury, the Advisory Board decided in favor of *Picnic* and honored William Inge with the Pulitzer Prize for drama.[115]

After watching and evaluating 26 plays the two jurors of 1954 (Oscar J. Campbell and Maurice J. Valency) faced a similar problem as in the previous year, and so they stated in their report: "Undoubtedly the best dramatic entertainment of the season was afforded by *The Caine Mutiny Court Martial* (by Herman Wouk). However, since the novel, upon which a part of this drama is based, has already received a Pulitzer Prize,[116] we feel that we cannot in all conscience recommend an excerpt from that novel for another Pulitzer Award. If this dramatization be excluded from consideration, we believe that the best play of the season is *The Teahouse of the August Moon* by John Patrick... This is an altogether delightful comedy, a fantasy about the impact of the East and West on each other... Second on our list but substantially lower we place *Tea and Sympathy* by Robert Anderson. The acting

112 Columbia University (Ed.), The Pulitzer Prizes, *op. cit.*, p. 55.

113 Cf. Heinz-D. Fischer/Erika J. Fischer (Eds.), The Pulitzer Prize Archive, Vol. 11: Poetry/Verse Awards 1918-1995, Munich 1997, pp. 43 ff.

114 Oscar J. Campbell/Maurice J. Valency, Report of the Pulitzer Prize Drama Jury, New York, March 31, 1953, pp. 1 f.

115 Columbia University (Ed.), The Pulitzer Prizes, *op. cit.*, p. 55.

116 Cf. Heinz-D. Fischer/Erika J. Fischer (Eds.), The Pulitzer Prize Archive, Vol. 10: Novel/Fiction Awards 1917-1994, Munich - New Providence - London - Paris 1997, pp. 135 ff.

JOHN PATRICK
The Teahouse of the August Moon
Martin Beck Theatre

Producer Maurice Evans, director Robert Lewis and playwright John Patrick discussing the production of *The Teahouse of the August Moon*

of the two principals in this play was as fine as any of the season. We feel," the jurors continued, "that in this report we should express our admiration for *In the Summer House* by Jane Bowles. It had qualities of insight and poetic imagination which might have made it the outstanding play of the year. But we do not believe that the new promising writer realized many of its dramatic and theatric potentialities."[117] Considering the arguments brought forward for the author ranking first the Advisory Board had no reservations in giving the award to John Patrick's *The Teahouse of the August Moon.*[118]

1955 turned out to be a remarkable year for the Pulitzer Prize for drama, because the award-winning production was picked in a rather unusual way. The jury (Oscar J. Campbell and Maurice J. Valency) shortlisted five out of the 35 plays produced on Broadway that season, namely: *The Bad Seed* by

117 Oscar J. Campbell/Maurice J. Valency, Report of the Pulitzer Prize Drama Jury, New York, March 31, 1954, pp. 1 f.

118 Columbia University (Ed.), The Pulitzer Prizes, *op. cit.*, p. 55.

Maxwell Anderson, *The Flowering Peach* by Clifford Odets, *The Desperate Hours* by Joseph Hayes, *Bus Stop* by William Inge and *Cat on a Hot Tin Roof* by Tennessee Williams. In an additional process of selection, it says in the jury-report, "the first to be eliminated was *Cat on a Hot Tin Roof*... The drama is amateurishly constructed, obscure in the solution of the principal problem, shows little intellectual grasp of the material and is from the stylistic points of view annoyingly pretentious. We do not believe that the author should be encouraged in this direction by the award of a Pulitzer Prize."[119] After crossing another two plays off their short-list the jurors stated: "We believe that both *The Bad Seed* and *The Flowering Peach* are greatly superior to the other plays of the season... We believe that *The Flowering Peach* is the strongest contender for the award."[120] But the Advisory Board was not willing to join the verdict of the drama jury. As Hohenberg relates, Joseph Pulitzer Jr., chairman of the Board, had "seen *Cat on a Hot Tin Roof* and thought it worthy of the drama prize. He had little patience with the arguments against its extravagant language and unpleasant sexual themes, but based himself entirely on its effectiveness as a piece of realistic theater. The... Board, after considerable discussion, went along with him and voted for *Cat on a Hot Tin Roof*,"[121] so that Tennessee Williams received his second Pulitzer Prize for drama.[122]

The two members (John M. Brown and Oscar J. Campbell) that made up the jury of 1956 anticipated a certain problem as they attempted to convincingly justify the dramatists ranking first on their list. "The play both of us feel is outstandingly meritorious," they wrote in their report, "is Frances Goodrich's and Albert Hackett's dramatization of *The Diary of Anne Frank*. We are well aware that, according to the terms of the award, the prize should go 'for the American play, preferably original in its source and dealing with American life,' etc., etc. *The Diary of Anne Frank*, we realize, does not deal with American life and is a dramatization. But we feel, and strongly feel, that its merits, sensitivity, and importance are such that they justify ignoring the qualifying clause that begins with 'preferably'... *The Diary of Anne Frank* is a tragedy that happens to be a comedy and a romance. More than being a brilliant and poignant reminder of the agonies through which the world has recently gone, it is a statement, courageous and immensely human, of the need of all of us in our daily lives to live not merely with death but above it.

119 Oscar J. Campbell/Maurice J. Valency, Report of the Pulitzer Prize Drama Jury, New York, March 31, 1955, pp. 1 f.

120 *Ibid.*, pp. 2 f.

121 John Hohenberg, The Pulitzer Prizes, *op. cit.*, p. 261.

122 Columbia University (Ed.), The Pulitzer Prizes, *op. cit.*, p. 55.

BARBARA BEL GEDDES
BURL IVES
in ELIA KAZAN'S
Cat on a Hot Tin Roof
by TENNESSEE WILLIAMS
with MILDRED DUNNOCK
MADELEINE SHERWOOD PAT HINGLE
and BEN GAZZARA
Scenery and Lighting by JO MIELZINER
Costumes by LUCINDA BALLARD
MOROSCO 45th st. West of B'Way · Mats. Wed. and Sat.

Should the Advisory Board feel that *The Diary of Anne Frank* is barred from consideration because of being a dramatization laid in a foreign land, ... (we) recommend *Inherit the Wind*... by Jerome Lawrence and Robert E. Lee... Third in our list of preferences is *Time Limit!*, a melodrama by Henry Denker and Ralph Berkey..."[123] Due to the fact that the vote for the play ranking first was brought forward with so much conviction, Hohenberg relates, "there was no dissent from the Board in 1956,"[124] and so the Pulitzer Prize went to Frances Goodrich and Albert Hackett for *The Diary of Anne Frank*.[125]

With the Pulitzer Prizes celebrating their fortieth anniversary in 1957, one juror, who had been member of the drama jury for several years, took stock. "Looking back over the forty years of its history," he summed up, "we can see that it has reflected the changes in the standards of public taste and that it has been an important factor in effecting these improvements. During these years the standards of the juries and the Advisory Board on Pulitzer Prizes have become increasingly more severe."[126] At that point in time 23 Broadway production were eligible, but the two jurors (John M. Brown and Oscar J. Campbell) were unanimously agreed that only one play should be considered for the award. "By far the most distinguished drama of the season," it can be read in the report, "is Eugene O'Neill's posthumous tragedy, *Long Day's Journey Into Night*. In spite of some of its blemishes – its great length, its tending to repeat and its heavy literary style – it richly deserves the award. In fact, it is the only play by an American author, presented during the current season, that can be regarded as a serious candidate. All competent judges agree that it is one of O'Neill's greatest plays; a few think it is his very greatest. In any case, it is an emotionally overwhelming tragedy. It is frankly autobiographical, for O'Neill faces with courage and tortured sympathy the mental and spiritual anguish of the life of his family during his young manhood."[127] Although *Orpheus Descending* by Tennessee Williams and *A Visit to a Small Planet* by Gore Vidal also made the list of finalists,[128] the Advisory Board also voted for *Long Day's Journey Into Night*, thus granting

123 John M. Brown/Oscar J. Campbell, Report of the Pulitzer Prize Drama Jury, New York, March 27, 1956, pp. 1 f.

124 John Hohenberg, The Pulitzer Prizes, *op. cit.*, p. 263.

125 Columbia University (Ed.), The Pulitzer Prizes, *op. cit.*, p. 55.

126 Oscar J. Campbell, Drama Awards, in: *Columbia Library Columns* (New York), Vol. VI/No. 3, May 1957, pp. 34 f.

127 John M. Brown/Oscar J. Campbell, Report of the Pulitzer Prize Drama Jury, New York, April 1, 1957, p. 1.

128 *Ibid.*, p. 2.

"A MASTERPIECE" —ATKINSON, N. Y. TIMES
"Sheer Magnificence" —CHAPMAN, N. Y. NEWS
LEIGH CONNELL, THEODORE MANN and JOSE QUINTERO
present
FREDRIC FLORENCE
MARCH · ELDRIDGE
in
EUGENE O'NEILL'S
Long Day's Journey Into Night
Directed by JOSÉ QUINTERO
with
JASON ROBARDS, Jr. · BRADFORD DILLMAN
KATHERINE ROSS
Scenery by DAVID HAYS · Lighting by THARON MUSSER · Costumes by MOTLEY
HELEN HAYES THEATRE
46th ST. WEST OF B'WAY
MONDAY THRU SATURDAY EVES. 7:30 (NO MAT. PERFS.)

Eugene O'Neill, several years after the death of the dramatist, his fourth Pulitzer Prize posthumously.[129]

The two jurors of 1958 (John M. Brown and John Gassner) did not find any opportunity to draw up a joint report, but nevertheless they both arrived at exactly the same suggestions in all points. "Just as *Long Day's Journey Into Night* towered above last season's new plays," one member of the jury stated, "so, it seems to me, *Look Homeward, Angel* towers above its competitors this year... It is with pleasure and deep conviction that I recommend Ketti Frings' dramatization of Thomas Wolfe's *Look Homeward, Angel.*"[130] The second juror also recommended "*Look Homeward, Angel* for the Pulitzer Prize as the most distinguished play of the season. It is not only a well written and ably organized work," he continued, "but a probing study of characters who carry much reality and conviction. The play, moreover, not only provides a vivid picture of the environment of one of America's leading literary figures but expresses the more or less universal dreams and tensions of youth in relation with its personal problems and aspirations."[131] Both jurors had as second choice on their list *The Dark at the Top of the Stairs* by William Inge, and both were also of the opinion that *Sunrise at Campobello* by Dore Schary should rank third.[132] The sound reasons given for choosing *Look Homeward, Angel* dispelled any doubts the Advisory Board might have had, and so the Pulitzer Prize was given to Ketti Frings.[133] "Neither the jury nor the Board," Hohenberg points out additionally, "considered Leonard Bernstein's musical evocation of the Romeo and Juliet theme in a New York setting, *West Side Story.*"[134]

129 Columbia University (Ed.), The Pulitzer Prizes, *op. cit.*, p. 55.
130 John M. Brown, Report, New York, March 24, 1958, pp. 1 f.
131 John Gassner, Report, New Haven, Ct., March 21, 1958, p. 1.
132 *Ibid.*
133 Columbia University (Ed.), The Pulitzer Prizes, *op. cit.*, p. 55.
134 John Hohenberg, The Pulitzer Prizes, *op. cit.*, p. 263.

O'NEILL's FIRST PULITZER REWARD

For *„Beyond the Horizon" (1920)*

One of the many Book Editions

The Play and its Public Reception

Eugene O'Neill had to wait until he was 31 years old for his first Broadway production, *Beyond the Horizon*, a tragedy in three acts. When O'Neill's first published play made it on the stage in early 1920, the following drama was presented to the audience in the Morosco Theatre: *Beyond the Horizon* tells the story of brothers Andrew (a farmer) and Robert (a poet). While Andrew plans to inherit the family farm and stay on the land, Robert - now recovered from a lengthy illness - will set sail with his uncle, and venture throughout the world. But before he leaves, Robert discovers his love for the girl-next-door, Ruth Atkins, the woman the families thought would marry Andrew. In newfound romance, Robert stays to farm, while Andrew leaves to the sea. Three years later, Andrew returns to a farm in ruins, his father dead, and Ruth bitter. While fully intending to fix his family, Andrew is called away and returns five years later to a farm even more desolate and in despair. Written in classic Eugene O'Neill style, *Beyond the Horizon* explores the bonds of brotherhood in the face of all adversity - even until the very end.

Most of the New York critics reacted with enthusiasm about the story and its performance. „The fare available for the New York theatergoers," the *New York Times* stated, „is immeasurably richer and more substantial because of a new play which was unfolded yesterday - an absorbing, significant and memorable tragedy, so full of meat that it makes most of the remaining fare seem like the merest meringue. The only reason for not calling *Beyond the Horizon* a great play is the natural gingerliness with which the reviewer uses that word. Certainly, despite a certain clumsiness and confusion in too luxurious multiplicity of scenes, the play has greatness in it, and marks O'Neill as one of our foremost playwrights." Similar feelings expressed the Pulitzer Prize Jurors in their report of May 11, 1920, saying: „The Committee is almost a unit in favor of *Beyond the Horizon*, Eugene O'Neill's play," several of the jury members „are very emphatic on the choice." Since the Advisory Board shared the jury's vote, O'Neill earned his first Pulitzer Prize in the Drama award category.

The play became very successful and reached more than 110 performances. In the words of historian John L. Toohey, the selection of O'Neill's play was „a fine decision, and a courageous one in a way, as the Pulitzer judges had been confronted with a type of art form that simply hadn't existed before. This was the first genuine tragedy that an American playwright had ever written."

THE WORK AND ITS NEW YORK PREMIERE

Beyond the Horizon is the "tale of the woman Ruth, who, faced by the choice between two brothers, marries the romantic Robert rather than the pragmatic Andrew and finds unhappiness," Samuel L. Leiter describes the play's content in short. And Edwin Bronner explains the story more in detail: "New England farmer Robert Mayo, filled with wanderlust and hating the farm on which he was born, is about to leave home on a long sea voyage. Ruth Atkins persuades Robert to stay and marry her, while Robert's prosaic brother Andrew, who really loves the farm, goes on the planned trip. All three fail in their search for meaning in life, none more cruelly than Robert, who dies without having seen beyond the horizon."

The first New York production of *Beyond the Horizon* opened with a special matinee at the Morosco Theatre on February 2, 1920. Following are a scene photo together with main portions of the program containing the original cast:

Mary Jeffery, Erville Alderson, Max Mitzel, Richard Bennett and Edward Arnold

Morosco Theatre

MESSRS. LEE AND J. J. SHUBERT, OWNERS
Forty-fifth Street, West of Broadway

OLIVER MOROSCO
Lessee and Manager

Telephone Bryant 230

THIS THEATRE, UNDER NORMAL CONDITIONS, WITH EVERY SEAT OCCUPIED, CAN BE EMPTIED IN LESS THAN THREE MINUTES. LOOK AROUND NOW, CHOOSE THE NEAREST EXIT TO YOUR SEAT, AND IN CASE OF DISTURBANCE OF ANY KIND, TO AVOID THE DANGERS OF PANIC, WALK (DO NOT RUN) TO THAT EXIT.
THOMAS J. DRENNAN, Fire Commissioner

SPECIAL MATINEE

FEBRUARY 3, 1920

JOHN D. WILLIAMS

Presents

A New American Tragedy in Three Acts

BEYOND THE HORIZON

By EUGENE G. O'NEILL

Cast of Characters
(In the order of their appearance)

ROBERT MAYO } *sons of James Mayo* { ......RICHARD BENNETT
ANDREW MAYO } { ....EDWARD ARNOLD
RUTH ATKINS........................HELEN MacKELLAR
MAX MITZEL
CAPT. DICK SCOTT, *Mrs. Mayo's brother, of the bark Sunda,*
MRS. KATE MAYO, *wife of James Mayo*..........MARY JEFFERY
JAMES MAYO, *a farmer*.................ERVILLE ALDERSON
MRS. ATKINS, *Ruth's widowed mother*....LOUISE CLOSSER HALE
MARY ....ELFIN FINN
BEN, *a farm hand*......................GEORGE HADDEN
DR. FAWCETT.........................GEORGE RIDDELL

(MISS HELEN MacKELLAR AND MESSRS. ARNOLD AND MITZEL, OF "THE STORM" COMPANY, APPEAR THROUGH THE COURTESY OF MR. GEORGE BROADHURST.)

Synopsis of Scenes

ACT I.

Scene 1—THE ROAD. *Sunset of a day in Spring.*

Scene 2—THE FARM HOUSE.. *The same night.*

ACT II.

Scene 1—THE FARM HOUSE. *Noon of a summer day. Several years later.*

Scene 2—THE TOP OF A HILL OVERLOOKING THE SEA. *The following day.*

ACT III.

THE FARM HOUSE. *Dawn of a day in late Fall. Five years later.*

Staged under the direction of HOMER SAINT-GAUDENS.

Scenery designed and painted by Hewlett & Basing; built by Philip Lennon.
Decorations by Mrs. Sidney Harris.

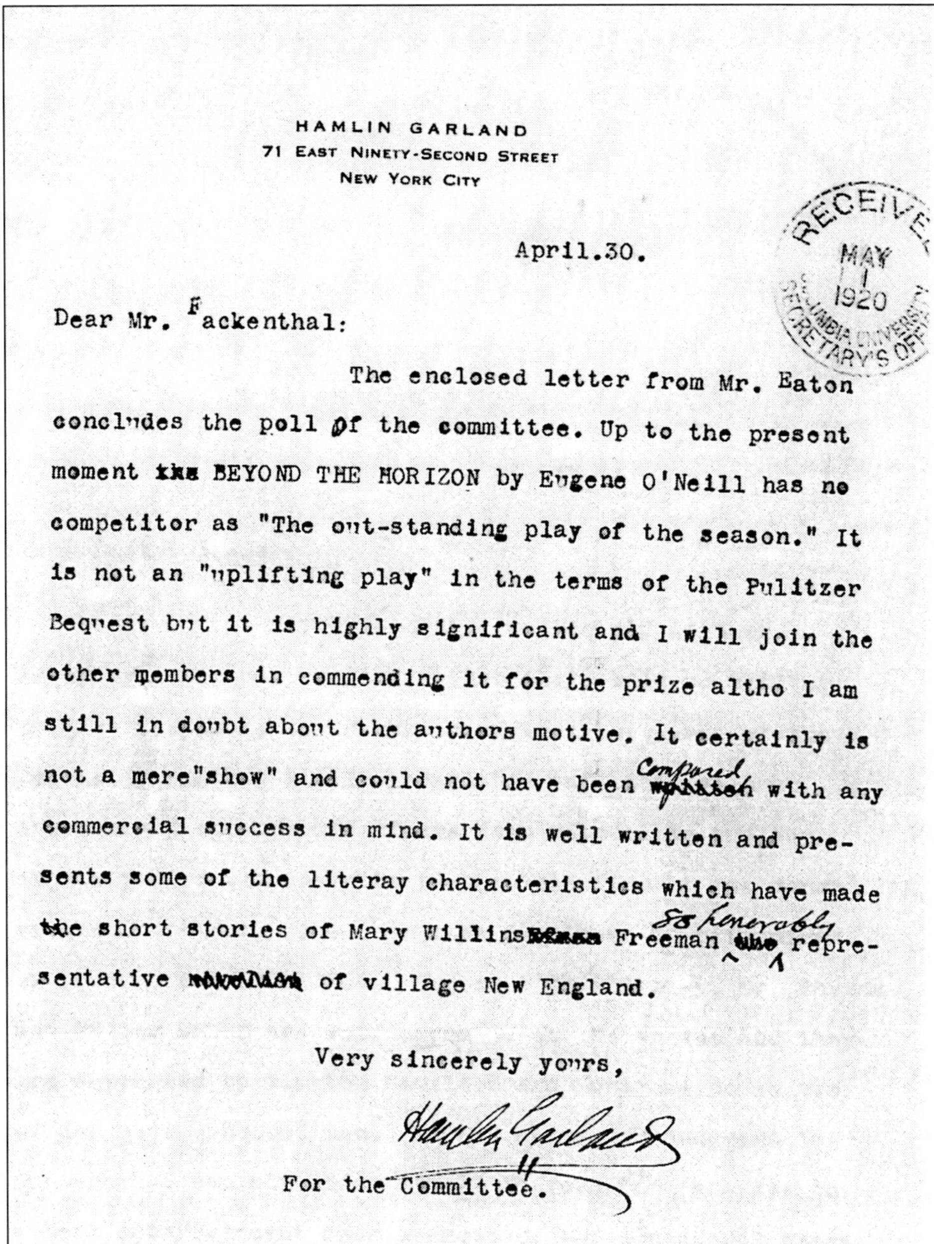
HAMLIN GARLAND
71 EAST NINETY-SECOND STREET
NEW YORK CITY

April.30.

Dear Mr. Fackenthal:

The enclosed letter from Mr. Eaton concludes the poll of the committee. Up to the present moment ~~the~~ BEYOND THE HORIZON by Eugene O'Neill has no competitor as "The out-standing play of the season." It is not an "uplifting play" in the terms of the Pulitzer Bequest but it is highly significant and I will join the other members in commending it for the prize altho I am still in doubt about the authors motive. It certainly is not a mere"show" and could not have been ~~written~~ compared with any commercial success in mind. It is well written and presents some of the literay characteristics which have made the short stories of Mary Willins ~~Eleanor~~ Freeman ~~the~~ so honorably representative ~~novelist~~ of village New England.

Very sincerely yours,

Hamlin Garland

For the Committee.

RECEIVED MAY 1 1920 COLUMBIA UNIVERSITY SECRETARY'S OFFICE

First Part of the Drama Jury Report of April 30, 1920

HAMLIN GARLAND
71 EAST NINETY-SECOND STREET
NEW YORK CITY

Passed

RECEIVED MAY 12 1920 COLUMBIA U. SECRETARY

May 11.

Dear Doctor Butler:

The Committee was deeply disturb-ed by my test query as to whether they would be willing to give the prize to Drinwater,prvided the terms of the Bequest permitted it. The Committee said that such an award would be a rebuff of American authorship and act in a way directly opposite to the intention of the donor of the Endowment. The committee is almost a unit in fav-or of BEYOND THE HORIZON, Eugene O'Neills play. Dr. Burton and Walter Eaton are very emphatic on the choice,and they are supported by Clayton Hamilton and Montrose Moses two of our best informed men. So far as my own judgment is concerned I can not bring myself to vote for a prize to a mere entertainment such as most of the successful plays are, and yet I can not regard O'Neills play as "Noble" or "Uplifting" which are I believe the expredded terms of the bequest. Nevertheless as it is the outstanding play of the season, thus far, I will join in the award.

Hoping this will answer the inquiries of your Advisor, I am very sincerely yours,

Hamlin Garland

Second Part of the Drama Jury Report of May 11, 1920

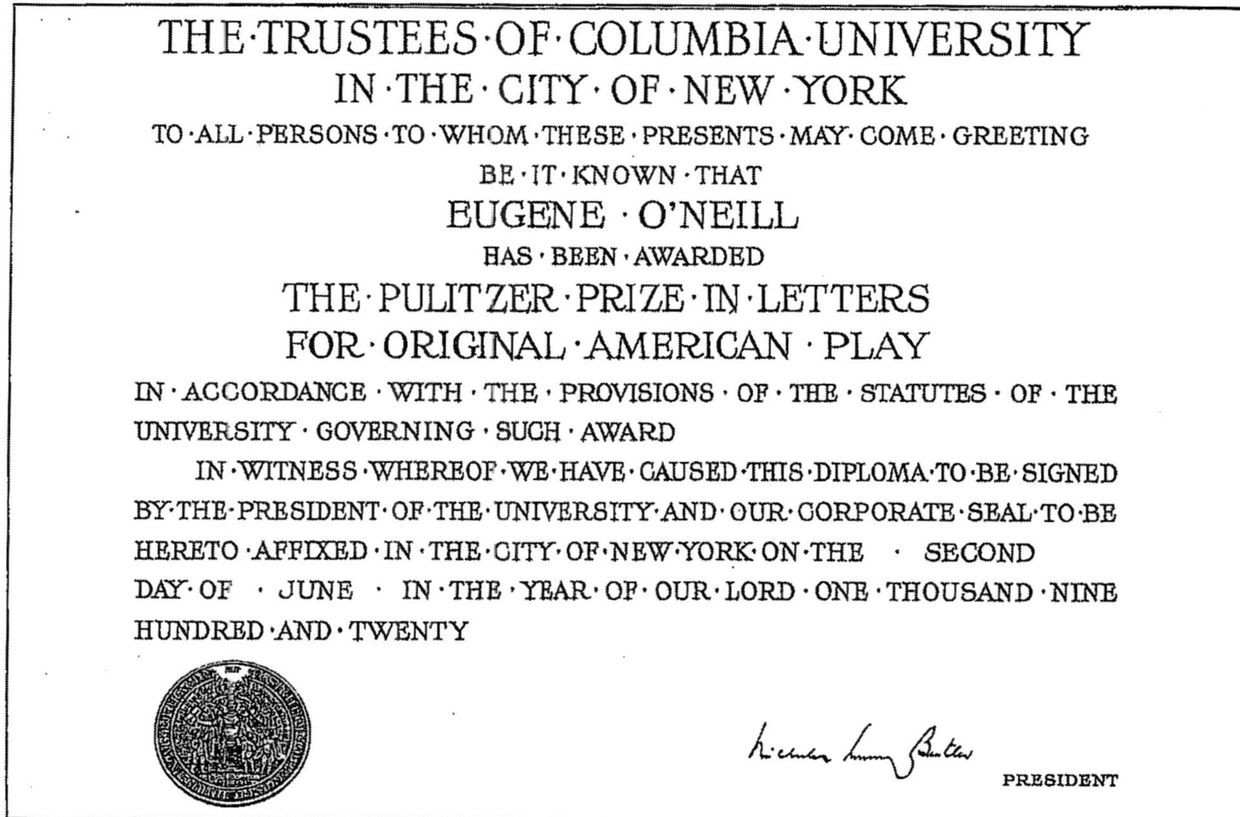

THE·TRUSTEES·OF·COLUMBIA·UNIVERSITY
IN·THE·CITY·OF·NEW·YORK
TO·ALL·PERSONS·TO·WHOM·THESE·PRESENTS·MAY·COME·GREETING
BE·IT·KNOWN·THAT
EUGENE · O'NEILL
HAS·BEEN·AWARDED
THE·PULITZER·PRIZE·IN·LETTERS
FOR·ORIGINAL·AMERICAN·PLAY

IN·ACCORDANCE·WITH·THE·PROVISIONS·OF·THE·STATUTES·OF·THE UNIVERSITY·GOVERNING·SUCH·AWARD

IN·WITNESS·WHEREOF·WE·HAVE·CAUSED·THIS·DIPLOMA·TO·BE·SIGNED BY·THE·PRESIDENT·OF·THE·UNIVERSITY·AND·OUR·CORPORATE·SEAL·TO·BE HERETO·AFFIXED·IN·THE·CITY·OF·NEW·YORK·ON·THE · SECOND DAY·OF · JUNE · IN·THE·YEAR·OF·OUR·LORD·ONE·THOUSAND·NINE HUNDRED·AND·TWENTY

Nicholas Murray Butler
PRESIDENT

Eugene O'Neill's first Pulitzer Prize Certificate for his Play „Beyond the Horizon“, signed by Columbia University President Nicholas Murray Butler on June 2, 1920

The Play's Act One

CHARACTERS

JAMES MAYO, *a farmer*
KATE MAYO, *his wife*
CAPTAIN DICK SCOTT, *of the bark* Sunda, *her brother*
ANDREW MAYO } *sons of James Mayo*
ROBERT MAYO }
RUTH ATKINS
MRS. ATKINS, *her widowed mother*
MARY
BEN, *a farm hand*
DOCTOR FAWCETT

ACT I

SCENE I: The Road. Sunset of a day in Spring.
SCENE II: The Farm House. The same night.

ACT II

(*Three years later*)

SCENE I: The Farm House. Noon of a Summer day.
SCENE II: The top of a hill on the farm overlooking the sea. The following day.

ACT III

(*Five years later*)

SCENE I: The Farm House. Dawn of a day in late Fall.
SCENE II: The Road. Sunrise.

Beyond the Horizon

ACT ONE

Scene One

A section of country highway. The road runs diagonally from the left, forward, to the right, rear, and can be seen in the distance winding toward the horizon like a pale ribbon between the low, rolling hills with their freshly plowed fields clearly divided from each other, checkerboard fashion, by the lines of stone walls and rough snake fences.

The forward triangle cut off by the road is a section of a field from the dark earth of which myriad bright-green blades of fall-sown rye are sprouting. A straggling line of piled rocks, too low to be called a wall, separates this field from the road.

To the rear of the road is a ditch with a sloping, grassy bank on the far side. From the center of this an old, gnarled apple tree, just budding into leaf, strains its twisted branches heavenwards, black against the pallor of distance. A snake-fence sidles from left to right along the top of the bank, passing beneath the apple tree.

The hushed twilight of a day in May is just beginning. The horizon hills are still rimmed by a faint line of flame, and the sky above them glows with the crimson flush of the sunset. This fades gradually as the action of the scene progresses.

At the rise of the curtain, Robert Mayo is discovered sitting on the fence. He is a tall, slender young man of twenty-three. There is a touch of the poet about him expressed in his high forehead and wide, dark eyes. His features are delicate and refined, leaning to weakness in the mouth and chin. He is dressed in gray corduroy trousers pushed into high laced boots, and a blue flannel shirt with a bright colored tie. He is reading a book by the fading sunset light. He shuts this, keeping a finger in to mark the place, and turns his head toward the horizon, gazing out over the fields and hills. His lips move as if he were reciting something to himself.

His brother Andrew comes along the road from the right, returning from his work in the fields. He is twenty-seven years old, an opposite type to Robert—husky, sun-bronzed, handsome in a large-featured, manly fashion—a son of the soil, intelligent in a shrewd way, but with nothing of the intellectual about him. He wears overalls, leather boots, a gray flannel shirt open at the neck, and a soft, mud-stained hat pushed back on his head. He stops to talk to Robert, leaning on the hoe he carries.

ANDREW—(*seeing Robert has not noticed his presence—in a loud shout*) Hey there! (*Robert turns with a start. Seeing who it is, he smiles.*) Gosh, you do take the prize for daydreaming! And I see you've toted one of the old books along with you. (*He crosses the ditch and sits on the fence near his brother.*) What is it this time—poetry, I'll bet. (*He reaches for the book.*) Let me see.

ROBERT—(*handing it to him rather reluctantly*) Look out you don't get it full of dirt.

ANDREW—(*glancing at his hands*) That isn't dirt—it's good clean earth. (*He turns over the pages. His eyes read something and he gives an exclamation of disgust.*) Hump! (*With a provoking grin at his brother he reads aloud in a doleful, sing-song voice*) "I have loved wind and light and the bright sea. But holy and most sacred night, not as I love and have loved thee." (*He hands the book back.*) Here! Take it and bury it. I suppose it's that year in college gave you a liking for that kind of stuff. I'm darn glad I stopped at High School, or maybe I'd been crazy too. (*He grins and slaps Robert on the back affectionately.*) Imagine me reading poetry and plowing at the same time! The team'd run away, I'll bet.

ROBERT—(*laughing*) Or picture me plowing.

ANDREW—You should have gone back to college last fall, like I know you wanted to. You're fitted for that sort of thing—just as I ain't.

ROBERT—You know why I didn't go back, Andy. Pa didn't like the idea, even if he didn't say so; and I know he wanted the money to use improving the farm. And besides, I'm not keen on being a student, just because you see me reading books all the time. What I want to do now is keep on moving so that I won't take root in any one place.

ANDREW—Well, the trip you're leaving on tomorrow will keep you moving all right. (*At this mention of the trip they both fall silent. There is a pause. Finally Andrew goes on, awkwardly, attempting to speak casually.*) Uncle says you'll be gone three years.

ROBERT—About that, he figures.

ANDREW—(*moodily*) That's a long time.

ROBERT—Not so long when you come to consider it. You know the *Sunda* sails around the Horn for Yokohama first, and that's a long voyage on a sailing ship; and if we go to any of the other places Uncle Dick mentions—India, or Australia, or South Africa, or South America—they'll be long voyages, too.

ANDREW—You can have all those foreign parts for all of me. (*after a pause*) Ma's going to miss you a lot, Rob.

ROBERT—Yes—and I'll miss her.

ANDREW—And Pa ain't feeling none too happy to have you go—though he's been trying not to show it.

ROBERT—I can see how he feels.

ANDREW—And you can bet that I'm not giving any cheers about it. (*He puts one hand on the fence near Robert.*)

ROBERT—(*putting one hand on top of Andrew's with a gesture almost of shyness*) I know that, too, Andy.

ANDREW—I'll miss you as much as anybody, I guess. You see, you and I ain't like most brothers—always fighting and separated a lot of the time, while we've always been together—just the two of us. It's different with us. That's why it hits so hard, I guess.

ROBERT—(*with feeling*) It's just as hard for me, Andy—believe that! I hate to leave you and the old folks—but—I feel I've got to. There's something calling me—(*He points to the horizon.*) Oh, I can't just explain it to you, Andy.

ANDREW—No need to, Rob. (*angry at himself*) Hell! You want to go—that's all there is to it; and I wouldn't have you miss this chance for the world.

ROBERT—It's fine of you to feel that way, Andy.

ANDREW—Huh! I'd be a nice son-of-a-gun if I didn't, wouldn't I? When I know how you need this sea trip to make a new man of you—in the body, I mean—and give you your full health back.

ROBERT—(*a trifle impatiently*) All of you seem to keep harping on my health. You were so used to seeing me lying around the house in the old days that you never will get over the notion that I'm a chronic invalid. You don't realize how

I've bucked up in the past few years. If I had no other excuse for going on Uncle Dick's ship but just my health, I'd stay right here and start in plowing.

ANDREW—Can't be done. Farming ain't your nature. There's all the difference shown in just the way us two feel about the farm. You—well, you like the home part of it, I expect; but as a place to work and grow things, you hate it. Ain't that right?

ROBERT—Yes, I suppose it is. For you it's different. You're a Mayo through and through. You're wedded to the soil. You're as much a product of it as an ear of corn is, or a tree. Father is the same. This farm is his life-work, and he's happy in knowing that another Mayo, inspired by the same love, will take up the work where he leaves off. I can understand your attitude, and Pa's; and I think it's wonderful and sincere. But I—well, I'm not made that way.

ANDREW—No, you ain't; but when it comes to understanding, I guess I realize that you've got your own angle of looking at things.

ROBERT—(*musingly*) I wonder if you do, really.

ANDREW—(*confidently*) Sure I do. You've seen a bit of the world, enough to make the farm seem small, and you've got the itch to see it all.

ROBERT—It's more than that, Andy.

ANDREW—Oh, of course. I know you're going to learn navigation, and all about a ship, so's you can be an officer. That's natural, too. There's fair pay in it, I expect, when you consider that you've always got a home and grub thrown in; and if you're set on traveling, you can go anywhere you're a mind to without paying fare.

ROBERT—(*with a smile that is half sad*) It's more than that, Andy.

ANDREW—Sure it is. There's always a chance of a good thing coming your way in some of those foreign ports or other. I've heard there are great opportunities for a young fellow with his eyes open in some of those new countries that are just being opened up. (*jovially*) I'll bet that's what you've been turning over in your mind under all your quietness! (*He slaps his brother on the back with a laugh.*) Well, if you get to be a millionaire all of a sudden, call 'round once in a while and I'll pass the plate to you. We could use a lot of money right here on the farm without hurting it any.

ROBERT—(*forced to laugh*) I've never considered that practical side of it for a minute, Andy.

ANDREW—Well, you ought to.

ROBERT—No, I oughtn't. (*pointing to the horizon—dreamily*) Supposing I was to tell you that it's just Beauty that's calling me, the beauty of the far off and unknown, the mystery and spell of the East which lures me in the books I've read, the need of the freedom of great wide spaces, the joy of wandering on and on—in quest of the secret which is hidden over there, beyond the horizon? Suppose I told you that was the one and only reason for my going?

ANDREW—I should say you were nutty.

ROBERT—(*frowning*) Don't, Andy. I'm serious.

ANDREW—Then you might as well stay here, because we've got all you're looking for right on this farm. There's wide space enough, Lord knows; and you can have all the sea you want by walking a mile down to the beach; and there's plenty of horizon to look at, and beauty enough for anyone, except in the winter. (*He grins.*) As for the mystery and spell, I haven't met 'em yet, but they're probably lying around somewheres. I'll have you understand this is a first class farm with all the fixings. (*He laughs.*)

ROBERT—(*joining in the laughter in spite of himself*) It's no use talking to you, you chump!

ANDREW—You'd better not say anything to Uncle Dick about spells and things when you're on the ship. He'll likely chuck you overboard for a Jonah. (*He jumps down from fence.*) I'd better run along. I've got to wash up some as long as Ruth's Ma is coming over for supper.

ROBERT—(*pointedly—almost bitterly*) And Ruth.

ANDREW—(*confused—looking everywhere except at Robert—trying to appear unconcerned*) Yes, Ruth'll be staying too. Well, I better hustle, I guess, and— (*He steps over the ditch to the road while he is talking.*)

ROBERT—(*who appears to be fighting some strong inward emotion—impulsively*) Wait a minute, Andy! (*He jumps down from the fence.*) There is something I want to— (*He stops abruptly, biting his lips, his face coloring.*)

ANDREW—(*facing him; half-defiantly*) Yes?

ROBERT—(*confusedly*) No— never mind—it doesn't matter, it was nothing.

ANDREW—(*after a pause, during which he stares fixedly at Robert's averted face*) Maybe I can guess—what you were going to say—but I guess you're right not to talk about it. (*He pulls Robert's hand from his side and grips it tensely; the two brothers stand looking into each other's eyes for a minute.*) We can't help those things, Rob. (*He turns away, suddenly releasing Robert's hand.*) You'll be coming along shortly, won't you?

ROBERT—(*dully*) Yes.

ANDREW—See you later, then. (*He walks off down the road to the left. Robert stares after him for a moment; then climbs to the fence rail again, and looks out over the hills, an expression of deep grief on his face. After a moment or so, Ruth enters hurriedly from the left. She is a healthy, blonde, out-of-door girl of twenty, with a graceful, slender figure. Her face, though inclined to roundness, is undeniably pretty, its large eyes of a deep blue set off strikingly by the sun-bronzed complexion. Her small, regular features are marked by a certain strength—an underlying, stubborn fixity of purpose hidden in the frankly-appealing charm of her fresh youthfulness. She wears a simple white dress but no hat.*)

RUTH—(*seeing him*) Hello, Rob!

ROBERT—(*startled*) Hello, Ruth!

RUTH—(*jumps the ditch and perches on the fence beside him*) I was looking for you.

ROBERT—(*pointedly*) Andy just left here.

RUTH—I know. I met him on the road a second ago. He told me you were here. (*tenderly playful*) I wasn't looking for Andy, Smarty, if that's what you mean. I was looking for you.

ROBERT—Because I'm going away tomorrow?

RUTH—Because your mother was anxious to have you come home and asked me to look for you. I just wheeled Ma over to your house.

ROBERT—(*perfunctorily*) How is your mother?

RUTH—(*a shadow coming over her face*) She's about the same. She never seems to get any better or any worse. Oh,

Rob, I do wish she'd try to make the best of things that can't be helped.

ROBERT—Has she been nagging at you again?

RUTH—(*nods her head, and then breaks forth rebelliously*) She never stops nagging. No matter what I do for her she finds fault. If only Pa was still living— (*She stops as if ashamed of her outburst.*) I suppose I shouldn't complain this way. (*She sighs.*) Poor Ma, Lord knows it's hard enough for her. I suppose it's natural to be cross when you're not able ever to walk a step. Oh, I'd like to be going away some place—like you!

ROBERT—It's hard to stay—and equally hard to go, sometimes.

RUTH—There! If I'm not the stupid body! I swore I wasn't going to speak about your trip—until after you'd gone; and there I go, first thing!

ROBERT—Why didn't you want to speak of it?

RUTH—Because I didn't want to spoil this last night you're here. Oh, Rob, I'm going to—we're all going to miss you so awfully. Your mother is going around looking as if she'd burst out crying any minute. You ought to know how I feel. Andy and you and I—why it seems as if we'd always been together.

ROBERT—(*with a wry attempt at a smile*) You and Andy will still have each other. It'll be harder for me without anyone.

RUTH—But you'll have new sights and new people to take your mind off; while we'll be here with the old, familiar place to remind us every minute of the day. It's a shame you're going—just at this time, in spring, when everything is getting so nice. (*with a sigh*) I oughtn't to talk that way when I know going's the best thing for you. You're bound to find all sorts of opportunities to get on, your father says.

ROBERT—(*heatedly*) I don't give a damn about that! I wouldn't take a voyage across the road for the best opportunity in the world of the kind Pa thinks of. (*He smiles at his own irritation.*) Excuse me, Ruth, for getting worked up over it; but Andy gave me an overdose of the practical considerations.

RUTH—(*slowly, puzzled*) Well, then, if it isn't— (*with sudden intensity*) Oh, Rob, why *do* you want to go?

ROBERT—(*turning to her quickly, in surprise—slowly*) Why do you ask that, Ruth?

RUTH—(*dropping her eyes before his searching glance*) Because— (*lamely*) It seems such a shame.

ROBERT—(*insistently*) Why?

RUTH—Oh, because—everything.

ROBERT—I could hardly back out now, even if I wanted to. And I'll be forgotten before you know it.

RUTH—(*indignantly*) You won't! I'll never forget— (*She stops and turns away to hide her confusion.*)

ROBERT—(*softly*) Will you promise me that?

RUTH—(*evasively*) Of course. It's mean of you to think that any of us would forget so easily.

ROBERT—(*disappointedly*) Oh!

RUTH—(*with an attempt at lightness*) But you haven't told me your reason for leaving yet?

ROBERT—(*moodily*) I doubt if you'll understand. It's difficult to explain, even to myself. Either you feel it, or you don't. I can remember being conscious of it first when I was only a kid—you haven't forgotten what a sickly specimen I was then, in those days, have you?

RUTH—(*with a shudder*) Let's not think about them.

ROBERT—You'll have to, to understand. Well, in those days, when Ma was fixing meals, she used to get me out of the way by pushing my chair to the west window and telling me to look out and be quiet. That wasn't hard. I guess I was always quiet.

RUTH—(*compassionately*) Yes, you always were—and you suffering so much, too!

ROBERT—(*musingly*) So I used to stare out over the fields to the hills, out there—(*he points to the horizon*) and somehow after a time I'd forget any pain I was in, and start dreaming. I knew the sea was over beyond those hills,—the folks had told me—and I used to wonder what the sea was like, and try to form a picture of it in my mind. (*with a smile*) There was all the mystery in the world to me then about that—far-off sea—and there still is! It called to me then just as it does now. (*after a slight pause*) And other times my eyes would follow this road, winding off into the distance, toward the hills, as if it, too, was searching for the sea. And I'd promise myself that when I grew up and was strong, I'd follow that road, and it and I would find the sea together. (*with a smile*) You see, my making this trip is only keeping that promise of long ago.

RUTH—(*charmed by his low, musical voice telling the dreams of his childhood*) Yes, I see.

ROBERT—Those were the only happy moments of my life then, dreaming there at the window. I liked to be all alone—those times. I got to know all the different kinds of sunsets by heart. And all those sunsets took place over there—(*he points*) beyond the horizon. So gradually I came to believe that all the wonders of the world happened on the other side of those hills. There was the home of the good fairies who performed beautiful miracles. I believed in fairies then. (*with a smile*) Perhaps I still do believe in them. Anyway, in those days they were real enough, and sometimes I could actually hear them calling to me to come out and play with them, dance with them down the road in the dusk in a game of hide-and-seek to find out where the sun was hiding himself. They sang their little songs to me, songs that told of all the wonderful things they had in their home on the other side of the hills; and they promised to show me all of them, if I'd only come, come! But I couldn't come then, and I used to cry sometimes and Ma would think I was in pain. (*He breaks off suddenly with a laugh.*) That's why I'm going now, I suppose. For I can still hear them calling. But the horizon is as far away and as luring as ever. (*He turns to her—softly*) Do you understand now, Ruth?

RUTH—(*spellbound, in a whisper*) Yes.

ROBERT—You feel it then?

RUTH—Yes, yes, I do! (*Unconsciously she snuggles close against his side. His arm steals about her as if he were not aware of the action.*) Oh, Rob, how could I help feeling it? You tell things so beautifully!

ROBERT—(*suddenly realizing that his arm is around her, and that her head is resting on his shoulder, gently takes his arm away.*

Ruth, brought back to herself, is overcome with confusion.) So now you know why I'm going. It's for that reason—that and one other.

RUTH—You've another? Then you must tell me that, too.

ROBERT—(*looking at her searchingly. She drops her eyes before his gaze.*) I wonder if I ought to! You'll promise not to be angry—whatever it is?

RUTH—(*softly, her face still averted*) Yes, I promise.

ROBERT—(*simply*) I love you. That's the other reason.

RUTH—(*hiding her face in her hands*) Oh, Rob!

ROBERT—I wasn't going to tell you, but I feel I have to. It can't matter now that I'm going so far away, and for so long—perhaps forever. I've loved you all these years, but the realization never came 'til I agreed to go away with Uncle Dick. Then I thought of leaving you, and the pain of that thought revealed to me in a flash—that I loved you, had loved you as long as I could remember. (*He gently pulls one of Ruth's hands away from her face.*) You mustn't mind my telling you this, Ruth. I realize how impossible it all is—and I understand; for the revelation of my own love seemed to open my eyes to the love of others. I saw Andy's love for you—and I knew that you must love him.

RUTH—(*breaking out stormily*) I don't! I don't love Andy! I don't! (*Robert stares at her in stupid astonishment. Ruth weeps hysterically.*) Whatever—put such a fool notion into—into your head? (*She suddenly throws her arms about his neck and hides her head on his shoulder.*) Oh, Rob! Don't go away! Please! You mustn't, now! You can't! I won't let you! It'd break my—my heart!

ROBERT—(*the expression of stupid bewilderment giving way to one of overwhelming joy. He presses her close to him—slowly and tenderly*) Do you mean that—that you love me?

RUTH—(*sobbing*) Yes, yes—of course I do—what d'you s'pose? (*She lifts up her head and looks into his eyes with a tremulous smile.*) You stupid thing! (*He kisses her.*) I've loved you right along.

ROBERT—(*mystified*) But you and Andy were always together!

RUTH—Because you never seemed to want to go any place with me. You were always reading an old book, and not paying any attention to me. I was too proud to let you see I cared because I thought the year you had away to college had made you stuck-up, and you thought yourself too educated to waste any time on me.

ROBERT—(*kissing her*) And I was thinking— (*with a laugh*) What fools we've both been!

RUTH—(*overcome by a sudden fear*) You won't go away on the trip, will you, Rob? You'll tell them you can't go on account of me, won't you? You can't go now! You can't!

ROBERT—(*bewildered*) Perhaps—you can come too.

RUTH—Oh, Rob, don't be so foolish. You know I can't. Who'd take care of ma? Don't you see I couldn't go—on her account? (*She clings to him imploringly.*) Please don't go—not now. Tell them you've decided not to. They won't mind. I know your mother and father'll be glad. They'll all be. They don't want you to go so far away from them. Please, Rob! We'll be so happy here together where it's natural and we know things. Please tell me you won't go!

ROBERT—(*face to face with a definite, final decision, betrays the conflict going on within him*) But—Ruth—I—Uncle Dick—

RUTH—He won't mind when he knows it's for your happiness to stay. How could he? (*As Robert remains silent she bursts into sobs again.*) Oh, Rob! And you said—you loved me!

ROBERT—(*conquered by this appeal—an irrevocable decision in his voice*) I won't go, Ruth. I promise you. There! Don't cry! (*He presses her to him, stroking her hair tenderly. After a pause he speaks with happy hopefulness.*) Perhaps after all Andy was right—righter than he knew—when he said I could find all the things I was seeking for here, at home on the farm. I think love must have been the secret—the secret that called to me from over the world's rim—the secret beyond every horizon; and when I did not come, it came to me. (*He clasps Ruth to him fiercely.*) Oh, Ruth, our love is sweeter than any distant dream! (*He kisses her passionately and steps to the ground, lifting Ruth in his arms and carrying her to the road where he puts her down.*)

RUTH—(*with a happy laugh*) My, but you're strong!

ROBERT—Come! We'll go and tell them at once.

RUTH—(*dismayed*) Oh, no, don't, Rob, not 'til after I've

gone. There'd be bound to be such a scene with them all together.

ROBERT—(*kissing her—gayly*) As you like—little Miss Common Sense!

RUTH—Let's go, then. (*She takes his hand, and they start to go off left. Robert suddenly stops and turns as though for a last look at the hills and the dying sunset flush.*)

ROBERT—(*looking upward and pointing*) See! The first star. (*He bends down and kisses her tenderly.*) *Our* star!

RUTH—(*in a soft murmur*) Yes. Our very own star. (*They stand for a moment looking up at it, their arms around each other. Then Ruth takes his hand again and starts to lead him away.*) Come, Rob, let's go. (*His eyes are fixed again on the horizon as he half turns to follow her. Ruth urges*) We'll be late for supper, Rob.

ROBERT—(*shakes his head impatiently, as though he were throwing off some disturbing thought—with a laugh*) All right. We'll run then. Come on! (*They run off laughing as*

The Curtain Falls)

SCENE TWO

The sitting room of the Mayo farm house about nine o'clock the same night. On the left, two windows looking out on the fields. Against the wall between the windows, an old-fashioned walnut desk. In the left corner, rear, a sideboard with a mirror. In the rear wall to the right of the sideboard, a window looking out on the road. Next to the window a door leading out into the yard. Farther right, a black horse-hair sofa, and another door opening on a bedroom. In the corner, a straight-backed chair. In the right wall, near the middle, an open doorway leading to the kitchen. Farther forward a double-heater stove with coal scuttle, etc. In the center of the newly carpeted floor, an oak dining-room table with a red cover. In the center of the table, a large oil reading lamp. Four chairs, three rockers with crocheted tidies on their backs, and one straight-backed, are placed about the table. The walls are papered a dark red with a scrolly-figured pattern.

Everything in the room is clean, well-kept, and in its exact place, yet there is no suggestion of primness about the whole. Rather the atmosphere is one of the orderly comfort of a simple, hard-earned prosperity, enjoyed and maintained by the family as a unit.

James Mayo, his wife, her brother, Captain Dick Scott, and Andrew are discovered. Mayo is his son Andrew over again in body and face—an Andrew sixty-five years old with a short, square, white beard. Mrs. Mayo is a slight, round-faced, rather prim-looking woman of fifty-five who had once been a school teacher. The labors of a farmer's wife have bent but not broken her, and she retains a certain refinement of movement and expression foreign to the Mayo part of the family. Whatever of resemblance Robert has to his parents may be traced to her. Her brother, the Captain, is short and stocky, with a weather-beaten, jovial face and a white mustache—a typical old salt, loud of voice and given to gesture. He is fifty-eight years old.

James Mayo sits in front of the table. He wears spectacles, and a farm journal which he has been reading lies in his lap. The Captain leans forward from a chair in the rear, his hands on the table in front of him. Andrew is tilted back on the straight-backed chair to the left, his chin sunk forward on his chest, staring at the carpet, preoccupied and frowning.

As the Curtain rises the Captain is just finishing the relation of some sea episode. The others are pretending an interest which is belied by the absent-minded expressions on their faces.

THE CAPTAIN—(*chuckling*) And that mission woman, she hails me on the dock as I was acomin' ashore, and she says—with her silly face all screwed up serious as judgment—"Captain," she says, "would you be so kind as to tell me where the sea-gulls sleeps at nights?" Blow me if them warn't her exact words! (*He slaps the table with the palm of his hands and laughs loudly. The others force smiles.*) Ain't that just like a fool woman's question? And I looks at her serious as I could, "Ma'm," says I, "I couldn't rightly answer that question. I ain't never seed a sea-gull in his bunk yet. The next time I hears one snorin'," I says, "I'll make a note of where he's turned in, and write you a letter 'bout it." And then she calls me a fool real spiteful and tacks away from me quick. (*He laughs again uproariously.*) So I got rid of her that way.

(The others smile but immediately relapse into expressions of gloom again.)

MRS. MAYO—*(absent-mindedly—feeling that she has to say something)* But when it comes to that, where *do* sea-gulls sleep, Dick?

SCOTT—*(slapping the table)* Ho! Ho! Listen to her, James. 'Nother one! Well, if that don't beat all hell—'scuse me for cussin', Kate.

MAYO—*(with a twinkle in his eyes)* They unhitch their wings, Katey, and spreads 'em out on a wave for a bed.

SCOTT—And then they tells the fish to whistle to 'em when it's time to turn out. Ho! Ho!

MRS. MAYO—*(with a forced smile)* You men folks are too smart to live, aren't you? *(She resumes her knitting. Mayo pretends to read his paper; Andrew stares at the floor.)*

SCOTT—*(looks from one to the other of them with a puzzled air. Finally he is unable to bear the thick silence a minute longer, and blurts out)* You folks look as if you was settin' up with a corpse. *(with exaggerated concern)* God A'mighty, there ain't anyone dead, be there?

MAYO—*(sharply)* Don't play the dunce, Dick! You know as well as we do there ain't no great cause to be feelin' chipper.

SCOTT—*(argumentatively)* And there ain't no cause to be wearin' mourning, either, I can make out.

MRS. MAYO—*(indignantly)* How can you talk that way, Dick Scott, when you're taking our Robbie away from us, in the middle of the night, you might say, just to get on that old boat of yours on time! I think you might wait until morning when he's had his breakfast.

SCOTT—*(appealing to the others hopelessly)* Ain't that a woman's way o' seein' things for you? God A'mighty, Kate, I can't give orders to the tide that it's got to be high just when it suits me to have it. I ain't gettin' no fun out o' missin' sleep and leavin' here at six bells myself. *(protestingly)* And the *Sunda* ain't an old ship—leastways, not very old—and she's good's she ever was.

MRS. MAYO—*(her lips trembling)* I wish Robbie weren't going.

MAYO—*(looking at her over his glasses—consolingly)* There, Katey!

MRS. MAYO—(*rebelliously*) Well, I *do* wish he wasn't!

SCOTT—You shouldn't be taking it so hard, 's far as I kin see. This vige'll make a man of him. I'll see to it he learns how to navigate, 'n' study for a mate's c'tificate right off—and it'll give him a trade for the rest of his life, if he wants to travel.

MRS. MAYO—But I don't want him to travel all his life. You've got to see he comes home when this trip is over. Then he'll be all well, and he'll want to—to marry—(*Andrew sits forward in his chair with an abrupt movement*)—and settle down right here. (*She stares down at the knitting in her lap—after a pause*) I never realized how hard it was going to be for me to have Robbie go—or I wouldn't have considered it a minute.

SCOTT—It ain't no good goin' on that way, Kate, now it's all settled.

MRS. MAYO—(*on the verge of tears*) It's all right for *you* to talk. You've never had any children. You don't know what it means to be parted from them—and Robbie my youngest, too. (*Andrew frowns and fidgets in his chair.*)

ANDREW—(*suddenly turning to them*) There's one thing none of you seem to take into consideration—that Rob wants to go. He's dead set on it. He's been dreaming over this trip ever since it was first talked about. It wouldn't be fair to him not to have him go. (*A sudden uneasiness seems to strike him.*) At least, not if he still feels the same way about it he did when he was talking to me this evening.

MAYO—(*with an air of decision*) Andy's right, Katey. That ends all argyment, you can see that. (*looking at his big silver watch*) Wonder what's happened to Robert? He's been gone long enough to wheel the widder to home, certain. He can't be out dreamin' at the stars his last night.

MRS. MAYO—(*a bit reproachfully*) Why didn't you wheel Mrs. Atkins back tonight, Andy? You usually do when she and Ruth come over.

ANDREW—(*avoiding her eyes*) I thought maybe Robert wanted to tonight. He offered to go right away when they were leaving.

MRS. MAYO—He only wanted to be polite.

ANDREW—(*gets to his feet*) Well, he'll be right back, I

guess. (*He turns to his father.*) Guess I'll go take a look at the black cow, Pa—see if she's ailing any.

MAYO—Yes—better had, son. (*Andrew goes into the kitchen on the right.*)

SCOTT—(*as he goes out—in a low tone*) There's the boy that would make a good, strong sea-farin' man—if he'd a mind to.

MAYO—(*sharply*) Don't you put no such fool notions in Andy's head, Dick—or you 'n' me's goin' to fall out. (*Then he smiles.*) You couldn't tempt him, no ways. Andy's a Mayo bred in the bone, and he's a born farmer, and a damn good one, too. He'll live and die right here on this farm, like I expect to. (*with proud confidence*) And he'll make this one of the slickest, best-payin' farms in the state, too, afore he gits through!

SCOTT—Seems to me it's a pretty slick place right now.

MAYO—(*shaking his head*) It's too small. We need more land to make it amount to much, and we ain't got the capital to buy it. (*Andrew enters from the kitchen. His hat is on, and he carries a lighted lantern in his hand. He goes to the door in the rear leading out.*)

ANDREW—(*opens the door and pauses*) Anything else you can think of to be done, Pa?

MAYO—No, nothin' I know of. (*Andrew goes out, shutting the door.*)

MRS. MAYO—(*after a pause*) What's come over Andy tonight, I wonder? He acts so strange.

MAYO—He does seem sort o' glum and out of sorts. It's 'count o' Robert leavin', I s'pose. (*to Scott*) Dick, you wouldn't believe how them boys o' mine sticks together. They ain't like most brothers. They've been thick as thieves all their lives, with nary a quarrel I kin remember.

SCOTT—No need to tell me that. I can see how they take to each other.

MRS. MAYO—(*pursuing her train of thought*) Did you notice, James, how queer everyone was at supper? Robert seemed stirred up about something; and Ruth was so flustered and giggly; and Andy sat there dumb, looking as if he'd lost his best friend; and all of them only nibbled at their food.

MAYO—Guess they was all thinkin' about tomorrow, same as us.

MRS. MAYO—(*shaking her head*) No. I'm afraid somethin's happened—somethin' else.

MAYO—You mean—'bout Ruth?

MRS. MAYO—Yes.

MAYO—(*after a pause—frowning*) I hope her and Andy ain't had a serious fallin'-out. I always sorter hoped they'd hitch up together sooner or later. What d'you say, Dick? Don't you think them two'd pair up well?

SCOTT—(*nodding his head approvingly*) A sweet, wholesome couple they'd make.

MAYO—It'd be a good thing for Andy in more ways than one. I ain't what you'd call calculatin' generally, and I b'lieve in lettin' young folks run their affairs to suit themselves; but there's advantages for both o' them in this match you can't overlook in reason. The Atkins farm is right next to ourn. Jined together they'd make a jim-dandy of a place, with plenty o' room to work in. And bein' a widder with only a daughter, and laid up all the time to boot, Mrs. Atkins can't do nothin' with the place as it ought to be done. She needs a man, a first-class farmer, to take hold o' things; and Andy's just the one.

MRS. MAYO—(*abruptly*) I don't think Ruth loves Andy.

MAYO—You don't? Well, maybe a woman's eyes is sharper in such things, but—they're always together. And if she don't love him now, she'll likely come around to it in time. (*as Mrs. Mayo shakes her head*) You seem mighty fixed in your opinion, Katey. How d'you know?

MRS. MAYO—It's just—what I feel.

MAYO—(*a light breaking over him*) You don't mean to say— (*Mrs. Mayo nods. Mayo chuckles scornfully.*) Shucks! I'm losin' my respect for your eyesight, Katey. Why, Robert ain't got no time for Ruth, 'cept as a friend!

MRS. MAYO—(*warningly*) Sss-h-h! (*The door from the yard opens, and Robert enters. He is smiling happily, and humming a song to himself, but as he comes into the room an undercurrent of nervous uneasiness manifests itself in his bearing.*)

MAYO—So here you be at last! (*Robert comes forward and sits on Andy's chair. Mayo smiles slyly at his wife.*) What have you been doin' all this time—countin' the stars to see if they all come out right and proper?

ROBERT—There's only one I'll ever look for any more, Pa.

MAYO—(*reproachfully*) You might've even not wasted time lookin' for that one—your last night.

MRS. MAYO—(*as if she were speaking to a child*) You ought to have worn your coat a sharp night like this, Robbie.

SCOTT—(*disgustedly*) God A'mighty, Kate, you treat Robert as if he was one year old!

MRS. MAYO—(*notices Robert's nervous uneasiness*) You look all worked up over something, Robbie. What is it?

ROBERT—(*swallowing hard, looks quickly from one to the other of them—then begins determinedly*) Yes, there *is* something—something I must tell you—all of you. (*As he begins to talk Andrew enters quietly from the rear, closing the door behind him, and setting the lighted lantern on the floor. He remains standing by the door, his arms folded, listening to Robert with a repressed expression of pain on his face. Robert is so much taken up with what he is going to say that he does not notice Andrew's presence.*) Something I discovered only this evening—very beautiful and wonderful—something I did not take into consideration previously because I hadn't dared to hope that such happiness could ever come to me. (*appealingly*) You must all remember that fact, won't you?

MAYO—(*frowning*) Let's get to the point, son.

ROBERT—(*with a trace of defiance*) Well, the point is this, Pa: I'm not going—I mean—I can't go tomorrow with Uncle Dick—or at any future time, either.

MRS. MAYO—(*with a sharp sigh of joyful relief*) Oh, Robbie, I'm so glad!

MAYO—(*astounded*) You ain't serious, be you, Robert? (*severely*) Seems to me it's a pretty late hour in the day for you to be upsettin' all your plans so sudden!

ROBERT—I asked you to remember that until this evening I didn't know myself. I had never dared to dream—

MAYO—(*irritably*) What is this foolishness you're talkin' of?

ROBERT—(*flushing*) Ruth told me this evening that—she loved me. It was after I'd confessed I loved her. I told her I hadn't been conscious of my love until after the trip had been arranged, and I realized it would mean—leaving her. That was the truth. I *didn't* know until then. (*as if justifying himself to the others*) I hadn't intended telling her anything but—suddenly—I felt I must. I didn't think it would matter, because I was going away. And I thought she loved—someone else. (*slowly—his eyes shining*) And then she cried and said it was I she'd loved all the time, but I hadn't seen it.

MRS. MAYO—(*rushes over and throws her arms about him*) I knew it! I was just telling your father when you came in—and, Oh, Robbie, I'm so happy you're not going!

ROBERT—(*kissing her*) I knew you'd be glad, Ma.

MAYO—(*bewilderedly*) Well, I'll be damned! You do beat all for gettin' folks' minds all tangled up, Robert. And Ruth too! Whatever got into her of a sudden? Why, I was thinkin'—

MRS. MAYO—(*hurriedly—in a tone of warning*) Never mind what you were thinking, James. It wouldn't be any use telling us that now. (*meaningly*) And what you were hoping for turns out just the same almost, doesn't it?

MAYO—(*thoughtfully—beginning to see this side of the argument*) Yes; I suppose you're right, Katey. (*scratching his head in puzzlement*) But how it ever come about! It do beat anything ever I heard. (*Finally he gets up with a sheepish grin and walks over to Robert.*) We're glad you ain't goin', your Ma and I, for we'd have missed you terrible, that's certain and sure; and we're glad you've found happiness. Ruth's a fine girl and'll make a good wife to you.

ROBERT—(*much moved*) Thank you, Pa. (*He grips his father's hand in his.*)

ANDREW—(*his face tense and drawn comes forward and holds out his hand, forcing a smile*) I guess it's my turn to offer congratulations, isn't it?

ROBERT—(*with a startled cry when his brother appears before him so suddenly*) Andy! (*confused*) Why—I—I didn't see you. Were you here when—

ANDREW—I heard everything you said; and here's wishing you every happiness, you and Ruth. You both deserve the best there is.

ROBERT—(*taking his hand*) Thanks, Andy, it's fine of you to— (*His voice dies away as he sees the pain in Andrew's eyes.*)

ANDREW—(*giving his brother's hand a final grip*) Good luck to you both! (*He turns away and goes back to the rear where he bends over the lantern, fumbling with it to hide his emotion from the others.*)

MRS. MAYO—(*to the Captain, who has been too flabbergasted by Robert's decision to say a word*) What's the matter, Dick? Aren't you going to congratulate Robbie?

SCOTT—(*embarrassed*) Of course I be! (*He gets to his feet and shakes Robert's hand, muttering a vague*) Luck to you, boy. (*He stands beside Robert as if he wanted to say something more but doesn't know how to go about it.*)

ROBERT—Thanks, Uncle Dick.

SCOTT—So you're not acomin' on the *Sunda* with me? (*His voice indicates disbelief.*)

ROBERT—I can't, Uncle—not now. I wouldn't miss it for anything else in the world under any other circumstances. (*He sighs unconsciously.*) But you see I've found—a bigger dream. (*then with joyous high spirits*) I want you all to understand one thing—I'm not going to be a loafer on your hands any longer. This means the beginning of a new life for me in every way. I'm going to settle right down and take a real interest in the farm, and do my share. I'll prove to you, Pa, that I'm as good a Mayo as you are—or Andy, when I want to be.

MAYO—(*kindly but skeptically*) That's the right spirit, Robert. Ain't none of us doubts your willin'ness, but you ain't never learned—

ROBERT—Then I'm going to start learning right away, and you'll teach me, won't you?

MAYO—(*mollifyingly*) Of course I will, boy, and be glad to, only you'd best go easy at first.

SCOTT—(*who has listened to this conversation in mingled consternation and amazement*) You don't mean to tell me you're goin' to let him stay, do you, James?

MAYO—Why, things bein' as they be, Robert's free to do as he's a mind to.

MRS. MAYO—*Let him!* The very idea!

SCOTT—(*more and more ruffled*) Then all I got to say is, you're a soft, weak-willed critter to be permittin' a boy—and women, too—to be layin' your course for you wherever they damn pleases.

MAYO—(*slyly amused*) It's just the same with me as 'twas with you, Dick. You can't order the tides on the seas to suit you, and I ain't pretendin' I can reg'late love for young folks.

SCOTT—(*scornfully*) Love! They ain't old enough to know love when they sight it! Love! I'm ashamed of you, Robert, to go lettin' a little huggin' and kissin' in the dark spile your chances to make a man out o' yourself. It ain't common sense—no siree, it ain't—not by a hell of a sight! (*He pounds the table with his fists in exasperation.*)

MRS. MAYO—(*laughing provokingly at her brother*) A fine one you are to be talking about love, Dick—an old cranky bachelor like you. Goodness sakes!

SCOTT—(*exasperated by their joking*) I've never been a damn fool like most, if that's what you're steerin' at.

MRS. MAYO—(*tauntingly*) Sour grapes, aren't they, Dick? (*She laughs. Robert and his father chuckle. Scott sputters with annoyance.*) Good gracious, Dick, you do act silly, flying into a temper over nothing.

SCOTT—(*indignantly*) Nothin'! You talk as if I wasn't concerned nohow in this here business. Seems to me I've got a right to have my say. Ain't I made all arrangements with the owners and stocked up with some special grub all on Robert's account?

ROBERT—You've been fine, Uncle Dick; and I appreciate it. Truly.

MAYO—'Course; we all does, Dick.

SCOTT—(*unplacated*) I've been countin' sure on havin' Robert for company on this vige—to sorta talk to and show things to, and teach, kinda, and I got my mind so set on havin' him I'm goin' to be double lonesome this vige. (*He pounds on the table, attempting to cover up this confession of weakness.*) Darn all this silly lovin' business, anyway. (*irritably*) But all this talk ain't tellin' me what I'm to do with that sta'b'd cabin I fixed up. It's all painted white, an' a bran new mattress on the bunk, 'n' new sheets 'n' blankets 'n' things. And Chips built in a book-case so's Robert could take his books along—with a slidin' bar fixed across't it, mind, so's they couldn't fall out no matter how she rolled. (*with excited consternation*) What d'you suppose my officers is goin' to think when there's no one comes aboard to occupy that sta'b'd cabin? And the men what did the work on it—what'll *they* think? (*He shakes his finger indignantly.*) They're liable as not to suspicion it was a *woman* I'd planned to ship along, and that she gave me the go-by at the last moment! (*He wipes his perspiring brow in anguish at this thought.*) Gawd A'mighty! They're only lookin' to have the laugh on me for something like that. They're liable to b'lieve anything, those fellers is!

MAYO—(*with a wink*) Then there's nothing to it but for you to get right out and hunt up a wife somewheres for that spick 'n' span cabin. She'll have to be a pretty one, too, to match it. (*He looks at his watch with exaggerated concern.*) You ain't got much time to find her, Dick.

SCOTT—(*as the others smile—sulkily*) You kin go to thunder, Jim Mayo!

ANDREW—(*comes forward from where he has been standing by the door, rear, brooding. His face is set in a look of grim determination.*) You needn't worry about that spare cabin, Uncle Dick, if you've a mind to take me in Robert's place.

ROBERT—(*turning to him quickly*) Andy! (*He sees at once the fixed resolve in his brother's eyes, and realizes immediately the reason for it—in consternation*) Andy, you mustn't!

ANDREW—You've made your decision, Rob, and now I've made mine. You're out of this, remember.

ROBERT—(*hurt by his brother's tone*) But Andy—

ANDREW—Don't interfere, Rob—that's all I ask. (*turning to his uncle*) You haven't answered my question, Uncle Dick.

SCOTT—(*clearing his throat, with an uneasy side glance at James Mayo who is staring at his elder son as if he thought he had suddenly gone mad*) O' course, I'd be glad to have you, Andy.

ANDREW—It's settled then. I can pack the little I want to take in a few minutes.

MRS. MAYO—Don't be a fool, Dick. Andy's only joking you.

SCOTT—(*disgruntedly*) It's hard to tell who's jokin' and who's not in this house.

ANDREW—(*firmly*) I'm not joking, Uncle Dick. (*as Scott looks at him uncertainly*) You needn't be afraid I'll go back on my word.

ROBERT—(*hurt by the insinuation he feels in Andrew's tone*) Andy! That isn't fair!

MAYO—(*frowning*) Seems to me this ain't no subject to joke over—not for Andy.

ANDREW—(*facing his father*) I agree with you, Pa, and I tell you again, once and for all, that I've made up my mind to go.

MAYO—(*dumbfounded—unable to doubt the determination in Andrew's voice—helplessly*) But why, son? Why?

ANDREW—(*evasively*) I've always wanted to go.

ROBERT—Andy!

ANDREW—(*half angrily*) You shut up, Rob! (*turning to his father again*) I didn't ever mention it because as long as Rob was going I knew it was no use; but now Rob's staying on here, there isn't any reason for me not to go.

MAYO—(*breathing hard*) No reason? Can you stand there and say that to me, Andrew?

MRS. MAYO—(*hastily—seeing the gathering storm*) He doesn't mean a word of it, James.

MAYO—(*making a gesture to her to keep silence*) Let me talk, Katey. (*in a more kindly tone*) What's come over you so sudden, Andy? You know's well as I do that it wouldn't be fair o' you to run off at a moment's notice right now when we're up to our necks in hard work.

ANDREW—(*avoiding his eyes*) Rob'll hold his end up as soon as he learns.

MAYO—Robert was never cut out for a farmer, and you was.

ANDREW—You can easily get a man to do my work.

MAYO—(*restraining his anger with an effort*) It sounds strange to hear you, Andy, that I always thought had good sense, talkin' crazy like that. (*scornfully*) Get a man to take your place! You ain't been workin' here for no hire, Andy, that you kin give me your notice to quit like you've done. The farm is your'n as well as mine. You've always worked on it with that understanding; and what you're sayin' you intend doin' is just skulkin' out o' your rightful responsibility.

ANDREW—(*looking at the floor—simply*) I'm sorry, Pa. (*after a slight pause*) It's no use talking any more about it.

MRS. MAYO—(*in relief*) There! I knew Andy'd come to his senses!

ANDREW—Don't get the wrong idea, Ma. I'm not backing out.

MAYO—You mean you're goin' in spite of—everythin'?

ANDREW—Yes. I'm going. I've got to. (*He looks at his father defiantly.*) I feel I oughn't to miss this chance to go out into the world and see things, and—I want to go.

MAYO—(*with bitter scorn*) So—you want to go out into the world and see thin's! (*his voice raised and quivering with anger*) I never thought I'd live to see the day when a son o' mine 'd look me in the face and tell a bare-faced lie! (*bursting out*) You're a liar, Andy Mayo, and a mean one to boot!

MRS. MAYO—James!

ROBERT—Pa!

SCOTT—Steady there, Jim!

MAYO—(*waving their protests aside*) He is and he knows it.

ANDREW—(*his face flushed*) I won't argue with you, Pa. You can think as badly of me as you like.

MAYO—(*shaking his finger at Andy, in a cold rage*) You know I'm speakin' truth—that's why you're afraid to argy! You lie when you say you want to go 'way—and see thin's! You ain't got no likin' in the world to go. I've watched you grow up, and I know your ways, and they're my ways. You're runnin' against your own nature, and you're goin' to be a'mighty sorry for it if you do. 'S if I didn't know your real reason for runnin' away! And runnin' away's the only words to fit it. You're runnin' away 'cause you're put out and riled 'cause your own brother's got Ruth 'stead o' you, and—

ANDREW—(*his face crimson—tensely*) Stop, Pa! I won't stand hearing that—not even from you!

MRS. MAYO—(*rushing to Andy and putting her arms about him protectingly*) Don't mind him, Andy dear. He don't mean a word he's saying! (*Robert stands rigidly, his hands clenched, his face contracted by pain. Scott sits dumbfounded and open-mouthed. Andrew soothes his mother who is on the verge of tears.*)

Mayo—(*in angry triumph*) It's the truth, Andy Mayo! And you ought to be bowed in shame to think of it!

Robert—(*protestingly*) Pa!

Mrs. Mayo—(*coming from Andrew to his father; puts her hands on his shoulders as though to try and push him back in the chair from which he has risen*) Won't you be still, James? Please won't you?

Mayo—(*looking at Andrew over his wife's shoulder—stubbornly*) The truth—God's truth!

Mrs. Mayo—Sh-h-h! (*She tries to put a finger across his lips, but he twists his head away.*)

Andrew—(*who has regained control over himself*) You're wrong, Pa, it isn't truth. (*with defiant assertiveness*) I don't love Ruth. I never loved her, and the thought of such a thing never entered my head.

Mayo—(*with an angry snort of disbelief*) Hump! You're pilin' lie on lie!

Andrew—(*losing his temper—bitterly*) I suppose it'd be hard for you to explain anyone's wanting to leave this blessed farm except for some outside reason like that. But I'm sick and tired of it—whether you want to believe me or not—and that's why I'm glad to get a chance to move on.

Robert—Andy! Don't! You're only making it worse.

Andrew—(*sulkily*) I don't care. I've done my share of work here. I've earned my right to quit when I want to. (*suddenly overcome with anger and grief; with rising intensity*) I'm sick and tired of the whole damn business. I hate the farm and every inch of ground in it. I'm sick of digging in the dirt and sweating in the sun like a slave without getting a word of thanks for it. (*tears of rage starting to his eyes—hoarsely*) I'm through, through for good and all; and if Uncle Dick won't take me on his ship, I'll find another. I'll get away somewhere, somehow.

Mrs. Mayo—(*in a frightened voice*) Don't you answer him, James. He doesn't know what he's saying. Don't say a word to him 'til he's in his right senses again. Please James, don't—

Mayo—(*pushes her away from him; his face is drawn and pale with the violence of his passion. He glares at Andrew as if he hated him.*) You dare to—you dare to speak like that to me? You talk like that 'bout this farm—the Mayo farm—where you was born—you—you— (*He clenches his fist above his head and advances threateningly on Andrew.*) You damned whelp!

MRS. MAYO—(*with a shriek*) James! (*She covers her face with her hands and sinks weakly into Mayo's chair. Andrew remains standing motionless, his face pale and set.*)

SCOTT—(*starting to his feet and stretching his arms across the table toward Mayo*) Easy there, Jim!

ROBERT—(*throwing himself between father and brother*) Stop! Are you mad?

MAYO—(*grabs Robert's arm and pushes him aside—then stands for a moment gasping for breath before Andrew. He points to the door with a shaking finger.*) Yes—go!—go!—You're no son o' mine—no son o' mine! You can go to hell if you want to! Don't let me find you here—in the mornin'—or—or—I'll *throw* you out!

ROBERT—Pa! For God's sake! (*Mrs. Mayo bursts into noisy sobbing.*)

MAYO—(*He gulps convulsively and glares at Andrew.*) You go—tomorrow mornin'—and by God—don't come back—don't dare come back—by God, not while I'm livin'—or I'll—I'll— (*He shakes over his muttered threat and strides toward the door rear, right.*)

MRS. MAYO—(*rising and throwing her arms around him—hysterically*) James! James! Where are you going?

MAYO—(*incoherently*) I'm goin'—to bed, Katey. It's late, Katey—it's late. (*He goes out.*)

MRS. MAYO—(*following him, pleading hysterically*) James! Take back what you've said to Andy. James! (*She follows him out. Robert and the Captain stare after them with horrified eyes. Andrew stands rigidly looking straight in front of him, his fists clenched at his sides.*)

SCOTT—(*the first to find his voice—with an explosive sigh*) Well, if he ain't the devil himself when he's roused! You oughtn't to have talked to him that way, Andy 'bout the damn farm, knowin' how touchy he is about it. (*with another sigh*) Well, you won't mind what he's said in anger. He'll be sorry for it when he's calmed down a bit.

ANDREW—(*in a dead voice*) You don't know him. (*defiantly*) What's said is said and can't be unsaid; and I've chosen.

ROBERT—(*with violent protest*) Andy! You can't go! This is all so stupid—and terrible!

ANDREW—(*coldly*) I'll talk to you in a minute, Rob. (*Crushed by his brother's attitude Robert sinks down into a chair, holding his head in his hands.*)

SCOTT—(*comes and slaps Andrew on the back*) I'm damned glad you're shippin' on, Andy. I like your spirit, and the way you spoke up to him. (*lowering his voice to a cautious whisper*) The sea's the place for a young feller like you that isn't half dead 'n' alive. (*He gives Andy a final approving slap.*) You 'n' me 'll get along like twins, see if we don't. I'm goin' aloft to turn in. Don't forget to pack your dunnage. And git some sleep, if you kin. We'll want to sneak out extra early b'fore they're up. It'll do away with more argyments. Robert can drive us down to the town, and bring back the team. (*He goes to the door in the rear, left.*) Well, good night.

ANDREW—Good night. (*Scott goes out. The two brothers remain silent for a moment. Then Andrew comes over to his brother and puts a hand on his back. He speaks in a low voice, full of feeling.*) Buck up, Rob. It ain't any use crying over spilt milk; and it'll all turn out for the best—let's hope. It couldn't be helped—what's happened.

ROBERT—(*wildly*) But it's a lie, Andy, a lie!

ANDREW—Of course it's a lie. You know it and I know it,—but that's all ought to know it.

ROBERT—Pa'll never forgive you. Oh, the whole affair is so senseless—and tragic. Why did you think you must go away?

ANDREW—You know better than to ask that. You know why. (*fiercely*) I can wish you and Ruth all the good luck in the world, and I do, and I mean it; but you can't expect me to stay around here and watch you two together, day after day—and me alone. I couldn't stand it—not after all the plans I'd made to happen on this place thinking—(*his voice breaks*) thinking she cared for me.

ROBERT—(*putting a hand on his brother's arm*) God! It's horrible! I feel so guilty—to think that I should be the cause of your suffering, after we've been such pals all our lives. If I could have foreseen what'd happen, I swear to you I'd have never said a word to Ruth. I swear I wouldn't have, Andy!

ANDREW—I know you wouldn't; and that would've been worse, for Ruth would've suffered then. (*He pats his brother's shoulder.*) It's best as it is. It had to be, and I've got to stand the gaff, that's all. Pa'll see how I felt—after a time. (*as Robert shakes his head*) —and if he don't—well, it can't be helped.

ROBERT—But think of Ma! God, Andy, you can't go! You can't!

ANDREW—(*fiercely*) I've got to go—to get away! I've got to, I tell you. I'd go crazy here, bein' reminded every second of the day what a fool I'd made of myself. I've got to get away and try and forget, if I can. And I'd hate the farm if I stayed, hate it for bringin' things back. I couldn't take interest in the work any more, work with no purpose in sight. Can't you see what a hell it'd be? You love her too, Rob. Put yourself in my place, and remember I haven't stopped loving her, and couldn't if I was to stay. Would that be fair to you or to her? Put yourself in my place. (*He shakes his brother fiercely by the shoulder.*) What'd you do then? Tell me the truth! You love her. What'd you do?

ROBERT—(*chokingly*) I'd—I'd go, Andy! (*He buries his face in his hands with a shuddering sob.*) God!

ANDREW—(*seeming to relax suddenly all over his body—in a low, steady voice*) Then you know why I got to go; and there's nothing more to be said.

ROBERT—(*in a frenzy of rebellion*) Why did this have to happen to us? It's damnable! (*He looks about him wildly, as if his vengeance were seeking the responsible fate.*)

ANDREW—(*soothingly—again putting his hands on his brother's shoulder*) It's no use fussing any more, Rob. It's done. (*forcing a smile*) I guess Ruth's got a right to have who she likes. She made a good choice—and God bless her for it!

ROBERT—Andy! Oh, I wish I could tell you half I feel of how fine you are!

ANDREW—(*interrupting him quickly*) Shut up! Let's go to bed. I've got to be up long before sun-up. You, too, if you're going to drive us down.

ROBERT—Yes. Yes.

ANDREW—(*turning down the lamp*) And I've got to pack yet. (*He yawns with utter weariness.*) I'm as tired as if I'd been plowing twenty-four hours at a stretch. (*dully*) I feel—dead. (*Robert covers his face again with his hands. Andrew shakes his head as if to get rid of his thoughts, and continues with a poor attempt at cheery briskness.*) I'm going to douse the light. Come on. (*He slaps his brother on the back. Robert does not move. Andrew bends over and blows out the lamp. His voice comes from the darkness.*) Don't sit there mourning, Rob. It'll all come out in the wash. Come on and get some sleep. Everything'll turn out all right in the end. (*Robert can be heard stumbling to his feet, and the dark figures of the two brothers can be seen groping their way toward the doorway in the rear as*

The Curtain Falls)

O'NEILL's SECOND PULITZER TROPHY

For „*Anna Christie*" *(1924)*

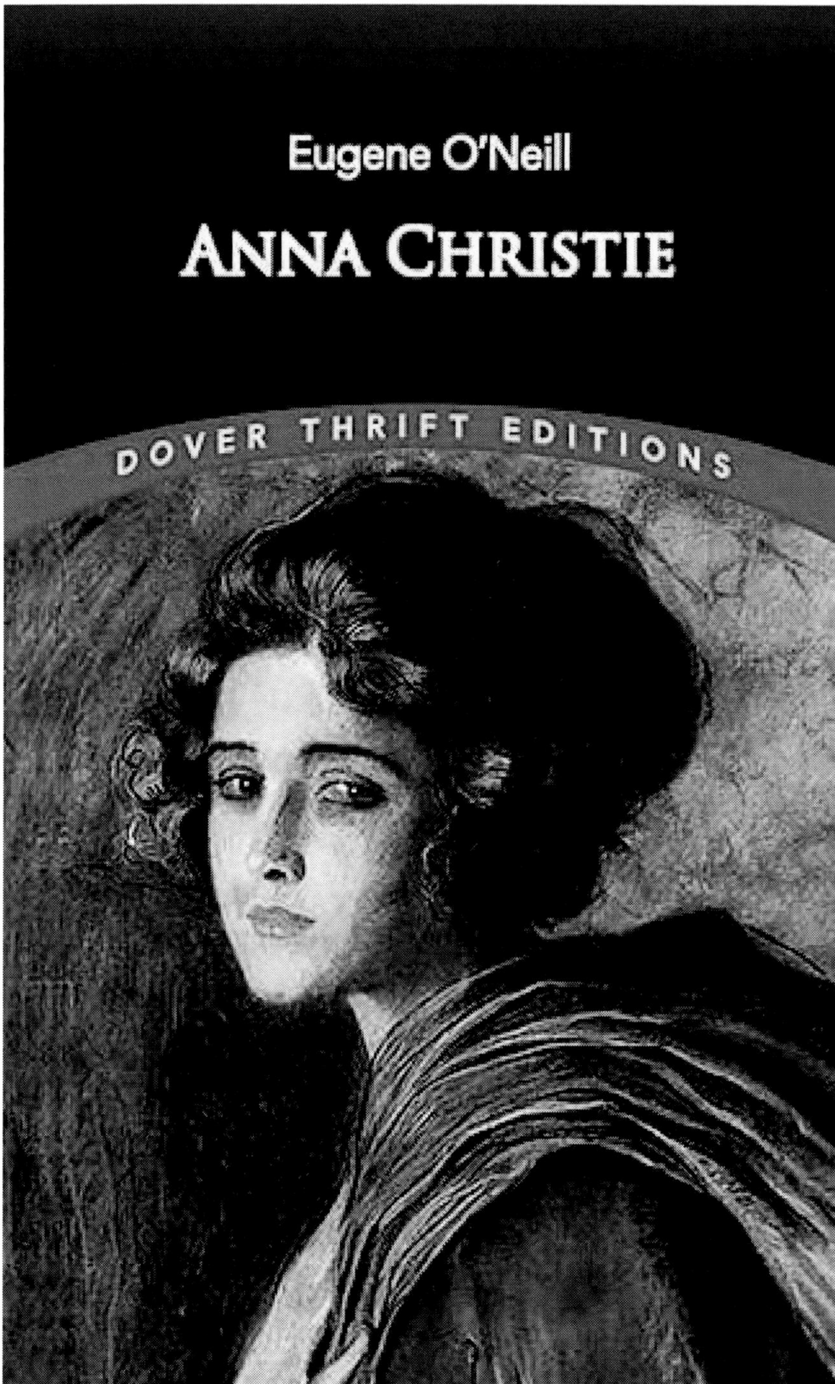

One of the many Book Editions

The Play and its Public Reception

About eighteen months after his first Pulitzer Prize for „Beyond the Horizon“ another play by Eugene O’Neill made it to a Broadway stage, a hard-hitting, yet humonous drama, „Anna Christie“. O’Neill had a great deal of trouble with the play, the first version under the title „Chris Christopherson,“about a nice young girl whose father didn’t want her to marry a sailnr. By the time he finished rewriting, Anna had to be transformed into a prostitute, making the play much more muscular.

Again, most of the New York critics praised the story and the performance. „*Anna Christie*“ ,the *Globe and Commercial Advertiser* stated, is a play of power, humor and understanding that searches its portion of life as no American drama has yet done. A production notable in vision, in writing and in acting.“ And the *New York Tribune* remarked: „If the gloomy trademark of Eugene O’Neill’s depressing product has kept you hitherto away from his plays, disregard it for an hour or two and go to see Anna Christie. The promise thus suggested is not that you will have a gay time in the observation of that drama, but that its veracious picture of some interesting characters in interesting circumstances Will appeal to your intelligence, while its ‘meaning’ will not in the last irritate you.“

But the *New York Times* was more critical by saying: „Anna Christie might be described as a work which towers above most of the plays in town, but which falls short of the stature and the perfection reached by Eugene O’Neill in some of his earlier work. The earlier work had established him as the nearest thing to a genius America has yet produced in the way of a playwright, and, though this *Anna Christie* of his has less directness and more dross and more moments of weak Violence than any of his forerunners, it is, nevertheless, a play written with that abundant imagination, that fresh and venturesorne mind and that sure instinct for the theatre which set this young author apart.“ Although the Pulitzer Prize jurors also had mixed feelings about O’NeillÂ°s work, they praised it in their report dated May lst, 1922, as “the best play of the year, and we have no second choice.“ The Advisory Board agreed and gave the Pulitzer decoration again to O’Neill.

The play made it to 177 performances. Audicnccs had an unfortunate habit of bursting into laughter near the end of the play, during the scene in which Anna swears on the crucifix that she will ever after live the good life. O’Ncill was inevitably stubbborn about scenes of this nature, in which he had overreached himself, with unintentionally ludicrous effect he would rcfusc to rewrite them, and would simply glower at audiencs‘ silly laugher. The ending of the play, with its clear implication that poor battcred Anna was somehow going tp be able to make a success of her marriage to Mat Burke, managed to irritate.“

THE WORK AND ITS NEW YORK PREMIERE

Anna Christie is called, by Samuel L. Leiter, a "fatalistic drama" which "concerns Old Chris, a Swedish coal-barge captain who blames the hardships... on 'dat ole davil sea.' Chris's daughter Anna, reared by relatives on a farm, has become a bedraggled prostitute. She goes East after fifteen years to find her father and soon becomes enmeshed in a torrential love affair with the shipwrecked Irish seaman Mat Burke... She reveals to Mat and her father the truth about her past. The men overcome their initial shock and disgust, but first they agree to be shipmates on a long voyage of forgetfulness, while Anna is to wait for them to be returned by 'dat ole davil sea.'"

The first New York production of *Anna Christie* opened at the Vanderbilt Theatre on November 2, 1921. Following are two scene photos together with main portions of the program containing the original cast:

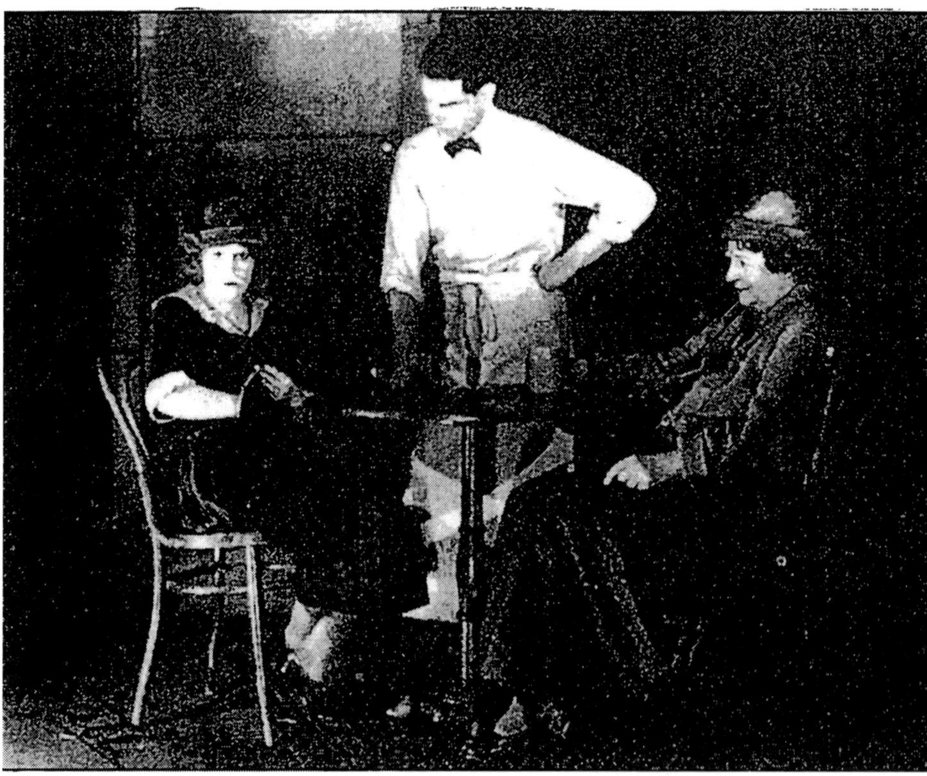

Pauline Lord, James C. Mack and Eugenie Blair

Vanderbilt Theatre

48th STREET, EAST OF BROADWAY

VANDERBILT AMUSEMENT CO............OWNERS
LYLE D. ANDREWS.....................MANAGER

FIRE NOTICE

Look around NOW and choose the nearest Exit to your seat. In case of fire walk (not run) to THAT Exit. Do not try to beat your neighbor to the street.

THOMAS J. DRENNAN, Fire Commissioner.

BEGINNING WEDNESDAY EVENING, NOVEMBER 2, 1921
Matinees Wednesday and Saturday

ARTHUR HOPKINS
Presents

ANNA CHRISTIE

—with—

PAULINE LORD

GEORGE MARION and FRANK SHANNON

A Play in Four Acts
By Eugene O'Neill
Fog Scene by Robert Edmond Jones
Staged by Arthur Hopkins

Characters
(In the order of appearance)

JOHNNY-THE-PRIEST..........................JAMES C. MACK
FIRST LONGSHOREMAN..........................G. O. TAYLOR
SECOND LONGSHOREMAN..........................JOHN HANLEY
A POSTMAN..........................WILLIAM AUGUSTIN
CHRIS. CHRISTOPHERSON..........................GEORGE MARION
MARTHY OWEN..........................EUGENIE BLAIR
ANNA CHRISTOPHERSON..........................PAULINE LORD
MAT BURKE..........................FRANK SHANNON
JOHNSON..........................OLE ANDERSON
THREE SAILORS....MESSRS. REILLY, HANSEN and KENNEDY

ACT ONE—Johnny-the-Priest's saloon near the Waterfront, New York City.

ACT TWO—The barge, Simeon Winthrop, at anchor in the harbor of Provincetown, Mass., ten days later.

ACT THREE—Cabin of the barge, at dock in Boston, a week later.

ACT FOUR—The same, two days later.

WM LYON PHELPS
LAMPSON PROFESSOR OF ENGLISH LITERATURE

YALE UNIVERSITY
NEW-HAVEN

1st May 1922

Dear Sir:-

Herewith I submit my report on the Pulitzer Prize for the best play of the year:-

Mr. Jesse Lynch Williams and I vote for <u>Anna Christie</u> by Eugene O'Neill. In our opinion this deserves the prize for the best play of the year, and we have no second choice; in fact we are quite strongly of the opinion that the prize should not be given to any other play.

Mr. Hamlin Garland has not seen <u>Anna Christie</u> but feels sure that he would not like it and will not vote for it. He has no other play to suggest and in his opinion the prize should not be given at all; he thinks that it would be better for the interests of the drama that no prize should be given this year. Mr. Williams and I feel, on the contrary, first, that it is exceedingly important that the prize should be given, and second, that it should be given to <u>Anna Christie</u>.

May I suggest, with all due deference, that when the drama prize was awarded last year very few people seemed to know about it. I mean, I wish that the award could be given in so public a manner in the newspapers that the Pulitzer prize would receive all the advertisement that it certainly merits.

Believe me,

Faithfully yours,

Chairman of the Prize Committee

Passed

Pulitzer Prize Drama Jury Report of May 1, 1922

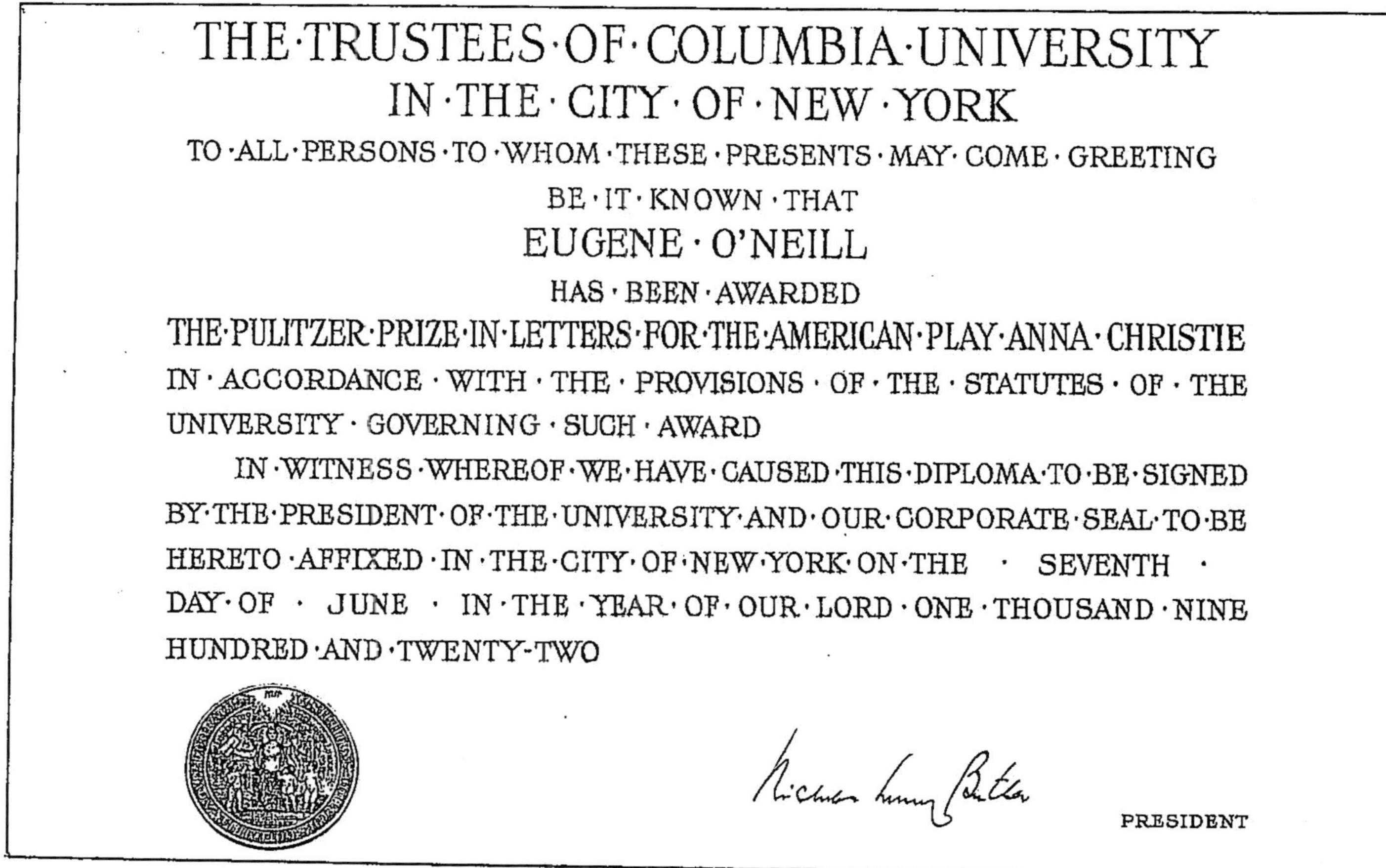
THE·TRUSTEES·OF·COLUMBIA·UNIVERSITY
IN·THE·CITY·OF·NEW·YORK
TO·ALL·PERSONS·TO·WHOM·THESE·PRESENTS·MAY·COME·GREETING
BE·IT·KNOWN·THAT
EUGENE·O'NEILL
HAS·BEEN·AWARDED
THE·PULITZER·PRIZE·IN·LETTERS·FOR·THE·AMERICAN·PLAY·ANNA·CHRISTIE
IN·ACCORDANCE·WITH·THE·PROVISIONS·OF·THE·STATUTES·OF·THE UNIVERSITY·GOVERNING·SUCH·AWARD
IN·WITNESS·WHEREOF·WE·HAVE·CAUSED·THIS·DIPLOMA·TO·BE·SIGNED BY·THE·PRESIDENT·OF·THE·UNIVERSITY·AND·OUR·CORPORATE·SEAL·TO·BE HERETO·AFFIXED·IN·THE·CITY·OF·NEW·YORK·ON·THE·SEVENTH· DAY·OF·JUNE·IN·THE·YEAR·OF·OUR·LORD·ONE·THOUSAND·NINE HUNDRED·AND·TWENTY-TWO
PRESIDENT

Eugen O'Neill's seond Pulitzer Prize Certificate for his Play „Anna Christie", signed by Columbia University President Nicholas Murray Butler on June 7,1922

The Play'sAct One

CHARACTERS

"Johnny-the-Priest"
Two Longshoremen
A Postman
Larry, *bartender*
Chris. Christopherson, *captain of the barge Simeon Winthrop*
Marthy Owen
Anna Christopherson, *Chris's daughter*
Three men of a steamer's crew
Mat Burke, *a stoker*
Johnson, *deckhand on the barge*

SCENES

Act I

"Johnny-the-Priest's" saloon near the waterfront, New York City.

Act II

The barge, *Simeon Winthrop*, at anchor in the harbor of Provincetown, Mass. Ten days later.

Act III

Cabin of the barge, at dock in Boston. A week later.

Act IV

The same. Two days later.

Time of the Play—About 1910.

Anna Christie

ACT I

SCENE—*"Johnny-the-Priest's" saloon near South Street, New York City. The stage is divided into two sections, showing a small back room on the right. On the left, forward, of the barroom, a large window looking out on the street. Beyond it, the main entrance—a double swinging door. Farther back, another window. The bar runs from left to right nearly the whole length of the rear wall. In back of the bar, a small showcase displaying a few bottles of case goods, for which there is evidently little call. The remainder of the rear space in front of the large mirrors is occupied by half-barrels of cheap whiskey of the "nickel-a-shot" variety, from which the liquor is drawn by means of spigots. On the right is an open doorway leading to the back room. In the back room are four round wooden tables with five chairs grouped about each. In the rear, a family entrance opening on a side street.*

It is late afternoon of a day in fall.

As the curtain rises, Johnny is discovered. "Johnny-the-Priest" deserves his nickname. With his pale, thin, clean-shaven face, mild blue eyes and white hair, a cassock would seem more suited to him than the apron he wears. Neither his voice nor his general manner dispel this illusion which has made him a personage of the water front. They are soft and bland. But beneath all his mildness one senses the man behind the mask—cynical, callous, hard as nails. He is lounging at ease behind the bar, a pair of spectacles on his nose, reading an evening paper.

Two longshoremen enter from the street, wearing their working aprons, the button of the union pinned conspicuously on the caps pulled sideways on their heads at an aggressive angle.

FIRST LONGSHOREMAN—(*as they range themselves at the bar*) Gimme a shock. Number Two. (*He tosses a coin on the bar.*)

SECOND LONGSHOREMAN—Same here. (*Johnny sets two glasses of barrel whiskey before them.*)

FIRST LONGSHOREMAN—Here's luck! (*The other nods. They gulp down their whiskey.*)

SECOND LONGSHOREMAN—(*putting money on the bar*) Give us another.

FIRST LONGSHOREMAN—Gimme a scoop this time—lager and porter. I'm dry.

SECOND LONGSHOREMAN—Same here. (*Johnny draws the lager and porter and sets the big, foaming schooners before them. They drink down half the contents and start to talk together hurriedly in low tones. The door on the left is swung open and Larry enters. He is a boyish, red-cheeked, rather good-looking young fellow of twenty or so.*)

LARRY—(*nodding to Johnny—cheerily*) Hello, boss.

JOHNNY—Hello, Larry. (*with a glance at his watch*) Just on time. (*Larry goes to the right behind the bar, takes off his coat, and puts on an apron.*)

FIRST LONGSHOREMAN—(*abruptly*) Let's drink up and get back to it. (*They finish their drinks and go out left. The postman enters as they leave. He exchanges nods with Johnny and throws a letter on the bar.*)

THE POSTMAN—Addressed care of you, Johnny. Know him?

JOHNNY—(*picks up the letter, adjusting his spectacles. Larry comes and peers over his shoulders. Johnny reads very slowly*) Christopher Christopherson.

THE POSTMAN—(*helpfully*) Square-head name.

LARRY—Old Chris—that's who.

JOHNNY—Oh, sure. I was forgetting Chris carried a hell of a name like that. Letters come here for him sometimes before, I remember now. Long time ago, though.

THE POSTMAN—It'll get him all right then?

JOHNNY—Sure thing. He comes here whenever he's in port.

THE POSTMAN—(*turning to go*) Sailor, eh?

JOHNNY—(*with a grin*) Captain of a coal barge.

THE POSTMAN—(*laughing*) Some job! Well, s'long.

JOHNNY—S'long. I'll see he gets it. (*The postman goes out. Johnny scrutinizes the letter.*) You got good eyes, Larry. Where's it from?

LARRY—(*after a glance*) St. Paul. That'll be in Minnesota, I'm thinkin'. Looks like a woman's writing, too, the old divil!

JOHNNY—He's got a daughter somewheres out West, I

think he told me once. (*He puts the letter on the cash register.*) Come to think of it, I ain't seen old Chris in a dog's age. (*Putting his overcoat on, he comes around the end of the bar.*) Guess I'll be gettin' home. See you to-morrow.

LARRY—Good-night to ye, boss. (*As Johnny goes toward the street door, it is pushed open and Christopher Christopherson enters. He is a short, squat, broad-shouldered man of about fifty, with a round, weather-beaten, red face from which his light blue eyes peer short-sightedly, twinkling with a simple good humor. His large mouth, overhung by a thick, drooping, yellow mustache, is childishly self-willed and weak, of an obstinate kindliness. A thick neck is jammed like a post into the heavy trunk of his body. His arms with their big, hairy, freckled hands, and his stumpy legs terminating in large flat feet, are awkwardly short and muscular. He walks with a clumsy, rolling gait. His voice, when not raised in a hollow boom, is toned down to a sly, confidential half-whisper with something vaguely plaintive in its quality. He is dressed in a wrinkled, ill-fitting dark suit of shore clothes, and wears a faded cap of gray cloth over his mop of grizzled, blond hair. Just now his face beams with a too-blissful happiness, and he has evidently been drinking. He reaches his hand out to Johnny.*)

CHRIS—Hello, Yohnny! Have drink on me. Come on, Larry. Give us drink. Have one yourself. (*putting his hand in his pocket*) Ay gat money—plenty money.

JOHNNY—(*shakes Chris by the hand*) Speak of the devil. We was just talkin' about you.

LARRY—(*coming to the end of the bar*) Hello, Chris. Put it there. (*They shake hands.*)

CHRIS—(*beaming*) Give us drink.

JOHNNY—(*with a grin*) You got a half-snootful now. Where'd you get it?

CHRIS—(*grinning*) Oder fallar on oder barge—Irish fallar—he gat bottle vhiskey and we drank it, yust us two. Dot vhiskey gat kick, by yingo! Ay yust come ashore. Give us drink, Larry. Ay vas little drunk, not much. Yust feel good. (*He laughs and commences to sing in a nasal, high-pitched quaver.*)

"My Yosephine, come board de ship. Long time Ay vait for
you.

De moon, she shi-i-i-ine. She looka yust like you.
Tchee-tchee, tchee-tchee, tchee-tchee, tchee-tchee."

(*To the accompaniment of this last he waves his hand as if he were conducting an orchestra.*)

JOHNNY—(*with a laugh*) Same old Yosie, eh, Chris?

CHRIS—You don't know good song when you hear him. Italian fallar on oder barge, he learn me dat. Give us drink. (*He throws change on the bar.*)

LARRY—(*with a professional air*) What's your pleasure, gentlemen?

JOHNNY—Small beer, Larry.

CHRIS—Vhiskey—Number Two.

LARRY—(*as he gets their drinks*) I'll take a cigar on you.

CHRIS—(*lifting his glass*) Skoal! (*He drinks.*)

JOHNNY—Drink hearty.

CHRIS—(*immediately*) Have oder drink.

JOHNNY—No. Some other time. Got to go home now. So you've just landed? Where are you in from this time?

CHRIS—Norfolk. Ve make slow voyage—dirty vedder—yust fog, fog, fog, all bloody time! (*There is an insistent ring from the doorbell at the family entrance in the back room. Chris gives a start—hurriedly*) Ay go open, Larry. Ay forgat. It vas Marthy. She come with me. (*He goes into the back room.*)

LARRY—(*with a chuckle*) He's still got that same cow livin' with him, the old fool!

JOHNNY—(*with a grin*) A sport, Chris is. Well, I'll beat it home. S'long. (*He goes to the street door.*)

LARRY—So long, boss.

JOHNNY—Oh—don't forget to give him his letter.

LARRY—I won't. (*Johnny goes out. In the meantime, Chris has opened the family entrance door, admitting Marthy. She might be forty or fifty. Her jowly, mottled face, with its thick red nose, is streaked with interlacing purple veins. Her thick, gray hair is piled anyhow in a greasy mop on top of her round head. Her figure is flabby and fat; her breath comes in wheezy gasps; she speaks in a loud, mannish voice, punctuated by explosions of hoarse laughter. But there still twinkles in her blood-shot blue eyes a youthful lust for life which hard usage has failed to stifle, a sense of humor mocking, but good-tempered. She wears a man's cap, double-breasted man's jacket, and a grimy, calico skirt. Her bare feet are encased in a man's brogans several sizes too large for her, which gives her a shuffling, wobbly gait.*)

MARTHY—(*grumblingly*) What yuh tryin' to do, Dutchy—keep me standin' out there all day? (*She comes forward and sits at the table in the right corner, front.*)

CHRIS—(*mollifyingly*) Ay'm sorry, Marthy. Ay talk to Yohnny. Ay forgat. What you goin' take for drink?

MARTHY—(*appeased*) Gimme a scoop of lager an' ale.

CHRIS—Ay go bring him back. (*He returns to the bar.*) Lager and ale for Marthy, Larry. Vhiskey for me. (*He throws change on the bar.*)

LARRY—Right you are. (*Then remembering, he takes the letter from in back of the bar.*) Here's a letter for you—from St. Paul, Minnesota—and a lady's writin'. (*He grins.*)

CHRIS—(*quickly—taking it*) Oh, den it come from my daughter, Anna. She live dere. (*He turns the letter over in his hands uncertainly.*) Ay don't gat letter from Anna—must be a year.

LARRY—(*jokingly*) That's a fine fairy tale to be tellin'—your daughter! Sure I'll bet it's some bum.

CHRIS—(*soberly*) No. Dis come from Anna. (*engrossed by the letter in his hand—uncertainly*) By golly, Ay tank Ay'm too drunk for read dis letter from Anna. Ay tank Ay sat down for a minute. You bring drinks in back room, Larry. (*He goes into the room on right.*)

MARTHY—(*angrily*) Where's my larger an' ale, yuh big stiff?

CHRIS—(*preoccupied*) Larry bring him. (*He sits down opposite her. Larry brings in the drinks and sets them on the table. He and Marthy exchange nods of recognition. Larry stands looking at Chris curiously. Marthy takes a long draught of her schooner and heaves a huge sigh of satisfaction, wiping her mouth with the back of her hand. Chris stares at the letter for a moment—slowly opens it, and, squinting his eyes, commences to read laboriously, his lips moving as he spells out the words. As he reads his face lights up with an expression of mingled joy and bewilderment.*)

LARRY—Good news?

MARTHY—(*her curiosity also aroused*) What's that yuh got—a letter, fur Gawd's sake?

CHRIS—(*pauses for a moment, after finishing the letter, as if to let the news sink in—then suddenly pounds his fist on the table with happy excitement*) Py yiminy! Yust tank, Anna say she's comin' here right avay! She gat sick on yob in St. Paul, she say. It's short letter, don't tal me much more'n dat. (*beaming*) Py golly, dat's good news all at one time for ole fallar! (*then turning to Marthy, rather shamefacedly*) You know, Marthy, Ay've tole you Ay don't see my Anna since she vas little gel in Sveden five year ole.

MARTHY—How old'll she be now?

CHRIS—She must be—lat me see—she must be twenty year ole, py Yo!

LARRY—(*surprised*) You've not seen her in fifteen years?

CHRIS—(*suddenly growing somber—in a low tone*) No. Ven she vas little gel, Ay vas bo'sun on vindjammer. Ay never gat home only few time dem year. Ay'm fool sailor fallar. My voman—Anna's mother—she gat tired vait all time Sveden for me ven Ay don't never come. She come dis country, bring Anna, dey go out Minnesota, live with her cousins on farm. Den ven her mo'der die ven Ay vas on voyage, Ay tank it's better dem cousins keep Anna. Ay tank it's better Anna live on farm, den she don't know dat ole davil, sea, she don't know fader like me.

LARRY—(*with a wink at Marthy*) This girl, now, 'll be marryin' a sailor herself, likely. It's in the blood.

CHRIS—(*suddenly springing to his feet and smashing his fist on the table in a rage*) No, py God! She don't do dat!

MARTHY—(*grasping her schooner hastily—angrily*) Hey, look out, yuh nut! Wanta spill my suds for me?

LARRY—(*amazed*) Oho, what's up with you? Ain't you a sailor yourself now, and always been?

CHRIS—(*slowly*) Dat's yust vhy Ay say it. (*forcing a smile*) Sailor vas all right fallar, but not for marry gel. No. Ay know dat. Anna's mo'der, she know it, too.

LARRY—(*as Chris remains sunk in gloomy reflection*) When is your daughter comin'? Soon?

CHRIS—(*roused*) Py yiminy, Ay forgat. (*reads through the letter hurriedly*) She say she come right avay, dat's all.

LARRY—She'll maybe be comin' here to look for you, I s'pose. (*He returns to the bar, whistling. Left alone with Marthy, who stares at him with a twinkle of malicious humor in her eyes, Chris suddenly becomes desperately ill-at-ease. He fidgets, then gets up hurriedly.)*

CHRIS—Ay gat speak with Larry. Ay be right back. (*mollifyingly*) Ay bring you oder drink.

MARTHY—(*emptying her glass*) Sure. That's me. (*As he retreats with the glass she guffaws after him derisively.*)

CHRIS—(*to Larry in an alarmed whisper*) Py yingo, Ay gat gat Marthy shore off barge before Anna come! Anna raise hell if she find dat out. Marthy raise hell, too, for go, py golly!

LARRY—(*with a chuckle*) Serve ye right, ye old divil—havin' a woman at your age!

CHRIS—(*scratching his head in a quandary*) You tal me lie for tal Marthy, Larry, so's she gat off barge quick.

LARRY—She knows your daughter's comin'. Tell her to get the hell out of it.

CHRIS—No. Ay don't like make her feel bad.

LARRY—You're an old mush! Keep your girl away from the barge, then. She'll likely want to stay ashore anyway. (*curiously*) What does she work at, your Anna?

CHRIS—She stay on dem cousins' farm 'till two year ago. Dan she gat yob nurse gel in St. Paul. (*then shaking his head resolutely*) But Ay don't vant for her gat yob now. Ay vant for her stay with me.

LARRY—(*scornfully*) On a coal barge! She'll not like that, I'm thinkin'.

MARTHY—(*shouts from next room*) Don't I get that bucket o' suds, Dutchy?

CHRIS—(*startled—in apprehensive confusion*) Yes, Ay come, Marthy.

LARRY—(*drawing the lager and ale, hands it to Chris—laughing*) Now you're in for it! You'd better tell her straight to get out!

CHRIS—(*shaking in his boots*) Py golly. (*He takes her drink in to Marthy and sits down at the table. She sips it in silence. Larry moves quietly close to the partition to listen, grinning with expectation. Chris seems on the verge of speaking, hesitates, gulps down his whiskey desperately as if seeking for courage. He attempts to whistle a few bars of "Yosephine" with careless bravado, but the whistle peters out futilely. Marthy stares at him keenly, taking in his embarrassment with a malicious twinkle of amusement in her eye. Chris clears his throat.*) Marthy—

MARTHY—(*aggressively*) Wha's that? (*then, pretending to fly into a rage, her eyes enjoying Chris' misery*) I'm wise to what's in back of your nut, Dutchy. Yuh want to git rid o' me, huh?—now she's comin'. Gimme the bum's rush ashore, huh? Lemme tell yuh, Dutchy, there ain't a square-head workin' on a boat man enough to git away with that. Don't start nothin' yuh can't finish!

CHRIS—(*miserably*) Ay don't start nutting, Marthy.

MARTHY—(*glares at him for a second—then cannot control a burst of laughter*) Ho-ho! Yuh're a scream, Square-head—an honest-ter-Gawd knockout! Ho-ho! (*She wheezes, panting for breath.*)

CHRIS—(*with childish pique*) Ay don't see nutting for laugh at.

MARTHY—Take a slant in the mirror and yuh'll see. Ho-ho! (*recovering from her mirth—chuckling, scornfully*) A square-head tryin' to kid Marthy Owen at this late day!—after me campin' with barge men the last twenty years. I'm wise to the game, up, down, and sideways. I ain't been born and dragged up on the water front for nothin'. Think I'd make trouble, huh? Not me! I'll pack up me duds an' beat it. I'm quittin' yuh, get me? I'm tellin' yuh I'm sick of stickin' with yuh, and I'm leavin' yuh flat, see? There's plenty of other guys on other barges waitin' for me. Always was, I always found. (*She claps the astonished Chris on the back.*) So cheer up, Dutchy! I'll be offen the barge before she comes. You'll be rid o' me for good—and me o' you—good riddance for both of us. Ho-ho!

CHRIS—(*seriously*) Ay don' tank dat. You vas good gel, Marthy.

MARTHY—(*grinning*) Good girl? Aw, can the bull! Well, yuh treated me square, yuhself. So it's fifty-fifty. Nobody's sore at nobody. We're still good frien's, huh? (*Larry returns to bar.*)

CHRIS—(*beaming now that he sees his troubles disappearing*) Yes, py golly.

MARTHY—That's the talkin'! In all my time I tried never to split with a guy with no hard feelin's. But what was yuh so scared about—that I'd kick up a row? That ain't Marthy's way. (*scornfully*) Think I'd break my heart to loose yuh? Commit suicide, huh? Ho-ho! Gawd! The world's full o' men if that's all I'd worry about! (*then with a grin, after emptying her glass*) Blow me to another scoop, huh? I'll drink your kid's health for yuh.

CHRIS—(*eagerly*) Sure tang. Ay go gat him. (*He takes the two glasses into the bar.*) Oder drink. Same for both.

LARRY—(*getting the drinks and putting them on the bar*) She's not such a bad lot, that one.

CHRIS—(*jovially*) She's good gel, Ay tal you! Py golly, Ay calabrate now! Give me vhiskey here at bar, too. (*He puts down money. Larry serves him.*) You have drink, Larry.

LARRY—(*virtuously*) You know I never touch it.

CHRIS—You don't know what you miss. Skoal! (*He drinks—then begins to sing loudly*)

"My Yosephine, come board de ship—"

(*He picks up the drinks for Marthy and himself and walks unsteadily into the back room, singing.*)

"De moon, she shi-i-i-ine. She looks yust like you.
Tche-tchee, tchee-tchee, tchee-tchee, tchee-tchee."

MARTHY—(*grinning, hands to ears*) Gawd!

CHRIS—(*sitting down*) Ay'm good singer, yes? Ve drink, eh? Skoal! Ay calabrate! (*He drinks.*) Ay calabrate 'cause Anna's coming home. You know, Marthy, Ay never write for her to come, 'cause Ay tank Ay'm no good for her. But all time Ay hope like hell some day she vant for see me and den she come. And dat's vay it happen now, py yiminy! (*his face beaming*) What you tank she look like, Marthy? Ay bet you she's fine, good, strong gel, pooty like hell! Living on farm made her like dat. And Ay bet you some day she marry good, steady land fallar here in East, have home all her own, have kits—and dan Ay'm ole grandfader, py golly! And Ay go visit dem every time Ay gat in port near! (*bursting with joy*) By yiminy crickens, Ay calabrate dat! (*shouts*) Bring oder drink, Larry! (*He smashes his fist on the table with a bang.*)

LARRY—(*coming in from bar—irritably*) Easy there! Don't be breakin' the table, you old goat!

CHRIS—(*by way of reply, grins foolishly and begins to sing*) "My Yosephine comes board de ship—"

MARTHY—(*touching Chris' arm persuasively*) You're soused to the ears, Dutchy. Go out and put a feed into you. It'll sober you up. (*then as Chris shakes his head obstinately*) Listen, yuh old nut! Yuh don't know what time your kid's liable to show up. Yuh want to be sober when she comes, don't yuh?

CHRIS—(*aroused—gets unsteadily to his feet*) Py golly, yes.

LARRY—That's good sense for you. A good beef stew'll fix you. Go round the corner.

CHRIS—All right. Ay be back soon, Marthy. (*Chris goes through the bar and out the street door.*)

LARRY—He'll come round all right with some grub in him.

MARTHY—Sure. (*Larry goes back to the bar and resumes his newspaper. Marthy sips what is left of her schooner reflectively. There is the ring of the family entrance bell. Larry comes to the door and opens it a trifle—then, with a puzzled expression, pulls it wide. Anna Christopherson enters. She is a tall, blond, fully-developed girl of twenty, handsome after a large, Viking-daughter fashion but now run down in health and plainly showing all the outward evidences of belonging to the world's oldest profession. Her youthful face is already hard and cynical beneath its layer of make-up. Her clothes are the tawdry finery of peasant stock turned prostitute. She comes and sinks wearily in a chair by the table, left front.*)

ANNA—Gimme a whiskey—ginger ale on the side. (*then, as Larry turns to go, forcing a winning smile at him*) And don't be stingy, baby.

LARRY—(*sarcastically*) Shall I serve it in a pail?

ANNA—(*with a hard laugh*) That suits me down to the ground. (*Larry goes into the bar. The two women size each other up with frank stares. Larry comes back with the drink which he sets before Anna and returns to the bar again. Anna downs her drink at a gulp. Then, after a moment, as the alcohol begins to rouse her, she turns to Marthy with a friendly smile.*) Gee, I needed that bad, all right, all right!

MARTHY—(*nodding her head sympathetically*) Sure—yuh look all in. Been on a bat?

ANNA—No—travelling—day and a half on the train. Had

to sit up all night in the dirty coach, too. Gawd, I thought I'd never get here!

MARTHY—(*with a start—looking at her intently*) Where'd yuh come from, huh?

ANNA—St. Paul—out in Minnesota.

MARTHY—(*staring at her in amazement—slowly*) So—yuh're— (*She suddenly bursts out into hoarse, ironical laughter.*) Gawd!

ANNA—All the way from Minnesota, sure. (*flaring up*) What you laughing at? Me?

MARTHY—(*hastily*) No, honest, kid. I was thinkin' of somethin' else.

ANNA—(*mollified—with a smile*) Well, I wouldn't blame you, at that. Guess I do look rotten—yust out of the hospital two weeks. I'm going to have another 'ski. What d'you say? Have something on me?

MARTHY—Sure I will. T'anks. (*She calls.*) Hey, Larry! Little service! (*He comes in.*)

ANNA—Same for me.

MARTHY—Same here. (*Larry takes their glasses and goes out.*)

ANNA—Why don't you come sit over here, be sociable. I'm a dead stranger in this burg—and I ain't spoke a word with no one since day before yesterday.

MARTHY—Sure thing. (*She shuffles over to Anna's table and sits down opposite her. Larry brings the drinks and Anna pays him.*)

ANNA—Skoal! Here's how! (*She drinks.*)

MARTHY—Here's luck! (*She takes a gulp from her schooner.*)

ANNA—(*taking a package of Sweet Caporal cigarettes from her bag*) Let you smoke in here, won't they?

MARTHY—(*doubtfully*) Sure. (*then with evident anxiety*) On'y trow it away if yuh hear someone comin'.

ANNA—(*lighting one and taking a deep inhale*) Gee, they're fussy in this dump, ain't they? (*She puffs, staring at the table top. Marthy looks her over with a new penetrating interest, taking in every detail of her face. Anna suddenly becomes conscious of this appraising stare—resentfully*) Ain't nothing wrong with me, is there? You're looking hard enough.

MARTHY—(*irritated by the other's tone—scornfully*) Ain't

got to look much. I got your number the minute you stepped in the door.

ANNA—(*her eyes narrowing*) Ain't you smart! Well, I got yours, too, without no trouble. You're me forty years from now. That's you! (*She gives a hard little laugh.*)

MARTHY—(*angrily*) Is that so? Well, I'll tell you straight, kiddo, that Marthy Owen never— (*She catches herself up short—with a grin*) What are you and me scrappin' over? Let's cut it out, huh? Me, I don't want no hard feelin's with no one. (*extending her hand*) Shake and forget it, huh?

ANNA—(*shakes her hand gladly*) Only too glad to. I ain't looking for trouble. Let's have 'nother. What d'you say?

MARTHY—(*shaking her head*) Not for mine. I'm full up. And you— Had anythin' to eat lately?

ANNA—Not since this morning on the train.

MARTHY—Then yuh better go easy on it, hadn't yuh?

ANNA—(*after a moment's hesitation*) Guess you're right. I got to meet someone, too. But my nerves is on edge after that rotten trip.

MARTHY—Yuh said yuh was just outa the hospital?

ANNA—Two weeks ago. (*leaning over to Marthy confidentially*) The joint I was in out in St. Paul got raided. That was the start. The judge give all us girls thirty days. The others didn't seem to mind being in the cooler much. Some of 'em was used to it. But me, I couldn't stand it. It got my goat right—couldn't eat or sleep or nothing. I never could stand being caged up nowheres. I got good and sick and they had to send me to the hospital. It was nice there. I was sorry to leave it, honest!

MARTHY—(*after a slight pause*) Did yuh say yuh got to meet someone here?

ANNA—Yes. Oh, not what you mean. It's my Old Man I got to meet. Honest! It's funny, too. I ain't seen him since I was a kid—don't even know what he looks like—yust had a letter every now and then. This was always the only address he give me to write him back. He's yanitor of some building here now—used to be a sailor.

MARTHY—(*astonished*) Janitor!

ANNA—Sure. And I was thinking maybe, seeing he ain't never done a thing for me in my life, he might be willing to stake me to a room and eats till I get rested up. (*wearily*) Gee, I sure need that rest! I'm knocked out. (*then resignedly*) But I ain't expecting much from him. Give you a kick when you're down, that's what all men do. (*with sudden passion*) Men, I hate 'em—all of 'em! And I don't expect he'll turn out no better than the rest. (*then with sudden interest*) Say, do you hang out around this dump much?

MARTHY—Oh, off and on.

ANNA—Then maybe you know him—my Old Man—or at least seen him?

MARTHY—It ain't old Chris, is it?

ANNA—Old Chris?

MARTHY—Chris Christopherson, his full name is.

ANNA—(*excitedly*) Yes, that's him! Anna Christopherson—that's my real name—only out there I called myself Anna Christie. So you know him, eh?

MARTHY—(*evasively*) Seen him about for years.

ANNA—Say, what's he like, tell me, honest?

MARTHY—Oh, he's short and—

ANNA—(*impatiently*) I don't care what he looks like. What kind is he?

MARTHY—(*earnestly*) Well, yuh can bet your life, kid, he's as good an old guy as ever walked on two feet. That goes!

ANNA—(*pleased*) I'm glad to hear it. Then you think's he'll stake me to that rest cure I'm after?

MARTHY—(*emphatically*) Surest thing you know. (*disgustedly*) But where'd yuh get the idea he was a janitor?

ANNA—He wrote me he was himself.

MARTHY—Well, he was lyin'. He ain't. He's captain of a barge—five men under him.

ANNA—(*disgusted in her turn*) A barge? What kind of a barge?

MARTHY—Coal, mostly.

ANNA—A coal barge! (*with a harsh laugh*) If that ain't a swell job to find your long lost Old Man working at! Gee, I knew something'd be bound to turn out wrong—always does with me. That puts my idea of his giving me a rest on the bum.

MARTHY—What d'yuh mean?

ANNA—I s'pose he lives on the boat, don't he?

MARTHY—Sure. What about it? Can't you live on it, too?

ANNA—(*scornfully*) Me? On a dirty coal barge! What d'you think I am?

MARTHY—(*resentfully*) What d'yuh know about barges, huh? Bet yuh ain't never seen one. That's what comes of his bringing yuh up inland—away from the old devil sea—where yuh'd be safe— Gawd! (*The irony of it strikes her sense of humor and she laughs hoarsely.*)

ANNA—(*angrily*) His bringing me up! Is that what he tells people! I like his nerve! He let them cousins of my Old Woman's keep me on their farm and work me to death like a dog.

MARTHY—Well, he's got queer notions on some things. I've heard him say a farm was the best place for a kid.

ANNA—Sure. That's what he'd always answer back—and a lot of crazy stuff about staying away from the sea—stuff I couldn't make head or tail to. I thought he must be nutty.

MARTHY—He is on that one point. (*casually*) So yuh didn't fall for life on the farm, huh?

ANNA—I should say not! The old man of the family, his wife, and four sons—I had to slave for all of 'em. I was only a poor relation, and they treated me worse than they dare treat a hired girl. (*after a moment's hesitation—somberly*) It was one of the sons—the youngest—started me—when I was sixteen. After that, I hated 'em so I'd killed 'em all if I'd stayed. So I run away—to St. Paul.

MARTHY—(*who has been listening sympathetically*) I've heard Old Chris talkin' about your bein' a nurse girl out there. Was that all a bluff yuh put up when yuh wrote him?

ANNA—Not on your life, it wasn't. It was true for two years. I didn't go wrong all at one jump. Being a nurse girl was yust what finished me. Taking care of other people's kids, always listening to their bawling and crying, caged in, when you're only a kid yourself and want to go out and see things. At last I got the chance—to get into that house. And you bet your life I took it! (*defiantly*) And I ain't sorry neither. (*after a pause—with bitter hatred*) It was all men's fault—the whole business. It was men on the farm ordering and beating me—and giving me the wrong start. Then when I was a nurse, it was men again hanging around, bothering me, trying to see what they could get. (*She gives a hard laugh.*) And now it's men all the time. Gawd, I hate 'em all, every mother's son of 'em! Don't you?

MARTHY—Oh, I dunno. There's good ones and bad ones, kid. You've just had a run of bad luck with 'em, that's all. Your Old Man, now—old Chris—he's a good one.

ANNA—(*sceptically*) He'll have to show me.

MARTHY—Yuh kept right on writing him yuh was a nurse girl still, even after yuh was in the house, didn't yuh?

ANNA—Sure. (*cynically*) Not that I think he'd care a darn.

MARTHY—Yuh're all wrong about him, kid. (*earnestly*) I know Old Chris well for a long time. He's talked to me 'bout you lots o' times. He thinks the world o' you, honest he does.

ANNA—Aw, quit the kiddin'!

MARTHY—Honest! Only, he's a simple old guy, see? He's got nutty notions. But he means well, honest. Listen to me, kid— (*She is interrupted by the opening and shutting of the street door in the bar and by hearing Chris's voice.*) Ssshh!

ANNA—What's up?

CHRIS—(*who has entered the bar. He seems considerably sobered up.*) Py golly, Larry, dat grub taste good. Marthy in back?

LARRY—Sure—and another tramp with her. (*Chris starts for the entrance to the back room.*)

MARTHY—(*to Anna in a hurried, nervous whisper*) That's him now. He's comin' in here. Brace up!

ANNA—Who? (*Chris opens the door.*)

MARTHY—(*as if she were greeting him for the first time*) Why hello, Old Chris. (*Then before he can speak, she shuffles hurriedly past him into the bar, beckoning him to follow her.*) Come here. I wanta tell yuh somethin'. (*He goes out to her. She speaks hurriedly in a low voice.*) Listen! I'm goin' to beat it down to the barge—pack up me duds and blow. That's her in there—your Anna—just come—waitin' for yuh. Treat her right, see? She's been sick. Well, s'long! (*She goes into the back room—to Anna*) S'long, kid. I gotta beat it now. See yuh later.

ANNA—(*nervously*) So long. (*Martha goes quickly out of the family entrance.*)

LARRY—(*looking at the stupefied Chris curiously*) Well, what's up now?

CHRIS—(*vaguely*) Nutting—nutting. (*He stands before the*

door to the back room in an agony of embarrassed emotion—then he forces himself to a bold decision, pushes open the door and walks in. He stands there, casts a shy glance at Anna, whose brilliant clothes, and, to him, high-toned appearance, awe him terribly. He looks about him with pitiful nervousness as if to avoid the appraising look with which she takes in his face, his clothes, etc—his voice seeming to plead for her forebearance.) Anna!

ANNA—(*acutely embarrassed in her turn*) Hello—father. She told me it was you. I yust got here a little while ago.

CHRIS—(*goes slowly over to her chair*) It's good—for see you—after all dem years, Anna. (*He bends down over her. After an embarrassed struggle they manage to kiss each other.*)

ANNA—(*a trace of genuine feeling in her voice*) It's good to see you, too.

CHRIS—(*grasps her arms and looks into her face—then overcome by a wave of fierce tenderness*) Anna lilla! Anna lilla! (*takes her in his arms*)

ANNA—(*shrinks away from him, half-frightened*) What's that—Swedish? I don't know it. (*then as if seeking relief from the tension in a voluble chatter*) Gee, I had an awful trip coming here. I'm all in. I had to sit up in the dirty coach all night—couldn't get no sleep, hardly—and then I had a hard job finding this place. I never been in New York before, you know, and—

CHRIS—(*who has been staring down at her face admiringly, not hearing what she says—impulsively*) You know you vas awful pooty gel, Anna? Ay bet all men see you fall in love with you, py yiminy!

ANNA—(*repelled—harshly*) Cut it! You talk same as they all do.

CHRIS—(*slowly*) Ay tank, after your mo'der die, ven Ay vas avay on voyage, it's better for you you don't never see me! (*He sinks down in the chair opposite her dejectedly—then turns to her—sadly*) Ay don't know, Anna, vhy Ay never come home Sveden in ole year. Ay vant come home end of every voyage. Ay vant see your mo'der, your two bro'der before dey vas drowned, you ven you vas born—but—Ay—don't go. Ay sign on oder ships—go South America, go Australia, go China, go every port all over world many times—but Ay never go aboard ship sail for Sveden. Ven Ay gat money for pay passage home as passenger den—(*he bows his head guiltily*) Ay forgat and Ay spend all money. Ven Ay tank again, it's too late. (*He sighs.*) Ay don't know vhy but dat's vay with most sailor fallar, Anna. Dat ole davil sea make dem crazy fools with her dirty tricks. It's so.

ANNA—(*who has watched him keenly while he has been speaking—with a trace of scorn in her voice*) Then you think the sea's to blame for everything, eh? Well, you're still workin' on it, ain't you, spite of all you used to write me about hating it. That dame was here told me you was captain of a coal barge—and you wrote me you was yanitor of a building!

CHRIS—(*embarrassed but lying glibly*) Oh, Ay work on land long time as yanitor. Yust short time ago Ay got dis yob cause Ay vas sick, need open air.

ANNA—(*sceptically*) Sick? You? You'd never think it.

CHRIS—And, Anna, dis ain't real sailor yob. Dis ain't real boat on sea. She's yust ole tub—like piece of land with house on it dat float. Yob on her ain't sea yob. No. Ay don't gat yob on sea, Anna, if Ay die first. Ay swear dat, ven your mo'der die. Ay keep my word, py yingo!

ANNA—(*perplexed*) Well, I can't see no difference. (*dismissing the subject*) Speaking of being sick, I been there myself—yust out of the hospital two weeks ago.

CHRIS—(*immediately all concern*) You, Anna? Py golly! (*anxiously*) You feel better now, dough, don't you? You look little tired, dat's all!

ANNA—(*wearily*) I am. Tired to death. I need a long rest and I don't see much chance of getting it.

CHRIS—What you mean, Anna?

ANNA—Well, when I made up my mind to come to see

you, I thought you was a yanitor—that you'd have a place where, maybe, if you didn't mind having me, I could visit a while and rest up—till I felt able to get back on the job again.

CHRIS—(*eagerly*) But Ay gat place, Anna—nice place. You rest all you want, py yiminy! You don't never have to vork as nurse gel no more. You stay with me, py golly!

ANNA—(*surprised and pleased by his eagerness—with a smile*) Then you're really glad to see me—honest?

CHRIS—(*pressing one of her hands in both of his*) Anna, Ay like see you like hell, Ay tal you! And don't you talk no more about gatting yob. You stay with me. Ay don't see you for long time, you don't forgat dat. (*His voice trembles.*) Ay'm gatting ole. Ay gat no one in vorld but you.

ANNA—(*touched—embarrassed by this unfamiliar emotion*) Thanks. It sounds good to hear someone—talk to me that way. Say, though—if you're so lonely—it's funny—why ain't you ever married again?

CHRIS—(*shaking his head emphatically—after a pause*) Ay love your mo'der too much for ever do dat, Anna.

ANNA—(*impressed—slowly*) I don't remember nothing about her. What was she like? Tell me.

CHRIS—Ay tal you all about everytang—and you tal me all tangs happen to you. But not here now. Dis ain't good place for young gel, anyway. Only no good sailor fallar come here for gat drunk. (*He gets to his feet quickly and picks up her bag.*) You come with me, Anna. You need lie down, gat rest.

ANNA—(*half rises to her feet, then sits down again*) Where're you going?

CHRIS—Come. Ve gat on board.

ANNA—(*disappointedly*) On board your barge, you mean? (*dryly*) Nix for mine! (*then seeing his crestfallen look—forcing a smile*) Do you think that's a good place for a young girl like me—a coal barge?

CHRIS—(*dully*) Yes, Ay tank. (*He hesitates—then continues more and more pleadingly.*) You don't know how nice it's on barge, Anna. Tug come and ve gat towed out on voyage—yust water all round, and sun, and fresh air, and good grub for make you strong, healthy gel. You see many tangs you don't see before. You gat moonlight at night, maybe; see steamer pass; see schooner make sail—see everytang dat's pooty. You need take rest like dat. You work too hard for young gel already. You need vacation, yes!

ANNA—(*who has listened to him with a growing interest—with an uncertain laugh*) It sounds good to hear you tell it. I'd sure like a trip on the water, all right. It's the barge idea has me stopped. Well, I'll go down with you and have a look—and maybe I'll take a chance. Gee, I'd do anything once.

CHRIS—(*picks up her bag again*) Ve go, eh?

ANNA—What's the rush? Wait a second. (*Forgetting the situation for a moment, she relapses into the familiar form and flashes one of her winning trade smiles at him.*) Gee, I'm thirsty.

CHRIS—(*sets down her bag immediately—hastily*) Ay'm sorry, Anna. What you tank you like for drink, eh?

ANNA—(*promptly*) I'll take a— (*then suddenly reminded—confusedly*) I don't know. What'a they got here?

CHRIS—(*with a grin*) Ay don't tank dey got much fancy drink for young gel in dis place, Anna. Yinger ale—sas'prilla, maybe.

ANNA—(*forcing a laugh herself*) Make it sas, then.

CHRIS—(*coming up to her—with a wink*) Ay tal you, Anna, ve calabrate, yes—dis one time because ve meet after many year. (*in a half whisper, embarrassedly*) Dey gat good port wine, Anna. It's good for you, Ay tank—little bit—for give you appetite. It ain't strong, neider. One glass don't go to your head, Ay promise.

ANNA—(*with a half hysterical laugh*) All right. I'll take port.

CHRIS—Ay go gat him. (*He goes out to the bar. As soon as the door closes, Anna starts to her feet.*)

ANNA—(*picking up her bag—half-aloud—stammeringly*) Gawd, I can't stand this! I better beat it. (*Then she lets her bag drop, stumbles over to her chair again, and covering her face with her hands, begins to sob.*)

LARRY—(*putting down his paper as Chris comes up—with a grin*) Well, who's the blond?

CHRIS—(*proudly*) Dat vas Anna, Larry.

LARRY—(*in amazement*) Your daughter, Anna? (*Chris nods. Larry lets a long, low whistle escape him and turns away embarrassedly.*)

CHRIS—Don't you tank she vas pooty gel, Larry?

LARRY—(*rising to the occasion*) Sure! A peach!

CHRIS—You bet you! Give me drink for take back—one port vine for Anna—she calabrate dis one time with me—and small beer for me.

LARRY—(*as he gets the drinks*) Small beer for you, eh? She's reformin' you already.

CHRIS—(*pleased*) You bet! (*He takes the drinks. As she hears him coming, Anna hastily dries her eyes, tries to smile. Chris comes in and sets the drinks down on the table—stares at her for a second anxiously—patting her hand*) You look tired, Anna. Vell, Ay make you take good long rest now. (*picking up his beer*) Come, you drink vine. It put new life in you. (*She lifts her glass—he grins.*) Skoal, Anna! You know dat Svedish word?

ANNA—Skoal! (*downing her port at a gulp like a drink of whiskey—her lips trembling*) Skoal? Guess I know that word, all right, all right!

(*The Curtain Falls*)

O'NEILL's THIRD PULITZER REWARD

For „Strange Interlude" *(1928)*

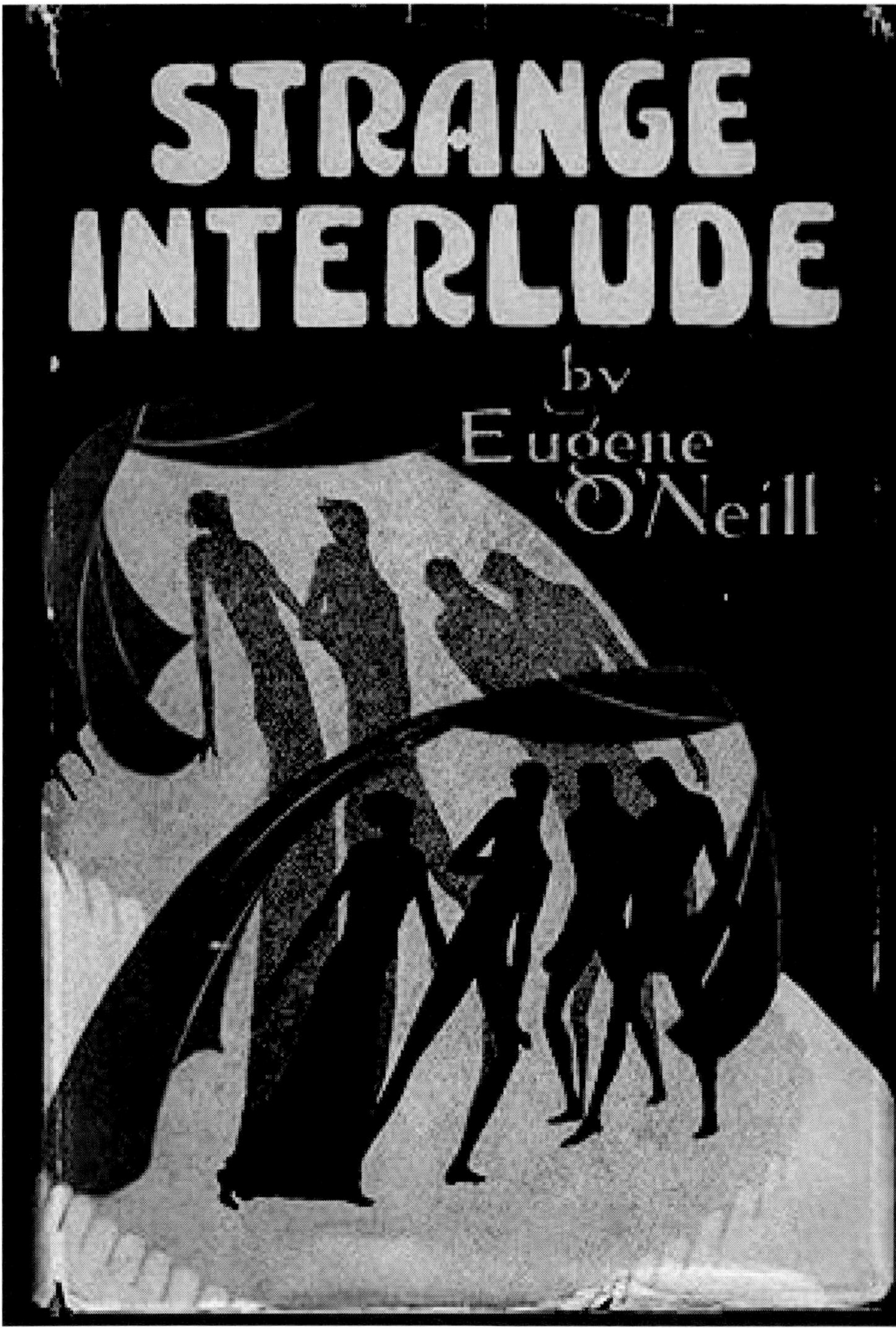

One of the many Book Editions

The Play and its Public Reception

Soon after earningi his second Pulitzer Prize fon Drama O'Neill began work on another play in early 1923, an experimental drama in nine acts, called Strange Include. He developed its scenario in 1925, and he wrote the play between May 1926 and the summer of 1927, and completed its text for publication in January 1928, during the final rehearsals for its premiere performance by the end of January.

The plot centers on Nina Leeds, Nina embarks on a series of sordid affairs before determining to marry an amiable fool, Sam Evans. While Nina is pregnant with Sam's child, she learns a horrifying secret known only to Sam's mother: insanity runs in the Evans family and could be inherited by any child of Sam's. Realizing that a child is essential to her own and to Sam's happiness, Nina decides on a „scientific" solution. She will abort Sam's child and conceive a child with the physician Ned Darrell, letting Sam believe that it is his.

The play's subject matter, very controversial for the 1920s, led to it being censored or banned in many cities outside New York, while the New York newspapers praised it, like the *New York Sun*: „*Strange Interlude* is inescapably O'Neill. It has the hugeness of mills of the gods. It builds up to such savagery of plot, such analytic slaying of its several people, that its last acts are soaked, strewn battleï¬ elds. But when one has done with *Strange Interlude* one has lived with it and its people a long, long while, completely, timelessly, as long as one lives with one's own secret self. And one has lived deep in the coils of a scheme of constant fascination, an enthralling and greatly affecting theme carried to furthest possible honesty and irony, to occasionally breath-taking beauty. It is a venture magniï¬ cent and a milestone to cleave the skyline of the future." _

According to their report dated March 17, 1928, the Pulitzer Prize jurors praised O'Nei1l's *Strange Interlude* in this way: „This play, by a man who has twice won the prize, repeats nothing of his former work. It develops a new technique to make possible a play of Freudian interpretations. It dramatizes the new psychology, and depicts the tragedy wrought in four lives because of the frustration of a woman's life due to the interference of a parent who thought (or pretended) he was acting for her good, when he was acting for his own selfish comfort. This drama of the subconscious and the frustration is sound and thoughtful in its developwent; but it also has great intensity of feeling, moments of beauty *Strange Interlude* gets its fingers deeply tangled in the web of human life, it has depth and intellectual power above any and all of its rivals. It is, in (the) jury's opinion, the logical recipient of the Pulitzer Prize for 1927-1928." So it happened and Eugene Of'Nei1l earned the prestigeous award for the third time. The play made it to 426 performances.

THE WORK AND ITS NEW YORK PREMIERE

Strange Interlude "zeroes in on four characters, chief among whom is the neurotic Nina. When her beloved, Gordon Shaw, died in the war before they could consummate their love, Nina consoled herself with the bodies of wounded soldiers, until she married Sam Evans, whom she did not love... A close friend... remains her lover through the years that follow," Samuel L. Leiter explains and continues: "Nina becomes the center of a circle of men: her husband, her lover, ... the mother-fixated novelist Charles Marsden, and her son. Her son develops into the heroic image of Gordon Shaw. She fails in her jealous attempts to disrupt the son's romance with Madeline Arnold. Sam dies; she marries Marsden."

The first New York production of *Strange Interlude* opened at the John Golden Theatre on January 30, 1928. Following are a scene photo together with main portions of the program containing the original cast:

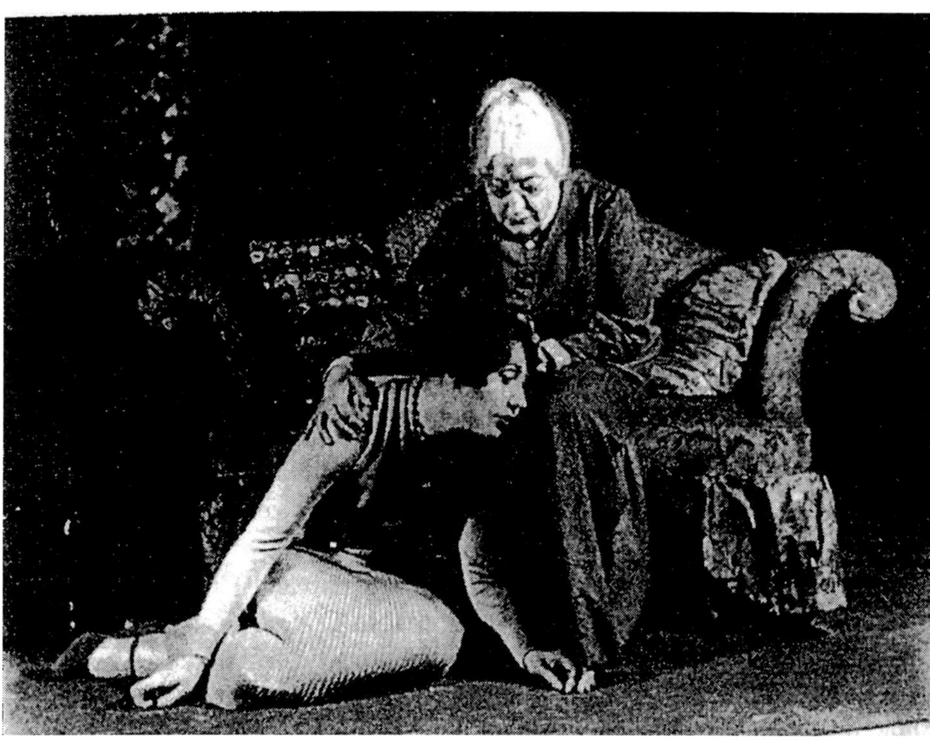

Lynn Fontanne and Helen Westley

THE NEW YORK MAGAZINE PROGRAM

John Golden Theatre

58th Street, Broadway and 7th Avenue

FIRE NOTICE: Look around NOW and choose the nearest Exit to your seat. In case of fire, walk (not run) to THAT Exit. Do not try to beat your neighbor to the street.

JOHN J. DORMAN, Fire Commissioner.

WEEK BEGINNING MONDAY EVENING, JUNE 18, 1928

FOURTH PRODUCTION OF THE TENTH SUBSCRIPTION SEASON

THE THEATRE GUILD

presents

STRANGE INTERLUDE

A Play in Nine Acts
By Eugene O'Neill

The Production directed by Philip Moeller
Settings by Jo Mielziner

CAST
(In the order of their appearance)

CHARLES MARSDEN	TOM POWERS
PROFESSOR LEEDS	PHILIP LEIGH
NINA LEEDS	LYNN FONTANNE
SAM EVANS	EARLE LARIMORE
EDMUND DARRELL	GLENN ANDERS
MRS. AMOS EVANS	HELEN WESTLEY
GORDON EVANS, as a boy	CHARLES WALTERS
MADELINE ARNOLD	ETHEL WESTLEY
GORDON EVANS, as a man	JOHN J. BURNS

SCENES

ACT 1

Library, Leeds' home in a small university town of New England.
An afternoon in late summer.

ACT 2

The same. Fall of the following year. Night.

ACT 3

Dining room of the Evans' homestead in northern New York State
Late spring of the next year. Morning.

ACT 4

The same as Acts 1 and 2. Fall of the same year. Evening.

ACT 5

Sitting room of small house Sam has rented at the Seashore near New York. The following April. Morning.

(DINNER INTERMISSION OF ONE HOUR)

ACT 6

The Same. A little over a year later. Evening.

ACT 7

Sitting room of the Evans' apartment on Park Avenue.
Nearly ten years later. Early afternoon.

ACT 8

Section of afterdeck of the Evans' cruiser anchored near the finish line at Poughkeepsie. Thirteen years later. Afternoon.

ACT 9

A terrace on the Evans' estate on Long Island.
Several months later. Late afternoon.

Stage Manager—Maurice McRae
Ass't Stage Manager—Eric Linden

Scenery built by Cleon Throckmorton, Inc. Painted by Robert Bergman.
Stockings by Van Raalte.

THE THEATRE GUILD, INC.

Board of Managers

Theresa Helburn, Philip Moeller, Maurice Wertheim
Lawrence Langner, Lee Simonson, Helen Westley

Executive Director: Theresa Helburn

Business Manager — Warren P. Munsell
Press Department — Robert F. Sisk

Play Reading Dept. — Courtenay Lemon

Reader of Foreign Plays—Anita Block

Technical Director — Kate Lawson
Counsel — Charles A. Riegelman
Subscription Secretary — Addie Williams

Address communications to the THEATRE GUILD, Inc.
245 West 52nd Street, New York City

Dr. Frank D. Fackenthal,
Secretary of Columbia University,
New York City.

Dear Sir:

Hereinunder is sent you the report of the Pulitzer prize drama Jury for the season of 1927-1928. It is a pleasure to report that the judgment of the jury is again unanimous, Messrs. Walter Prichard Eaton and Clayton Hamilton, the other two members of the Jury, being in entire agreement with myself.

Of the plays which by general consent and your jury's observation were candidates of standing for the Pulitzer prize this year, the following were the leaders;-

"The Royal Family", by Ferber and Kauffman--seems too confined to the comedy of stage folk to meet the terms of the award;

"The Racket" by Bartlett Cormack, praisworthy in its veracious detail, but a "crook" melodrama lacking sufficient dignity for this prize;

"Behold The Bridegroom" by George Kelly, already a Pulitzer prize winner; this play inferior to his winning work, which alone should rule it out;

"The Trial Of Mary Dugan" by Bayard Veiller, expertly contrived and admirably written, but also a melodrama of crime and the courts, made upon a lower level than various other candidates for this prize;

"Paris Bound", by Philip Barry, a clever and well written comedy of manners, with seriousness behind its levity: worth consideration;

"Coquette", by Ann Preston Bridgers and George Abbott, a play of the new South opposed to the old South, in the clash of two generations; for two acts significant drama, then becoming too arbitrary and losing itself in "theatre"

"Four Walls" by Dana Burnett and Geo. Abbott, a play about a N. Y. gangster, who learns that himself and his environment are prison walls, not the bars of Sing Sing; a play with a serious idea, logically worked out, and full of spiritual value, would be the second choice of your jury,

First page of the Pulitzer Prize Drama Jury Report of March 17, 1928

Passed

"Strange Interlude", by Eugene O'Neill. This play, by a man who has twice won the prize, repeats nothing of his former work. It develops a new technique to make possible a play of Freudian interpretations. It dramatizes the new psychology, and depicts the tragedy wrought in four lives because of the frustration of a woman's life due to the interference of a parent who thought (or pretended) he was acting for her good, when he was acting for his own selfish comfort. This drama of the subconscious and of frustration is sound and thoughtful in its development; but it also has great intensity of feeling, moments of beauty, and above all it shows dramatically that the conscious emotions, which give us dignity in our own eyes as individuals, cannot be ignored. In spite of too great length, some pretentiousness, and the abnormality of the "case" studied, "Strange Interlude" gets its fingers deeply tangled in the web of human life, it has depth and intellectual power above any and all of its rivals. It is, in your jury's opinion, the logical recipient of the Pulitzer prize for 1927-1928.

Very sincerely

A. E. Thomas

Chairman.

Second page of the Pulitzer Prize Drama Jury Report of March 17, 1928

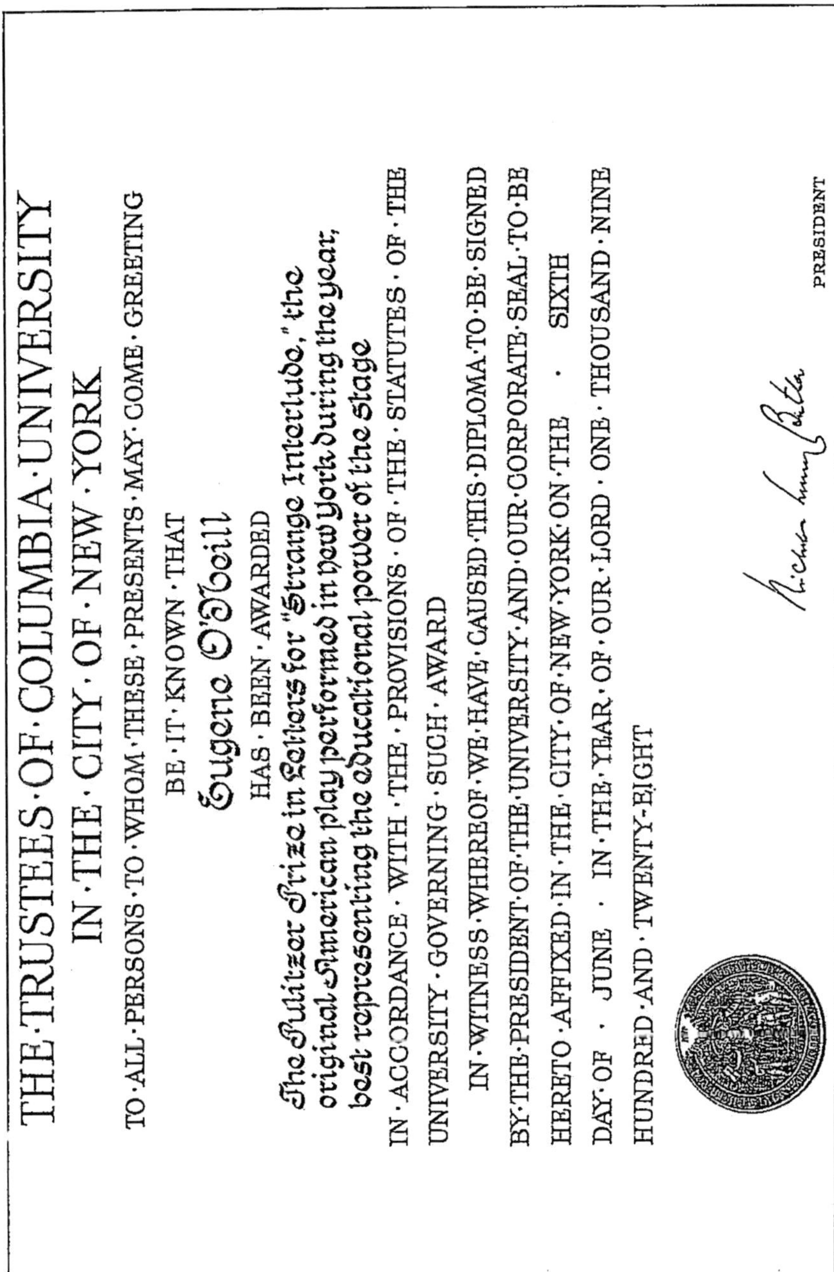

THE·TRUSTEES·OF·COLUMBIA·UNIVERSITY
IN·THE·CITY·OF·NEW·YORK

TO·ALL·PERSONS·TO·WHOM·THESE·PRESENTS·MAY·COME·GREETING

BE·IT·KNOWN·THAT

Eugene O'Neill

HAS·BEEN·AWARDED

The Pulitzer Prize in Letters for "Strange Interlude," the original American play performed in New York during the year, best representing the educational power of the stage

IN·ACCORDANCE·WITH·THE·PROVISIONS·OF·THE·STATUTES·OF·THE UNIVERSITY·GOVERNING·SUCH·AWARD

IN·WITNESS·WHEREOF·WE·HAVE·CAUSED·THIS·DIPLOMA·TO·BE·SIGNED BY·THE·PRESIDENT·OF·THE·UNIVERSITY·AND·OUR·CORPORATE·SEAL·TO·BE HERETO·AFFIXED·IN·THE·CITY·OF·NEW·YORK·ON·THE · SIXTH DAY·OF · JUNE · IN·THE·YEAR·OF·OUR·LORD·ONE·THOUSAND·NINE HUNDRED·AND·TWENTY-EIGHT

PRESIDENT

Eugene O'Neill's third Pulitzer Prize Certificate for his Play „Strange Interlude", signed by Columbia University President Nicholas Murray Butler on June 6, 1928

CHARACTERS

Charles Marsden
Professor Henry Leeds
Nina Leeds, *his daughter*
Edmund Darrell
Sam Evans
Mrs. Amos Evans, *Sam's mother*
Gordon Evans
Madeline Arnold

SCENES

First Part

Act One

Library, the Leeds' home in a small university town of New England—an afternoon in late summer.

Act Two

The same. Fall of the following year. Night.

Act Three

Dining room of the Evans' homestead in northern New York state—late spring of the next year. Morning.

Act Four

The same as Acts One and Two. Fall of the same year. Evening.

Act Five

Sitting room of small house Evans has rented in a seashore suburb near New York. The following April. Morning.

Second Part

Act Six

The same. A little over a year later. Evening.

Act Seven

Sitting room of the Evans' apartment on Park Avenue. Nearly eleven years later. Early afternoon.

Strange Interlude

FIRST PART

ACT ONE

SCENE—*The library of Professor Leeds' home in a small university town in New England. This room is at the front part of his house with windows opening on the strip of lawn between the house and the quiet residential street. It is a small room with a low ceiling. The furniture has been selected with a love for old New England pieces. The walls are lined almost to the ceiling with glassed-in bookshelves. These are packed with books, principally editions, many of them old and rare, of the ancient classics in the original Greek and Latin, of the later classics in French and German and Italian, of all the English authors who wrote while* s *was still like an* f *and a few since then, the most modern probably being Thackeray. The atmosphere of the room is that of a cosy, cultured retreat, sedulously built as a sanctuary where, secure with the culture of the past at his back, a fugitive from reality can view the present safely from a distance, as a superior with condescending disdain, pity, and even amusement.*

There is a fair-sized table, a heavy armchair, a rocker, and an old bench made comfortable with cushions. The table, with the Professor's armchair at its left, is arranged toward the left of the room, the rocker is at center, the bench at right.

There is one entrance, a door in the right wall, rear.

It is late afternoon of a day in August. Sunshine, cooled and dimmed in the shade of trees, fills the room with a soothing light.

The sound of a maid's voice—a middle-aged woman—explaining familiarly but respectfully from the right, and Marsden enters. He is a tall thin man of thirty-five, meticulously well-dressed in tweeds of distinctly English tailoring, his appearance that of an Anglicized New England gentleman. His face is too long for its width, his nose is high and narrow, his forehead broad, his mild blue eyes those of a dreamy self-analyst, his thin lips ironical and a bit sad. There is an indefinable feminine quality about him, but it is nothing apparent in either appearance or act. His manner is cool and poised. He speaks with a careful ease as one who listens to his own conversation. He has long fragile hands, and the stoop to his shoulders of a man weak muscularly, who has never liked athletics and has always been regarded as of delicate constitution. The main point about his personality is a quiet charm, a quality of appealing, inquisitive friendliness, always willing to listen, eager to sympathize, to like and to be liked.

MARSDEN—(*standing just inside the door, his tall, stooped figure leaning back against the books—nodding back at the maid and smiling kindly*) I'll wait in here, Mary. (*His eyes follow her for a second, then return to gaze around the room slowly with an appreciative relish for the familiar significance of the books. He smiles affectionately and his amused voice recites the words with a rhetorical resonance.*) Sanctum Sanctorum! (*His voice takes on a monotonous musing quality, his eyes stare idly at his drifting thoughts.*)

How perfectly the Professor's unique haven! . . .

(*He smiles.*)

Primly classical . . . when New Englander meets Greek! . . .

(*looking at the books now*)

He hasn't added one book in years . . . how old was I when I first came here? . . . six . . . with my father . . . father . . . how dim his face has grown! . . . he wanted to speak to me just before he died . . . the hospital . . . smell of iodoform in the cool halls . . . hot summer . . . I bent down . . . his voice had withdrawn so far away . . . I couldn't understand him . . . what son can ever understand? . . . always too near, too soon, too distant or too late! . . .

(*His face has become sad with a memory of the bewildered suffering of the adolescent boy he had been at the time of his father's death. Then he shakes his head, flinging off his thoughts, and makes himself walk about the room.*)

What memories on such a smiling afternoon! . . . this pleasant old town after three months . . . I won't go to Europe again . . . couldn't write a line there . . . how answer the fierce question of all those dead and maimed? . . . too big a job for me! . . .

(*He sighs—then self-mockingly*)

But back here . . . it is the interlude that gently questions . . . in this town dozing . . . decorous bodies moving with circumspection through the afternoons . . . their habits affectionately chronicled . . . an excuse for weaving amusing words . . . my novels . . . not of cosmic importance, hardly . . .

(*then self-reassuringly*)

but there is a public to cherish them, evidently . . . and I can write! . . . more than one can say of these modern sex-yahoos! . . . I must start work tomorrow . . . I'd like to use the Professor in a novel sometime . . . and his wife . . . seems impossible she's been dead six years . . . so aggressively his wife! . . . poor Professor! now it's Nina who bosses him . . . but that's different . . . she has bossed me, too, ever since she was a baby . . . she's a woman now . . . known love and death . . . Gordon brought down in flames . . . two days before the armistice . . . what fiendish irony! . . . his wonderful athlete's body . . . her lover . . . charred bones in a cage of twisted steel . . . no wonder she broke down . . . Mother said she's become quite queer lately . . . Mother seemed jealous of my concern . . . why have I never fallen in love with Nina? . . . could I? . . . that way . . . used to dance her on my knee . . . sit her on my lap . . . even now she'd never think anything about it . . . but sometimes the scent of her hair and skin . . . like a dreamy drug . . . dreamy! . . . there's the rub! . . . all dreams with me! . . . my sex life among the phantoms! . . .

(*He grins torturedly.*)

Why? . . . oh, this digging in gets nowhere . . . to the devil with sex! . . . our impotent pose of today to beat the loud drum on fornication! . . . boasters . . . eunuchs parading with the phallus! . . . giving themselves away . . . whom do they fool? . . . not even themselves! . . .

(*his face suddenly full of an intense pain and disgust*)

Ugh! . . . always that memory! . . . why can't I ever forget? . . . as sickeningly clear as if it were yesterday . . . prep school . . . Easter vacation . . . Fatty Boggs and Jack Frazer . . . that house of cheap vice

. . . one dollar! . . . why did I go? . . . Jack, the dead game sport . . . how I admired him! . . . afraid of his taunts . . . he pointed to the Italian girl . . . "Take her!" . . . daring me . . . I went . . . miserably frightened . . . what a pig she was! . . . pretty vicious face under caked powder and rouge . . . surly and contemptuous . . . lumpy body . . . short legs and thick ankles . . . slums of Naples . . . "What you gawkin' about? Git a move on, kid" . . . kid! . . . I *was* only a kid! . . . sixteen . . . test of manhood . . . ashamed to face Jack again unless . . . fool! . . . I might have lied to him! . . . but I honestly thought that wench would feel humiliated if I . . . oh, stupid kid! . . . back at the hotel I waited till they were asleep . . . then sobbed . . . thinking of Mother . . . feeling I had defiled her . . . and myself . . . forever! . . .

(*mocking bitterly*)

"Nothing half so sweet in life as love's young dream," what? . . .

(*He gets to his feet impatiently.*)

Why does my mind always have to dwell on that? . . . too silly . . . no importance really . . . an incident such as any boy of my age . . .

(*He hears someone coming quickly from the right and turns expectantly. Professor Leeds enters, a pleased relieved expression fighting the flurried worry on his face. He is a small, slender man of fifty-five, his hair gray, the top of his head bald. His face, prepossessing in spite of its too-small, over-refined features, is that of a retiring, studious nature. He has intelligent eyes and a smile that can be ironical. Temperamentally timid, his defense is an assumption of his complacent, superior manner of the classroom toward the world at large. This defense is strengthened by a natural tendency toward a prim provincialism where practical present-day considerations are concerned (though he is most liberal—even radical—in his tolerant understanding of the manners and morals of Greece and Imperial Rome!). This classroom poise of his, however, he cannot quite carry off outside the classroom. There is an unconvincing quality about it that leaves his larger audience—and particularly the Professor himself—subtly embarrassed. As*

Marsden is one of his old students, whom, in addition, he has known from childhood, he is perfectly at ease with him.)

MARSDEN—(*holding out his hand—with unmistakable liking*) Here I am again, Professor!

PROFESSOR LEEDS—(*shaking his hand and patting him on the back—with genuine affection*) So glad to see you, Charlie! A surprise, too! We didn't expect you back so soon! (*He sits in his chair on the left of the table while Marsden sits in the rocker. Looking away from Marsden a moment, his face now full of selfish relief as he thinks*)

Fortunate, his coming back . . . always calming influence on Nina . . .

MARSDEN—And I never dreamed of returning so soon. But Europe, Professor, is the big casualty they were afraid to set down on the list.

PROFESSOR LEEDS—(*his face clouding*) Yes, I suppose you found everything completely changed since before the war. (*He thinks resentfully*)

The war . . . Gordon! . . .

MARSDEN—Europe has "gone west"—(*he smiles whimsically*) to America, let's hope! (*then frowningly*) I couldn't stand it. There were millions sitting up with the corpse already, who had a family right to be there— (*then matter-of-factly*) I was wasting my time, too. I couldn't write a line. (*then gaily*) But where's Nina? I must see Nina!

PROFESSOR LEEDS—She'll be right in. She said she wanted to finish thinking something out— You'll find Nina changed, Charlie, greatly changed! (*He sighs—thinking with a trace of guilty alarm*)

The first thing she said at breakfast . . . "I dreamed of Gordon" . . . as if she wanted to taunt me! . . . how absurd! . . . her eyes positively glared! . . .

(*suddenly blurting out resentfully*) She dreams about Gordon.

MARSDEN—(*looking at him with amused surprise*) Well, I'd hardly call that a change, would you?

PROFESSOR LEEDS—(*thinking, oblivious to this remark*)

But I must constantly bear in mind that she's not herself . . . that she's a sick girl . . .

MARSDEN—(*thinking*)

The morning news of Gordon's death came . . . her

face like gray putty . . . beauty gone . . . no face can afford intense grief . . . it's only later when sorrow . . .

(*with concern*) Just what do you mean by changed, Professor? Before I left she seemed to be coming out of that horrible numbed calm.

PROFESSOR LEEDS—(*slowly and carefully*) Yes, she has played a lot of golf and tennis this summer, motored around with her friends, and even danced a good deal. And she eats with a ravenous appetite. (*thinking frightenedly*)

Breakfast . . . "dreamed of Gordon" . . . what a look of hate for me in her eyes! . . .

MARSDEN—But that sounds splendid! When I left she wouldn't see anyone or go anywhere. (*thinking pityingly*)

Wandering from room to room . . . her thin body and pale lost face . . . gutted, love-abandoned eyes! . . .

PROFESSOR LEEDS—Well, now she's gone to the opposite extreme! Sees everyone—bores, fools—as if she'd lost all discrimination or wish to discriminate. And she talks interminably, Charlie—intentional nonsense, one would say! Refuses to be serious! Jeers at everything!

MARSDEN—(*consolingly*) Oh, that's all undoubtedly part of the effort she's making to forget.

PROFESSOR LEEDS—(*absent-mindedly*) Yes. (*arguing with himself*)

Shall I tell him? . . . no . . . it might sound silly . . . but it's terrible to be so alone in this . . . if Nina's mother had lived . . . my wife . . . dead! . . . and for a time I actually felt released! . . . wife! . . . helpmeet! . . . now I need help! . . . no use! . . . she's gone! . . .

MARSDEN—(*watching him—thinking with a condescending affection*)

Good little man . . . he looks worried . . . always fussing about something . . . he must get on Nina's nerves. . . .

(*reassuringly*) No girl could forget Gordon in a hurry, especially after the shock of his tragic death.

PROFESSOR LEEDS—(*irritably*) I realize that. (*thinking resentfully*)

Gordon . . . always Gordon with everyone! . . .

MARSDEN—By the way, I located the spot near Sedan where Gordon's machine fell. Nina asked me to, you know.

PROFESSOR LEEDS—(*irritated—expostulatingly*) For heaven's sake, don't remind her! Give her a chance to forget if you want to see her well again. After all, Charlie, life must be lived and Nina can't live with a corpse forever! (*trying to control his irritation and talk in an objective tone*) You see, I'm trying to see things through clearly and unsentimentally. If you'll remember, I was as broken up as anyone over Gordon's death. I'd become so reconciled to Nina's love for him—although, as you know, I was opposed at first, and for fair reasons, I think, for the boy, for all his good looks and prowess in sport and his courses, really came of common people and had no money of his own except as he made a career for himself.

MARSDEN—(*a trifle defensively*) I'm sure he would have had a brilliant career.

PROFESSOR LEEDS—(*impatiently*) No doubt. Although you must acknowledge, Charlie, that college heroes rarely shine brilliantly in after life. Unfortunately, the tendency to spoil them in the university is a poor training—

MARSDEN—But Gordon was absolutely unspoiled, I should say.

PROFESSOR LEEDS—(*heatedly*) Don't misunderstand me, Charlie! I'd be the first to acknowledge— (*a bit pathetically*) It isn't Gordon, Charlie. It's his memory, his ghost, you might call it, haunting Nina, whose influence I have come to dread because of the terrible change in her attitude toward me. (*His face twitches as if he were on the verge of tears—he thinks desperately*)

> I've got to tell him . . . he will see that I acted for the best . . . that I was justified. . . .

(*He hesitates—then blurts out*) It may sound incredible, but Nina has begun to act as if she hated me!

MARSDEN—(*startled*) Oh, come now!

PROFESSOR LEEDS—(*insistently*) Absolutely! I haven't wanted to admit it. I've refused to believe it, until it's become too appallingly obvious in her whole attitude toward me! (*His voice trembles.*)

MARSDEN—(*moved—expostulating*) Oh, now you're becoming morbid! Why, Nina has always idolized you! What possible reason—?

PROFESSOR LEEDS—(*quickly*) I can answer that, I think. She has a reason. But why she should blame me when she must know I acted for the best— You probably don't know, but just before he sailed for the front Gordon wanted their marriage to take place, and Nina consented. In fact, from the insinuations she lets drop now, she must have been most eager, but at the time— However, I felt it was ill-advised and I took Gordon aside and pointed out to him that such a precipitate marriage would be unfair to Nina, and scarcely honorable on his part.

MARSDEN—(*staring at him wonderingly*) You said that to Gordon? (*thinking cynically*)

> A shrewd move! . . . Gordon's proud spot, fairness and honor! . . . but was it honorable of you? . . .

PROFESSOR LEEDS—(*with a touch of asperity*) Yes, I said it, and I gave him my reason. There *was* the possibility he might be killed, in the flying service rather more than a possibility, which needless to say, I did not point out, but which Gordon undoubtedly realized, poor boy! If he were killed, he would be leaving Nina a widow, perhaps with a baby, with no resources, since he was penniless, except what pension she might get from the government; and all this while she was still at an age when a girl, especially one of Nina's charm and beauty, should have all of life before her. Decidedly, I told him, in justice to Nina, they must wait until he had come back and begun to establish his position in the world. That was the square thing. And Gordon was quick to agree with me!

MARSDEN—(*thinking*)

> The square thing! . . . but we must all be crooks where happiness is concerned! . . . steal or starve! . . .

(*then rather ironically*) And so Gordon told Nina he'd suddenly realized it wouldn't be fair to her. But I gather he didn't tell her it was your scruple originally?

PROFESSOR LEEDS—No, I asked him to keep what I said strictly confidential.

MARSDEN—(*thinking ironically*)

Trusted to his honor again! . . . old fox! . . . poor Gordon! . . .

But Nina suspects now that you—?

PROFESSOR LEEDS—(*startled*) Yes. That's exactly it. She knows in some queer way. And she acts toward me exactly as if she thought I had deliberately destroyed her happiness, that I had hoped for Gordon's death and been secretly overjoyed when the news came! (*His voice is shaking with emotion.*) And there you have it, Charlie—the whole absurd mess! (*thinking with a strident accusation*)

And it's true, you contemptible . . . !

(*then miserably defending himself*)

No! . . . I acted unselfishly . . . for her sake! . . .

MARSDEN—(*wonderingly*) You don't mean to tell me she has accused you of all this?

PROFESSOR LEEDS—Oh, no, Charlie! Only by hints—looks—innuendos. She knows she has no real grounds, but in the present state of her mind the real and the unreal become confused—

MARSDEN—(*thinking cynically*)

As always in all minds . . . or how could men live? . . .

(*soothingly*) That's just what you ought to bear in your mind—the state of hers—and not get so worked up over what I should say is a combination of imagination on both your parts. (*He gets to his feet as he hears voices from the right.*) Buck up! This must be Nina coming. (*The Professor gets to his feet, hastily composing his features into his bland, cultured expression.*)

MARSDEN—(*thinking self-mockingly but a bit worried about himself*)

My heart pounding! . . . seeing Nina again! . . . how sentimental . . . how she'd laugh if she knew! . . . and quite rightly . . . absurd for me to react as if I loved . . . that way . . . her dear old Charlie . . . ha! . . .

(*He smiles with bitter self-mockery.*)

PROFESSOR LEEDS—(*thinking worriedly*)

I hope she won't make a scene . . . she's seemed on

the verge all day . . . thank God, Charlie's like one of the family . . . but what a life for me! . . . with the opening of the new term only a few weeks off! . . . I can't do it . . . I'll have to call in a nerve specialist . . . but the last one did her no good . . . his outrageous fee . . . he can take it to court . . . I absolutely refuse . . . but if he should bring suit? . . . what a scandal . . . no, I'll have to pay . . . somehow . . . borrow . . . he has me in a corner, the robber! . . .

NINA—(*enters and stands just inside the doorway looking directly at her father with defiant eyes, her face set in an expression of stubborn resolve. She is twenty, tall with broad square shoulders, slim strong hips and long beautifully developed legs—a fine athletic girl of the swimmer, tennis player, golfer type. Her straw-blond hair, framing her sunburned face, is bobbed. Her face is striking, handsome rather than pretty, the bone structure prominent, the forehead high, the lips of her rather large mouth clearly modelled above the firm jaw. Her eyes are beautiful and bewildering, extraordinarily large and a deep greenish blue. Since Gordon's death they have a quality of continually shuddering before some terrible enigma, of being wounded to their depths and made defiant and resentful by their pain. Her whole manner, the charged atmosphere she gives off, is totally at variance with her healthy outdoor physique. It is strained, nerve-racked, hectic, a terrible tension of will alone maintaining self-possession. She is dressed in smart sport clothes. Too preoccupied with her resolve to remember or see Marsden, she speaks directly to her father in a voice tensely cold and calm.*) I have made up my mind, Father.

PROFESSOR LEEDS—(*thinking distractedly*)

What does she mean? . . . oh, God help me! . . .

(*flustered—hastily*) Don't you see Charlie, Nina?

MARSDEN—(*troubled—thinking*)

She has changed . . . what has happened? . . .

(*He comes forward toward her—a bit embarrassed but affectionately using his pet name for her.*) Hello, Nina Cara Nina! Are you trying to cut me dead, young lady?

NINA—(*turning her eyes to Marsden, holding out her hand for him to shake, in her cool, preoccupied voice*) Hello, Charlie. (*Her eyes immediately return to her father.*) Listen, Father!

MARSDEN—(*standing near her, concealing his chagrin*)

That hurts! . . . I mean nothing! . . . but she's a sick girl . . . I must make allowance . . .

PROFESSOR LEEDS—(*thinking distractedly*)

That look in her eyes! . . . hate! . . .

(*with a silly giggle*) Really, Nina, you're absolutely rude! What has Charlie done?

NINA—(*in her cool tone*) Why, nothing. Nothing at all. (*She goes to him with a detached, friendly manner.*) Did I seem rude, Charlie? I didn't mean to be. (*She kisses him with a cool, friendly smile.*) Welcome home. (*thinking wearily*)

What has Charlie done? . . . nothing . . . and never will . . . Charlie sits beside the fierce river, immaculately timid, cool and clothed, watching the burning, frozen naked swimmers drown at last. . . .

MARSDEN—(*thinking torturedly*)

Cold lips . . . the kiss of contempt! . . . for dear old Charlie! . . .

(*forcing a good-natured laugh*) Rude? Not a bit! (*banteringly*) As I've often reminded you, what can I expect when the first word you ever spoke in this world was an insult to me. "Dog" you said, looking right at me—at the age of one! (*He laughs. The Professor laughs nervously. Nina smiles perfunctorily.*)

NINA—(*thinking wearily*)

The fathers laugh at little daughter Nina . . . I must get away! . . . nice Charlie doggy . . . faithful . . . fetch and carry . . . bark softly in books at the deep night. . . .

PROFESSOR LEEDS—(*thinking*)

What is she thinking? . . . I can't stand living like this! . . .

(*giggle gone to a twitching grin*) You are a cool one, Nina! You'd think you'd just seen Charlie yesterday!

NINA—(*slowly—coolly and reflectively*) Well, the war is over. Coming back safe from Europe isn't such an unusual feat now, is it?

MARSDEN—(*thinking bitterly*)

A taunt . . . I didn't fight . . . physically unfit . . . not like Gordon . . . Gordon in flames . . . how she must resent my living! . . . thinking of me, scribbling in press bureau . . . louder and louder lies . . . drown the guns and the screams . . . deafen the world with lies . . . hired choir of liars! . . .

(*forcing a joking tone*) Little you know the deadly risks I ran, Nina! If you'd eaten some of the food they gave me on my renovated transport, you'd shower me with congratulations! (*The Professor forces a snicker.*)

NINA—(*coolly*) Well, you're here, and that's that. (*then suddenly expanding in a sweet, genuinely affectionate smile*) And I *am* glad, Charlie, always glad you're here! You know that.

MARSDEN—(*delighted and embarrassed*) I hope so, Nina!

NINA—(*turning on her father—determinedly*) I must finish what I started to say, Father. I've thought it all out and decided that I simply must get away from here at once—or go crazy! And I'm going on the nine-forty tonight. (*She turns to Marsden with a quick smile.*) You'll have to help me pack, Charlie! (*thinking with weary relief*)

Now that's said . . . I'm going . . . never come back . . . oh, how I loathe this room! . . .

MARSDEN—(*thinking with alarm*)

What's this? . . . going? . . . going to whom? . . .

PROFESSOR LEEDS—(*thinking—terrified*)

Going? . . . never come back to me? . . . no! . . .

(*desperately putting on his prim severe manner toward an unruly pupil*) This is rather a sudden decision, isn't it? You haven't mentioned before that you were considering—in fact, you've led me to believe that you were quite contented here—that is, of course I mean for the time being, and I really think—

MARSDEN—(*looking at Nina—thinking with alarm*)

Going away to whom? . . .

(*then watching the Professor with a pitying shudder*)

He's on the wrong tack with his professor's manner . . . her eyes seeing cruelly through him . . . with what terrible recognition! . . . God, never bless me with children! . . .

NINA—(*thinking with weary scorn*)

The Professor of Dead Languages is talking again . . . a dead man lectures on the past of living . . . since I was born I have been in his class, loving-attentive, pupil-daughter Nina . . . my ears numb with spiritless messages from the dead . . . dead words droning on . . . listening because he is my cultured father . . . a little more inclined to deafness than the rest (let me be just) because he is my father . . . father? . . . what is father? . . .

PROFESSOR LEEDS—(*thinking—terrified*)

I must talk her out of it! . . . find the right words! . . . oh, I know she won't hear me! . . . oh, wife, why did you die, you would have talked to her, she would have listened to you! . . .

(*continuing in his professor's superior manner*) —and I really think, in justice to yourself above all, you ought to consider this step with great care before you definitely commit yourself. First and foremost, there is your health to be taken into consideration. You've been very ill, Nina, how perilously so perhaps you're not completely aware, but I assure you, and Charlie can corroborate my statement, that six months ago the doctors thought it might be years before—and yet, by staying home and resting and finding healthy outdoor recreation among your old friends, and keeping your mind occupied with the routine of managing the household—(*he forces a prim playful smile*) and managing me, I might add!—you have wonderfully improved and I think it most ill-advised in the hottest part of August, while you're really still a convalescent—

NINA—(*thinking*)

Talking! . . . his voice like a fatiguing dying tune droned on a beggar's organ . . . his words arising from the tomb of a soul in puffs of ashes . . .

(*torturedly*)

Ashes! . . . oh, Gordon, my dear one! . . . oh, lips on my lips, oh, strong arms around me, oh, spirit so brave and generous and gay! . . . ashes dissolving into mud! . . . mud and ashes! . . . that's all! . . . gone! . . . gone forever from me! . . .

PROFESSOR LEEDS—(*thinking angrily*)

Her eyes . . . I know that look . . . tender, loving . . . not for me . . . damn Gordon! . . . I'm glad he's dead! . . .

(*a touch of asperity in his voice*) And at a couple of hours' notice to leave everything in the air, as it were— (*then judicially*) No, Nina, frankly, I can't see it. You know I'd gladly consent to anything in the world to benefit you, but—surely, you can't have reflected!

NINA—(*thinking torturedly*)

> Gordon darling, I must go away where I can think of you in silence! . . .

(*She turns on her father, her voice trembling with the effort to keep it in control—icily*) It's no use talking, Father. I *have* reflected and I am going!

PROFESSOR LEEDS—(*with asperity*) But I tell you it's quite impossible! I don't like to bring up the money consideration but I couldn't possibly afford— And how will you support yourself, if I may ask? Two years in the University, I am sorry to say, won't be much use to you when applying for a job. And even if you had completely recovered from your nervous breakdown, which it's obvious to anyone you haven't, then I most decidedly think you should finish out your science course and take your degree before you attempt— (*thinking desperately*)

> No use! . . . she doesn't hear . . . thinking of Gordon . . . she'll defy me . . .

NINA—(*thinking desperately*)

> I must keep calm . . . I mustn't let go or I'll tell him everything . . . and I mustn't tell him . . . he's my father . . .

(*with the same cold calculating finality*) I've already had six months' training for a nurse. I will finish my training. There's a doctor I know at a sanitarium for crippled soldiers—a friend of Gordon's. I wrote to him and he answered that he'll gladly arrange it.

PROFESSOR LEEDS—(*thinking furiously*)

> Gordon's friend . . . Gordon again! . . .

(*severely*) You seriously mean to tell me you, in your condition, want to nurse in a soldiers' hospital! Absurd!

MARSDEN—(*thinking with indignant revulsion*)

> Quite right, Professor! . . . her beauty . . . all those men . . . in their beds . . . it's too revolting! . . .

(*with a persuasive quizzing tone*) Yes, I must say I can't see you as a peace-time Florence Nightingale, Nina!

NINA—(*coolly, struggling to keep control, ignoring these remarks*) So you see, Father, I've thought of everything and there's not the slightest reason to worry about me. And I've been teaching Mary how to take care of you. So you won't need me at all. You can go along as if nothing had happened—and really, nothing will have happened that hasn't already happened.

PROFESSOR LEEDS—Why, even the manner in which you address me—the tone you take—proves conclusively that you're not yourself!

NINA—(*her voice becoming a bit uncanny, her thoughts breaking through*) No, I'm not myself yet. That's just it. Not all myself. But I've been becoming myself. And I must finish!

PROFESSOR LEEDS—(*with angry significance—to Marsden*) You hear her, Charlie? She's a sick girl!

NINA—(*slowly and strangely*) I'm not sick. I'm too well. But they are sick and I must give my health to help them to live on, and to live on myself. (*with a sudden intensity in her tone*) I must pay for my cowardly treachery to Gordon! You should understand this, Father, you who— (*She swallows hard, catching her breath. Thinking desperately*)

> I'm beginning to tell him! . . . I mustn't! . . . he's my father! . . .

PROFESSOR LEEDS—(*in a panic of guilty fear, but defiantly*) What do you mean? I am afraid you're not responsible for what you're saying.

NINA—(*again with the strange intensity*) I must pay! It's my plain duty! Gordon is dead! What use is my life to me or anyone? But I must make it of use—by giving it! (*fiercely*) I must learn to give myself, do you hear—give and give until I can make that gift of myself for a man's happiness without scruple, without fear, without joy except in his joy! When I've accomplished this I'll have found myself, I'll know how to start in living my own life again! (*appealing to them with a desperate impatience*) Don't you see? In the name of the commonest decency and honor, I owe it to Gordon!

PROFESSOR LEEDS—(*sharply*) No, I can't see—nor anyone else! (*thinking savagely*)

> I hope Gordon is in hell! . . .

MARSDEN—(*thinking*)

Give herself? . . . can she mean her body? . . . beautiful body . . . to cripples? . . . for Gordon's sake? . . . damn Gordon! . . .

(*coldly*) What do you mean, you owe it to Gordon, Nina?

PROFESSOR LEEDS—(*bitterly*) Yes, how ridiculous! It seems to me when you gave him your love, he got more than he could ever have hoped—

NINA—(*with fierce self-contempt*) I gave him? What did I give him? It's what I didn't give! That last night before he sailed—in his arms until my body ached—kisses until my lips were numb—knowing all that night—something in me knowing he would die, that he would never kiss me again—knowing this so surely yet with my cowardly brain lying, no, he'll come back and marry you, you'll be happy ever after and feel his children at your breasts looking up with eyes so much like his, possessing eyes so happy in possessing you! (*then violently*) But Gordon never possessed me! I'm still Gordon's silly virgin! And Gordon is muddy ashes! And I've lost my happiness forever! All that last night I knew he wanted me. I knew it was only the honorable code-bound Gordon, who kept commanding from his brain, no, you mustn't, you must respect her, you must wait till you have a marriage license! (*She gives a mocking laugh.*)

PROFESSOR LEEDS—(*shocked*) Nina! This is really going too far!

MARSDEN—(*repelled—with a superior sneer*) Oh, come now, Nina! You've been reading books. Those don't sound like your thoughts.

PROFESSOR LEEDS—(*thinking—furiously*)

What an animal! . . . and my daughter! . . . she doesn't get it from me! . . . was her mother like that? . . .

(*distractedly*) Nina! I really can't listen!

NINA—(*savagely*) And that's exactly what my father did say! Wait, he told Gordon! Wait for Nina till the war's over, and you've got a good job and can afford a marriage license!

PROFESSOR LEEDS—(*crumbling pitifully*) Nina! I—!

MARSDEN—(*flurriedly—going to him*) Don't take her seriously, Professor! (*thinking with nervous repulsion*)

Nina has changed . . . all flesh now . . . lust . . . who would dream she was so sensual? . . . I wish I were out of this! . . . I wish I hadn't come here today! . . .

NINA—(*coldly and deliberately*) Don't lie any more, Father! Today I've made up my mind to face things. I know now why Gordon suddenly dropped all idea of marriage before he left, how unfair to me he suddenly decided it would be! Unfair to me! Oh, that's humorous! To think I might have had happiness, Gordon, and now Gordon's child— (*then directly accusing him*) You told him it'd be unfair, you put him on his honor, didn't you?

PROFESSOR LEEDS—(*collecting himself—woodenly*) Yes. I did it for your sake, Nina.

NINA—(*in the same voice as before*) It's too late for lies!

PROFESSOR LEEDS—(*woodenly*) Let us say then that I *persuaded* myself it was for your sake. That may be true. You are young. You think one can live with truth. Very well. It is also true I was jealous of Gordon. I was alone and I wanted to keep your love. I hated him as one hates a thief one may not accuse nor punish. I did my best to prevent your marriage. I was glad when he died. There. Is that what you wish me to say?

NINA—Yes. Now I begin to forget I've hated you. You were braver than I, at least.

PROFESSOR LEEDS—I wanted to live comforted by your love until the end. In short, I am a man who happens to be your father. (*He hides his face in his hands and weeps softly.*) Forgive that man!

MARSDEN—(*thinking timidly*)

In short, forgive us our possessing as we forgive those who possessed before us . . . Mother must be wondering what keeps me so long . . . it's time for tea . . . I must go home . . .

NINA—(*sadly*) Oh, I forgive you. But do you understand now that I must somehow find a way to give myself to Gordon still, that I must pay my debt and learn to forgive myself?

PROFESSOR LEEDS—Yes.

NINA—Mary will look after you.

PROFESSOR LEEDS—Mary will do very well, I'm sure.

MARSDEN—(*thinking*)

Nina has changed . . . this is no place for me . . . Mother is waiting tea. . . .

(*then venturing on an uncertain tone of pleasantry*) Quite so, you two. But isn't this all nonsense? Nina will be back with us in a month, Professor, what with the depressing heat and humidity, and the more depressing halt and the lame!

PROFESSOR LEEDS—(*sharply*) She must stay away until she gets well. This time I do speak for her sake.

NINA—I'll take the nine-forty. (*turning to Marsden—with a sudden girlishness*) Come on upstairs, Charlie, and help me pack! (*She grabs him by the hand and starts to pull him away.*)

MARSDEN—(*shrugging his shoulders—confusedly*) Well—I don't understand this!

NINA—(*with a strange smile*) But some day I'll read it all in one of your books, Charlie, and it'll be so simple and easy to understand that I won't be able to recognize it, Charlie, let alone understand it! (*She laughs teasingly.*) Dear old Charlie!

MARSDEN—(*thinking in agony*)

God damn in hell . . . dear old Charlie! . . .

(*then with a genial grin*) I'll have to propose, Nina, if you continue to be my severest critic! I'm a stickler for these little literary conventions, you know!

NINA—All right. Propose while we pack. (*She leads him off, right.*)

PROFESSOR LEEDS—(*blows his nose, wipes his eyes, sighs, clears his throat, squares his shoulders, pulls his coat down in front, sets his tie straight, and starts to take a brisk turn about the room. His face is washed blandly clean of all emotion.*)

Three weeks now . . . new term . . . I will have to be looking over my notes. . . .

(*He looks out of window, front.*)

Grass parched in the middle . . . Tom forgotten the sprinkler . . . careless . . . ah, there goes Mr. Davis of the bank . . . bank . . . my salary will go farther now . . . books I really need . . . all bosh two can live as cheaply as one . . . there are worse things than being a trained nurse . . . good background of discipline . . . she needs it . . . she may meet rich fellow there . . . mature . . . only students here for her . . . and their fathers never approve if they have anything. . . .

(*He sits down with a forced sigh of peace.*)

I am glad we had it out . . . his ghost will be gone now . . . no more Gordon, Gordon, Gordon, love and praise and tears, all for Gordon! . . . Mary will do very well by me . . . I will have more leisure and peace of mind . . . and Nina will come back home . . . when she is well again . . . the old Nina! . . . my little Nina! . . . she knows and she forgave me . . . she said so . . . said! . . . but could she really? . . . don't you imagine? . . . deep in her heart? . . . she still must hate? . . . oh, God! . . . I feel cold! . . . alone! . . . this home is abandoned! . . . the house is empty and full of death! . . . there is a pain about my heart! . . .

(*He calls hoarsely, getting to his feet*) Nina!

NINA'S VOICE—(*Her voice, fresh and girlish, calls from upstairs*) Yes, Father. Do you want me?

PROFESSOR LEEDS—(*struggling with himself—goes to door and calls with affectionate blandness*) No. Never mind. Just wanted to remind you to call for a taxi in good time.

NINA'S VOICE—I won't forget.

PROFESSOR LEEDS—(*looks at his watch*)

Five-thirty just . . . nine-forty, the train . . . then . . . Nina no more! . . . four hours more . . . she'll be packing . . . then good-bye . . . a kiss . . .

nothing more ever to say to each other . . . and I'll die in here some day . . . alone . . . gasp, cry out for help . . . the president will speak at the funeral . . . Nina will be here again . . . Nina in black . . . too late! . . .

(*He calls hoarsely*) Nina! (*There is no answer.*)

In other room . . . doesn't hear . . . just as well . . .

(*He turns to the bookcase and pulls out the first volume his hands come on and opens it at random and begins to read aloud sonorously like a child whistling to keep up his courage in the dark.*)

"Stetit unus in arcem
Erectus capitis victorque ad sidera mittit
Sidereos oculos propiusque adspectat Olympum
Inquiritque Iovem;" . . .

(*Curtain*)

O'NEILL's NOBEL LITERATURE PRIZE

For „*Original Concept of Tragedy*" (1936)

EUGENE
O'NEILL
THE COLLECTED WORKS
OF EUGENE O'NEILL

O'Neill's Additional Pulitzer Chances

After Eugene O'Neill had earned his third Pulitzer Prize in 1928, he several times was listed as a finalist in other Pulitzer jury reports. For example, in 1932 his play „Mourning Becomes Electraâ" was „seriously considered" for his next Pulitzer award but the jurors hesitated to select him because of the three decorations in the past. The same reservation by the Jury may have happened two years later when O'Neill's play „Ah Wildernis" also became a ffinalist but the committee did not have the courage to give him his fourth Pulitzer Prize.

It is interesting that just about the time O'Neill had completed „Mouring Becomes Electra" which was instrumental later in earning him th Nobel Prize, his name was being mentioned as a contender for that honor. In November, 1929, an article in the Paris edition of the *New York Herald-Tribune* had listed him as possible recipient of the Noble recognition. „Which mention," O'Neill said to a friend at the time, „is at least a step forward for us Yanks!" He observed, however, that the award was more likely to go to Thomas Mann. „I hope so," he added; „he deserves it. l think his work, with a few exceptions, is great stuff."

After the Nobel Prize was given to Thomas Mann, O'Neill's reaction was this: „On careful consideration - and no sour grapes about it because I have had no hopes - I think the Nobel Prize, until you become very old and childlike, costs more than it's worth. It's an anchor around one's neck that one would never he able to shake off." Despite O'Neill's estimate of European chauvinism, the Nobel award was bestowed on Sinclair Lewis the following year and received it in Stockholm on December 12, 1930.

In the following years O'Neill repeatedly was nominated for the Nobel Prize but others did win: in 1951 it was Erik Axel Karlfeldt from Sweden, followed by John Galsworthy from Enghand in 1932. The Russian Ivan Bunin was successful in 1933, followed by the Italian Luigi Pirandello in 1934. The 1935 Nobel Prize in Literature was not awarded after the Swedish Academy decided that no author in the fiel of literature was a suitable candidate. The Nobel Committee had received 52 nominations for 38 authors.

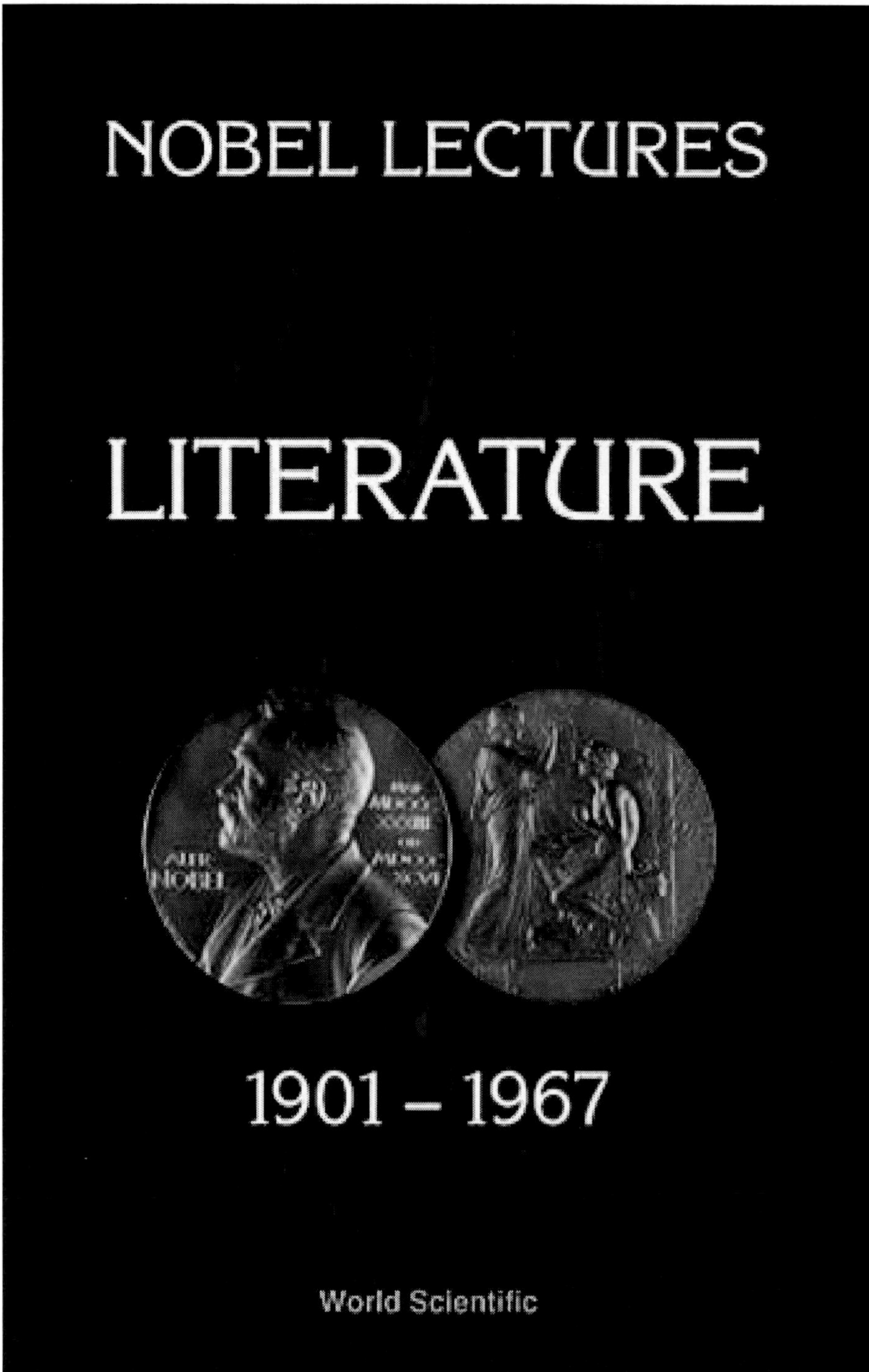
NOBEL LECTURES
LITERATURE
1901 – 1967
World Scientific

O'Neill's Noble Competitors of the Year

In 1936 the Nobel Committe received 47 nominations for 27 writers including Paul Valery from France, Ludwig Klages and Sigmund Freud from Germany and the American Eugene O'Neill who finally did win „for the power, hosesty and deep-felt emotions of his dramatic works, which embody an original concept of tragedy." He was the second American to become a Nobel literature laureate after Sinclair Lewis six years ago. while O'Neill and his wife Carlotta lived in Seattle, it was Carlotta who brought him the news on the morning of of November 12, 1936, after she had received a telephone call.

Reporters asked for and got some interviews From the Nobel Laureate. Later in the day, when O'Neill received official notification of the award from the Swedish consul, he said he would not be able to arrange his affaire in time to be in Stockholm for the presentation. O'Neill did very little work during the next few weeks. Answering the letters and telegrams of ongratulation that poured in took up much of ONeill's time between November 12 and the second week of December, when et Stockholm e annual Nobel Prize festivities started.

As the Laureate was unable to be present at the Noble Banouet at the City Hall in Stockholm on December 10, 1956, O'Neill had written an acceptance speech that was read by James E. Brown Jr., the American Charge d'Affairs at the U.S. Embassy in the Swedish capital. But before Brown could read O'Neill's speech, the ceremony was opened with a „Presentation Speech" by Per Hallström, Permanent Secretary of the Swedish Academy who praised O'Neill's works.

Prior to the speech, Robert Fries, Director of the Bergius Foundation, remarked: «It is difficult to explain the vital processes in the living organism; it is difficult to interpret the inmost essence of matter, but it is perhaps most difficult to sound the human mind and to understand the soul in it: shifting phases. With passionate intensity and impulsive genius Eugene O'Neill has done this in dramas, and one cannot but be captivated by the masterly way in which he deals with the great problems of life.« Then followed Hallström's O'Neill laudatio.

O'Neill praised by the Swedish Academy

Eugene O'Neill's dramatic production has been of a sombre character from the very first, and for him life as a whole quite early came to signify tragedy.

This has been attributed to the bitter experiencces of his youth, more especially to what he underwent as a sailor. The legendary nimbus that gathers around celebrities in his case took the form of heroic events created out of his

Eugene O'Neill and his wife Carlotta in Seattle, 1936, after hearing of the Nobel Prize

background. With his contempt for publicity, O'Neill straightway put a stop to all such attempts; there was no glamour to be derived from his drab hardships and toils. We may indeed conclude that the stern experiences were not uncongenial to his spirit, tending as they did to afford release of certain chaotic forces within him.

His pessimism was presumably on the one hand an innate trait of his being, on the other an offshoot of the literary current of the age, though possibly it is rather to be interpreted as the reaction of a profound personality to the American optimism of old tradition. Whatever the source of his pessimism may have been, however, the line of his development was marked out, and O'Neill became by degrees the uniquely and fiercely tragic dramatist that the world has come to know. The conception of life that he presents is not a product of elaborate thinking, but it has the genuine stamp of something lived through. It is based upon an exceedingly intense, one might say, heart-rent, realization of the austerity of life, side by side with a kind of rapture at the beauty of human destinies shaped in the struggle against odds.

A primitive sense of tragedy, as we see, lacking moral backing and achieving no inner victory – merely the bricks and mortar for the temple of tragedy in the grand and ancient style. By his very primitiveness, however, this modern tragedian has reached the well-spring of this form of creative art, a naive and simple belief in fate. At certain stages it has contributed a stream of pulsating life-blood to his work.

That was, however, at a later period. In his earliest dramas O'Neill was a strict and somewhat arid realist; those works we may here pass by. Of more moment were a series of one-act plays, based upon material assembled during his years at sea. They brought to the theatre something novel, and hence he attracted attention.

Those plays were not, however, dramatically notable; properly speaking, merely short stories couched in dialogue-form; true works of art, however, of their type, and heart-stirring in their simple, rugged delineation. In one of them, *The Moon of the Caribbees* (1918), he attains poetic heights, partly by the tenderness in depicting the indigence of a sailor's life with its naive illusions of joy, and pertly by the artistic background of the play: dirge-like Negro songs coming from a white coral shore beneath metallically glittering palms and the great moon of the Caribbean Sea. Altogether it is a mystical weave of melancholy, primitive savagery, yearning, lunar effulgence, and oppressive desolateness.

The drama *Anna Christie* (1921) achieves its most striking effect through the description of sailors' life ashore in and about waterfront saloons. The first act is O'Neill's masterpiece in the domain of strict realism, each character being depicted with supreme sureness and mastery. The content is the raising of a fallen Swedish girl to respectable human status by the strong and wholesome influences of the sea; for once pessimism is left out of the picture, the play having what is termed a happy ending.

With his drama *The Hairy Ape* (1922), also concerned with sailors' lives, O'Neill launches into that expressionism which sets its stamp upon his «ideadramas». The aim of expressionism in literature and the plastic arts is difficult to determine; nor need we discuss it, since for practical purposes a brief description suffices. It endeavours to produce its effects by a sort of mathematical method; it may be said to extract the square root of the complex phenomena of reality, and build with those abstractions a new world on an enormously magnified scale. The procedure is an irksome one and can hardly be said to achieve mathematical exactitude; for a long time, however, it met with great success throughout the world.

The Hairy Ape seeks to present on a monumental scale the rebellious slave of steam power, intoxicated with his force and with superman ideas. Outwardly he is a relapse to primitive man, and he presents himself as a kind of beast, suffering from yearning for genius. The play depicts his tragical discomfiture and ruin on being brought up against cruel society.

Subsequently O'Neill devoted himself for a number of years to a boldly expressionistic treatment of ideas and social questions. The resulting plays have little connection with real life; the poet and dreamer isolates himself, becoming absorbed in feverishly pursued speculation and phantasy.

The Emperor Jones (1920), as an artistic creation, stands rather by itself; through it the playwright first secured any considerable celebrity. The theme embraces the mental breakdown of a Negro despot who rules over a Negro-populated island in the West Indies. The despot perishes on the flight from his glory, hunted in the dead of night by the troll-drums of his pursuers and by recollections of the past shaping themselves as paralyzing visions. These memories stretch back beyond his own life to the dark continent of Africa. Here lies concealed the theory of the individual's unconscious inner life being the carrier of the successive stages in the evolution of the race. As to the rightness of the theory we need form no opinion; the play takes so strong a hold upon our nerves and senses that our attention is entirely absorbed.

The «dramas of ideas» proper are too numerous and too diversified to be included in a brief survey. Their themes derive from contemporary life or from sagas and legends; all are metamorphosed by the author's fancy. They play on emotional chords all tightly strung, give amazing decorative effects, and manifest a never-failing dramatic energy. Practically speaking, everything in human life in the nature of struggle or combat has here been used as a subject for creative treatment, solutions being sought for and tried out of the spiritual or mental riddles presented. One favourite theme is the cleavage of personality that arises when an individual's true character is driven in upon itself by pressure from the world without, having to yield place to a make-believe character, its own live traits being hidden behind a mask. The dramatist's musings are apt to delve so deep that what he evolves has an urge, like deep-sea fauna, to burst asunder on being brought into the light of day. The results he achieves, however, are never without poetry; there is an abundant flow of passionate, pregnant words. The action, too, yields evidence in every case of the never-slumbering energy that is one of O'Neill's greatest gifts.

Underneath O'Neill's fantastic love of experimenting, however, is a hint of a yearning to attain the monumental simplicity characteristic of ancient drama. In his *Desire Under the Elms* (1924) he made an attempt in that irection, drawing his motif from the New England farming community, hardened in te progress of generations into a type of Puritanism that had gradually come to forfeit its idealistic inspiration. The course embarked upon was to be followed with more success in the «Electra» trilogy.

In between appeared *A Play; Strange Interlude* (1928), which won high praise and became renowned. It is rightly termed «A Play», for with its broad and loose-knit method of presentation it cannot be regarded as a tragedy; it would rather seem most aptly defined as a psychological novel in scenes. To its subtitle, «Strange Interlude», a direct clue is given in the course of the play: «Life, the present, is the strange interlude between the past and what is to come.» The author tries to make his idea clear, as far as possible, by resorting to a peculiar device: on the one hand, the characters speak and reply as the action of the play demands; on the other, they reveal their real natures and their recollections in the form of monologues, inaudible to the other characters upon the stage. Once again, the element of masking!

Regarded as a psychological novel, up to the point at which it becomes too improbable for any psychology, the work is very notable for its wealth of analytical and above all intuitive acumen, and for the profound insight it displays into the inner workings of the human spirit. The training bore fruit in the real tragedy that followed, the author's grandest work: *Mourning Becomes Electra* (1931). Both in the story it unfolds and in the destiny-charged atmosphere enshrouding it, this play keeps close to the tradition of the ancient drama, though in both respects it is adjusted to modern life and to modern lines of thought. The scene of this tragedy of the modern-time house of Atreus is laid in the period of the great Civil War, America's *Iliad*. That choice lends the drama the clear perspective of the past and yet provides it with a background of intellectual life and thought sufficiently close to the present day. The most remarkable feature in the drama is the way in which the element of fate has been further developed. It is based upon up-to-date hypotheses, primarily upon the natural-scientific determinism of the doctrine of heredity, and also upon the Freudian omniscience concerning the unconscious, the nightmare dream of perverse family emotions.

These hypotheses are not, as we know, established beyond dispute, but the all-important point regarding this drama is that its author has embraced and applied them with unflinching consistency, constructing upon their foundation a chain of events as inescapable as if they had been proclaimed by the Sphinx of Thebes herself; Thereby he has achieved a masterly example of constructive ability and elaborate motivation of plot, and one that is surely without a counterpart in the whole range of latter-day drama. This applies especially to the first two parts of the trilogy.

Two dramas, wholly different and of a new type for O'Neill, followed. They constitute a characteristic illustration of the way he has of never resting content with a result achieved, no matter what success it may have met with. They also gave evidence of his courage, for in them he launched a challenge to a considerable section of those whose favourable opinions he had won, and even to the dictators of those opinions. Though it may not at the present time be dangerous to defy natural human feelings and conceptions, it is not by any means free from risk to prick the sensitive conscience of critics. In Ah, Wilderness (1933) the esteemed writer of tragedies astonished his admirers by presenting them with an idyllic middle-class comedy and carried his audiences with him. In its depiction of the spiritual life of young people the play contains a good deal of poetry, while its gayer scenes display unaffected humour and comedy; it is, moreover, throughout simple and human in its appeal.

In *Days Without End* (1934) the dramatist tackled the problem of religion, one that he had until then touched upon only superficially, without identifying himself with it, and merely from the natural scientist's combative standpoint. In this play he showed that he had an eye for the irrational, felt the need of absolute values, and was alive to the danger of spiritual impoverishment in the empty space that will be all that is left over the hard and solid world of rationalism. The form the work took was that of a modern miracle play, and perhaps, as with his tragedies of fate, the temptation to experiment was of great importance in its origination. Strictly observing the conventions of the drama form chosen, he adopted medieval naiveté in his presentation of the struggle of good against evil, introducing, however, novel and bold features of stage technique. The principal character he cleaves into two parts, white and black, not only inwardly but also corporeally, each half leading its own independent bodily life – a species of Siamese twins contradicting each other. The result is a variation upon earlier experiments. Notwithstanding the risk attendant upon that venture, the drama is sustained by the author's rare mastery of scenic treatment, while in the spokesman of religion, a Catholic priest, O'Neill has created one of his most lifelike characters. Whether that circumstance may be interpreted as indicating a decisive change in his outlook upon life remains to be seen in the future.

O'Neill's dramatic production has been extraordinarily comprehensive in scope, versatile in character, and abundantly fruitful in new departures; and still its originator is at a stage of vigorous development. Yet in essential matters, he himself has always been the same in the exuberant end unrestrainably lively play of his imagination, in his never-wearying delight in giving shape to the ideas, whether emanating from within or without, that have jostled one another in the depths of his contemplative nature, and, perhaps first and foremost, in his possession of a proudly and ruggedly independent character.

In choosing Eugene O'Neill as the recipient of the 1936 Nobel Prize in Literature, the Swedish Academy can express its appreciation of his peculiar and rare literary gifts and also express their homage to his personality in these words: the Prize has been awarded to him for dramatic works of vital energy, sincerity, and intensity of feeling, stamped with an original conception of tragedy."

O'Neill's Banquet Speech in Stockholm

„It is an extraordinary privilege that has come to me to take before this gathering of eminent persons the place of my fellow-countryman, Mr. Eugene O'Neill, recipient of the Nobel Prize in Literature, who unfortunately is unable to be present here today.

It is an extraordinary privilege because the significance and true worth of the Nobel Prizes are fully recognized in all advanced parts of the world. The Prizes are justly held in honor and esteem, for it is well known that they are awarded without prejudice of any kind by the several committees whose members generously devote much time and thought to the task in their charge.

In addition to being a stimulus to endeavour and a high recognition of achievement, the Prizes are valuable in another respect. Owing to the complete absence of partiality in the awarding of them, they induce people of all countries to think in terms of the world and mankind, heedless of classifications or boundaries of any character. The good influence of such conspicuous recognition of a particular achievement thus spreads far beyond its special purpose.

Mr. O'Neill has been prevented from being here today principally because the state of his health, damaged by overwork, has forced him to follow his doctor's orders to live absolutely quietly for several months. It is his hope, and I follow his own words in a letter to me, that all those connected with the festival will accept in good faith his statement of the impossibility of his attending, and not put it down to arbitrary temperament, or anything of the sort.

In view of his inability to attend, he promptly sent a speech to be read on his behalf on this occasion. Mr. O'Neill in a letter to me said regarding his speech, «It is no mere artful gesture to please a Swedish audience. It is a plain statement of fact and my exact feeling, and I am glad of this opportunity to get it said and on record.» It affords me great pleasure to read now the speech addressed to this gathering by Mr. Eugene O'Neill.

«First, I wish to express again to you my deep regret that circumstances have made it impossible for me to visit Sweden in time for the festival, and to be present at this banquet to tell you in person of my grateful appreciation.

It is difficult to put into anything like adequate words the profound gratitude I feel for the greatest honor that my work could ever hope to attain, the award of the Nobel Prize. This highest of distinctions is all the more grateful to me because I feel so deeply that it is not only my work which is being honored, but the work of all my colleagues in America – that this Nobel Prize is a symbol of the recognition by Europe of the coming-of-age of the American theatre. For my plays are merely, through luck of time and circumstance, the most widely-known examples of the work done by American playwrights in the years since the World War – work that has finally made modern American drama in its finest aspects an achievement of which Americans can be justly proud, worthy at last to claim kinship with the modern drama of Europe, from which our original inspiration so surely derives.

This thought of original inspiration brings me to what is, for me, the greatest happiness this occasion affords, and that is the opportunity it gives me to acknowledge, with gratitude and pride, to you and to the people of Sweden, the debt my work owes to that greatest genius of all modern dramatists, your August Strindberg.

It was reading his plays when I first started to write back in the winter of 1913-14 that, above all else, first gave me the vision of what modern drama could be, and first inspired me with the urge to write for the theatre myself. If there is anything of lasting worth in my work, it is due to that original impulse from him, which has continued as my inspiration down all the years since then – to the ambition I received then to follow in the footsteps of his genius as worthily as my talent might permit, and with the same integrity of purpose.

Of course, it will be no news to you in Sweden that my work owes much to the influence of Strindberg. That influence runs clearly through more than a few of my plays and is plain for everyone to see. Neither will it be news for anyone who has ever known me, for I have always stressed it myself. I have never been one of those who are so timidly uncertain of their own contribution that they feel they cannot afford to admit ever having been influenced, lest they be discovered as lacking all originality.

No, I am only too proud of my debt to Strindberg, only too happy to have this opportunity of proclaiming it to his people. For me, he remains, as Nietzsche remains in his sphere, the Master, still to this day more modern than any of us, still our leader. And it is my pride to imagine that perhaps his spirit, musing over this year's Nobel award for literature, may smile with a little satisfaction, and find the follower not too unworthy of his Master.»

Prior to the speech, Robert Fries, Director of the Bergius Foundation, remarked: «It is difficult to explain the vital processes in the living organism; it is difficult to interpret the inmost essence of matter, but it is perhaps most difficult to sound the human mind and to understand the soul in its shifting phases. With passionate intensity and impulsive genius Eugene O'Neill has done this in his dramas, and one cannot but be captivated by the masterly way in which he deals with the great problems of life."

O'Neill's Nobel Prize Diploma Facsimile

The final act of the ceremonies of honor came on February 17, 1937, while O'Neill was a patient in Oakland Merritt Hospital for an appendectomy operation: Carl E. Wallerstedt, the Swedish consul in San Francisco, visited the hospital to present O'Neill with the Alfred Nobel Gold Medal and embossed diploma that represented the Nobel Prize. Besides of the consul, no one attended the only five minutes ceremony except 'O'Neill's physician and his nurse. Wallerstedt told O'Neill: „It is customary for Nobel Prize winners to go to Sweden to receive their awards, and only on rare occasions is the order reversed. This is one time when custom must give way to emergency, as my nation no longer seeks to defer honor to a man who has won the highest_award which can be made in his chosen field of endeavor.

The added that he hoped O'Neill would soon be well enough to make his promised trip to Sweden. "Thank you. I will go as soon as I am able", murmured O'Neill, unawar that a world war and, later, his own invalidism would prevent his ever making the trip. He was so weak that his knees shook as he rose from his chair to receive the medal and scroll, and his hands tremble as he accepted them. The scroll, embossed with characters sybolizing O'Neill's work, had been designed especially for him and the gold medal was a replica

Eugene O'Neill's

Nobel Diploma

of all the others awarded in the field of literature.

The diploma stated in Swedish that O'Neill was chosen from all playwrights in the world for 1936 literature honors by the Swedish Academy „for his creative drama, for characters marked by virility, honesty end strong emotions as well as for depth of interpretation." Not long after moving with bis wife Carlotta into a rented home he inscribed the Nobel Prize edition of his plays, recentky published by Random House, to Carlotta, „the Noblest Prize of alli" with, „as always," all his love.

O'Neill's Critical Voices from Abroad

„Anyone familiar with drama and theatre knows the name of Eugene O'Neill," Horst Franz and Susan Tuch stated in their book Eugene O'Neill's Critics - Voices from Abroad, and they continue: „There is hardly a country in which his plays have not been performed and very few languages into which at least certain of his works have not been translated. Various outstanding stage productions have helped to establish O'Neill's international reputation. Since 1922, when Hugo von Hofmannsthal's evaluation appeared in Das Tagebuch, there has been a outpouring of opinions about O'Neill the man, his experimental work, his universal qualities, his philosophical and psychological probings, his language, his dramatic method, and his forerunners in the theatre, American as well as foreign.

O'Neill has been called a naturalist, an expressionist, a realist, a romantic. Critics have found in his plays the imprints of Schopenhauer, Nietzsche, Freud, and Jung and have declared him to be a „transplanted" European. Other critics point to Melville, Poe, and Hawthorne and emphasize the playWright's American roots. Still others have directed attention to O'Neill's kinship with Oriental thought, particularly Taoism. Audiences accustomed to viewing and reading the works of such dramatists as the Scandinavians Ibsen and Strindberg, the Germans Wedekind and Kaiser, the Irishmen Shaw and Synge, the Chinese Hung Shen and Ts'ao Yü, and the Russians Gorky and Chekhov had no difficulty in adjusting to O'Neill.

Who was responsible for introducing O'Neill to foreign audiences? His early European admirers included Alfred Kerr, the spirited drama critic of the *Berliner Tageblatt*; Firmin Gemier, the director of the Odeon, the second national theatre of France; the British producer Basil Dean, who wanted to stage the controversial *Desire Under the Elms*; and the versatile Czech dramaturge Frank Tetauer, who translated a number of O'Neill's plays for the Municipal Theatre of Prague.

It was unfortunate for O'Neill's reputation in Europe that the pioneer Work in his behalf was accompanied by a number of ill-fated first productions, which made Europeans wonder about the achievements of the „foremost" American playwright. A colorless translation, a static interpretation of the title role, an oversentimentalized story, and a melodramatic ending did little to recommend the 1923 presentation of *Anna Christie* in Berlin at the Deutsches Theatre. The production of the second O'Neill play in Germany also suffered from technical inadequacies.

The high mark of O'Neill's career was the Nobel Prize, whic was presented by Per Hallström in 1936. The .award brought the dramaturgist wider international recognition, a considerable increase in foreign productions, and more attention from the literar crities. In France for example, where there had not been a genuine interest in O'Neill, the Nobel Prize accounted for a number of serious investigation into the literary qualities of his work. O'Neill's eventual acceptance as American playwright as a master of tragedy followed.

France was not the only country to show increase O'Neill after he received the Nobel Prize. Even in Germany, where he had become *persona non grata* with the rise of the Nazi régime, afull 1ength study and various essays appeared. In Italy, when the war interfered with the productions of American („enemy") plays, O'Neill was declared an Irishman and his plays were imported from Dublin, and continued to be presented on the Italian stage. Immediate after World War II, O'Neill once again dominated the theatres of Western Europe and, after some years of hesitation, East European countries relented and included O'Neill in the repertoire of their theatres.

Though O'Neill's influence has not been particularly stron on the dramatic traditions of Poland and Hungary, quite the opposite is true in the Soviet Union. In that country, no other foreign dramatist has played as important arole. An early (1924) production of *Anna Christie* had a surprisingly successful run at the Comedia Theatre in Moscow, but O'Neill's name was not really well-known in the Soviet Union until Alexander Tairov and his Kamerny Theatre showed an interest in the American's work. Beginning in 1926, Tairov presented O'Neill's plays not only in Russia but on tour in Europe and South America. Tairov was a brilliant interpreter of the technical requirements of O'Neill's plays.

Although the Kamerny Theatre's tour did not extend to Japan, Tairov s friendship with actor Yoshi Hijikata helped to acquaint that country with O'Neill's work. His plays were included in performances given by the Tsukiji Little Theatre, which aimed to encourage the production of an advanced drama worthy of a new generation, to make possible experiments in the arts of the theatre, and to create a permanent stage where „edifying" plays would be offered. From 1924 to 1929, the Tsukiji included in its repertoire Shakespeare, important European playwrights such as Ibsen and Chekhov, some contemporary writers such as Capek and Kaiser, modern Japanese plays, and American drama (mostly O'Neill).

No discussion of O'Neill is complete without mention of the Royal Dramatic Theatre in Stockholm, the Dramaten, which since 1923 has demonstrated a devoted artistic interest in the American playwright. This theatre has contributed decisively to the realization and stabilization of O'Neill's acceptance in Europe. It became the only stage on which O'Neill's plays were performed consistently as part of the standard repertoire. And, as is well known, O'Neill's last four plays were first produced not in New York but in Stockholm. For these reasons, the Dramaten has appropriately been called O'Neill's Bayreuth. O'Neill has been influential in other parts of Scandinavia as well.

The remarkable record of international O'Neill productions during a period of six decades proves that the opinion of this dramatist prevailed. O'Neill's popularity is indicated, too, by the staggering number of translations that have been made of his plays and by the numerous books and articles, written by foreign scholars, devoted to the playwright. A bibliography, of O'Neill biograhy and work interpretations reflects the world-wide attention the American dramatist has commanded. The foreign reception of his dramas proves that, for the most part, O'Neill speaks a language that is truly universal."

O'NEILLS's FOURTH PULITZER DECORATION

For „Long Day's Journey into Night" (1957)

First Book edition with O'Neill photo

The Play and its Public Reception

On November 29, 1945, Eugene O'Neill, a sick, weary and aging man, took a manuscript of a play to Random House publishers. It had been finished for some time, since 1941, and it had been two years in the writing. Its title was *Long Day's Journey Into Night*; it was plainly autobiographical in nature. When O'Neill gave the manuscript to the publishing house, he wanted to seal it up. He insisted it be done with red sealing wax. O'Neill then dictated a covering letter, expressing: „I am this day depositing with you, on condition that it not be opened by you until twenty-five years after my death, a sealed copy of the manuscript of an original play which I have written, entitled *Long Day's Journey Into Night*. „Never before", as John L. Toohey has written, such mumbo-jumbo surrounded the script of any play, but O'Neill was not playing childish games. He had scraped *Long Day's Journey Into Night* right out of his bones, and had put himself and his family into it with deepest sympathy and understanding, but with absolutely naked candor. It had been a cruelly difficult play for him to write."

Some two years after O'Neill's death in November 1953, his widow Carlotta took the manusript of *Long Day's Journey Into Night* away from Random House and turned it over to Yale University Press. Almost simultaneously, she allowed the play to be given its first public performance, in Stockholm, where it was done with great success by the Royal Dramatic Theatre in February of 1956. Under the terms of O'Neill's will, Carlotta O'Neill was given full control of all of his plays, and consequently had every legal right to countermand O'Neill's twenty-five-year ban. For a while she considered denying the play an American production, at least for a few years, but finally she agreed and gave the American rights to a production that started in November 1956 in New York City at the Helen Hayes Theatre.

The play takes place on a single day in August 1912, from around 8:30 a.m., to midnight. The setting is the seaside Connecticut home of the Tyrones, Monte Cristo Cottage. The four main characters are the semi-autobiographical representations of O'Neill himself, his older brother, and their parents. This play portrays a family in a ferociously negative light as the parents and two sons express accusations, blame, and resentments - qualities that are often paired with pathetic and self-defeating attempts at affection, encouragement, tenderness, and yearnings for things to be otherwise. The pain of this family is made worse by their depth of self-understanding and self-analysis, combined with a brutal honesty, as they see it, and an ability to boldly express themselves. The story deals with the mother's addiction to morphine, the family's addiction to whiskey, the father's miserliness, the older brother's licentiousness, and younger brother's illness.

Long Day's Journey Into Night

Royal Dramatic Theatre, Stockholm

Opened: Thursday, February 02, 1956

Producer: Karl Ragnar Gierow   Director: Bengt Ekerot

Original production

James Tyrone - Lars Hanson
Mary Tyrone - Inga Tidblad
James Tyrone, Jr. - Ulf Palme
Edmund Tyrone - Jarl Kulle
Cathleen - Caterine Westerlund

New York Times Review, February 19, 1956

Very positive reactions about the production of *Long Day's Journey Into Night* came from all New York newspapers. The *Evening Post* called the performance „magnificent and shattering ... Eugene O'Neill's autobiographical drama broods with unsparing candor over some of the most pitiful and terrible personal concerns that a playwright ever tore out of his youthful memories and transforms them into a masterpiece of understanding, compassion and dark, tormented beauty." And the *New York Times* added: „With the production of *Long Day's Journey Into Night* the American theatre aquires size and stature. The play is like a Dostoevsky novel in which Strindberg had written the dialogue. *Long Day's Journey Into Night* has been worth waiting for. It restores the drama to literature and the theatre to art." The *Daily News* remarked about the play: „It was given a magnificent performance. It exploded like a dazzling skyrocket over the humdrum of Broadway theatricals. This is O'Neill's most beautiful play - perhaps the only beautiful one he ever wrote. And it is one of the great dramas of any time."

When the Pulitzer Prize jurors of next year's competition met, they had to evaluate 23 theatre productions eligible for the drama award of the 1956-57 season. In their report, dated April 1, 1957, they made this recommendation: „By far the most distinguished drama of the Season is Eugene O'Neill's posthumous tragedy *Long Day's Journey Into Night*. In spite of some of its blemishes - its great length, its tending to repeat and its heavy literary style - it richly deserves the award. In fact, it is the only play by an American author, presented during the current season, that can regarded as a serious candidate. All competent judges agree that it is one of O'Neill's greatest plays; a few think it his very gratest."

„In any case," the jury report continued, „it is an emotionally overwhelming tragedy. It is frankly autobiographical... Fortunately, the action does not leave the audience in an atmosphere of unrelieved gloom. The last act serves as a kind of benediction of pity and understanding upon the doomed character. The acting of all four protagonists is among the best of the season... In brief, we believe that the Pulitzer award has seldom gone to so great a play as *Long Day's Journey Into Night*." So, close to four years after his death, Eugene O'Neill was given the 1957 Pulitzer Prize for Drama, it was his fourth recognition of that type. The play made it for 390 performances.

THE WORK AND ITS NEW YORK PREMIERE

Long Day's Journey Into Night is described by John L. Toohey as follows: "The entire action of the play takes place in the New England summer home of the Tyrones, on an August day and night in 1912. James Tyrone is an aging actor... His wife, Mary, is gentle and nervous, and obviously in poor health. They have two sons: Jamie, a robust rakehell of 34, and Edmund, 23, thin and sick. As the long day passes, and finally blends into the night, the members of this tortured family savage each other interminably, and the bitter truth about each one emerges... Exhausted, the Tyrones are simply staring at each other."

The first New York production of *Long Day's Journey Into Night* opened at the Helen Hayes Theatre on November 7, 1956. Following are a scene photo together with main portions of the program containing the original cast:

Florence Eldridge and Fredric March

Helen Hayes Theatre

FIRE NOTICE: The exit indicated by a red light and sign nearest to the seat you occupy is the shortest route to the street. In the event of fire please do not run—WALK TO THAT EXIT.
EDW. F. CAVANAGH, JR.
FIRE COMMISSIONER

Thoughtless persons annoy patrons and distract actors and endanger the safety of others by lighting matches during the performance and intermissions. This violates a city ordinance and renders the offender liable to ARREST. It is urged that all patrons refrain from lighting matches in the auditorium of this theatre.

THE · PLAYBILL · A · WEEKLY · PUBLICATION · OF · PLAYBILL · INCORPORATED

Week beginning Monday, January 28, 1957 • No Matinees

IN THE EVENT OF AN AIR RAID ALARM REMAIN IN YOUR SEATS AND OBEY THE INSTRUCTIONS OF THE MANAGEMENT.—ROBERT E. CONDON, DIRECTOR OF CIVIL DEFENSE.

Leigh Connell, Theodore Mann and José Quintero

present

Fredric MARCH in **Florence ELDRIDGE**

EUGENE O'NEILL'S
LONG DAY'S JOURNEY INTO NIGHT

Directed by **Jose Quintero**

with

JASON ROBARDS, JR. **BRADFORD DILLMAN**
KATHERINE ROSS

Setting by DAVID HAYS
Lighting by THARON MUSSER
Costumes by MOTLEY

CAST
(In order of appearance)

JAMES TYRONE .... FREDRIC MARCH

MARY CAVAN TYRONE .... FLORENCE ELDRIDGE

JAMES TYRONE, JR., their elder son..JASON ROBARDS, JR.

EDMUND TYRONE, their younger son..BRADFORD DILLMAN

CATHLEEN, second girl .... KATHERINE ROSS

The Management is not responsible for personal apparel or property of patrons unless properly checked with the theatre attendant. Patrons are advised to take their coats and wraps with them whenever they leave their seats. • Ladies are requested to remove their hats.

JOHN MASON BROWN
17 EAST 89th STREET
NEW YORK 28, N. Y.

March 26, 1957

Advisory Board on Pulitzer Prizes
Columbia University
New York 27, N. Y.

Dear Sirs:

I have met with Professor Campbell and I have reported to him, as I am reporting to you, that my recommendation, an inevitable one, for this year's Pulitzer Prize Play is Eugene O'Neill's *Long Day's Journey into Night*. I say inevitable because, as has not been the case in many recent seasons, no other American play has been produced which is by any stretch of the imagination a near second.

Mr. O'Neill's intensely autobiographical work has its obvious shortcomings. It is too long by at least an hour for its own good. Its repetitions at a few moments, more than being bothersome, become laughable. And its dialogue often has the commonplaceness that cursed O'Neill's writing throughout his lonely and magnificent career. These lacks, however, in *Long Day's Journey* must be measured against the play's merits. It is a monumental work overwhelming in its power. No matter how the dialogue may read, it adjusts itself (as was so often the case in O'Neill's writing) admirably to the speaking needs of actors. Moreover, O'Neill faces the anguishes of a period in his own family life with the same unblinking courage with which throughout his career he faced the tragic sorrows of the world. In many years of theatregoing I must confess I have never seen a play more nakedly autobiographical than this one. Inevitably, its exploration of the misery of O'Neill's own life adds to its fascination. Although it does not rise in its final scene to the exaltation achieved by O'Neill in the concluding moments of *Desire* and *Mourning Becomes Electra*, the heat and force of its dramatic drive are beyond denying and communicate themselves even in the printed script without the benefit of the excellent production *Journey* has been given...

First Drama Jury Report of March 26, 1957

Columbia University IN THE CITY OF NEW YORK

NEW YORK 27, NEW YORK

Telephone · UNiversity 5-4000, Extension 2653

April 1, 1957

Advisory Board on Pulitzer Prizes
518 Journalism

Gentlemen:

I present herewith my recommendation for the Pulitzer Prize in the drama for the season extending from April 1, 1956 to April 1, 1957. I enclose also a list of the twenty-three plays and musicals eligible for the prize. The members of your jury have seen all of these plays, have read the texts when they were available and have conferred whenever it seemed appropriate.

By far the most distinguished drama of the season is Eugene O'Neill's posthumous tragedy, Long Day's Journey Into Night. In spite of some of its blemishes - its great length, its tending to repeat and its heavy literary style - it richly deserves the award. In fact, it is the only play by an American author, presented during the current season, that can be regarded as a serious candidate. All competent judges agree that it is one of O'Neill's greatest plays; a few think it his very greatest. In any case, it is an emotionally overwhelming tragedy. It is frankly autobiographical, for O'Neill faces with courage and tortured sympathy the mental and spiritual anguish of the life of his family during his young manhood. But the bitter afflictions of the Tyrone family, starkly presented, are symbols of what O'Neill believed were the dark forces of fate that shape the destinies of all human beings. Fortunately, the action does not leave the audience in an atmosphere of unrelieved gloom. The last act serves as a kind of benediction of pity and understanding upon the doomed character.

The acting of all four protagonists is among the best of the

Second Drama Jury Report of April 1, 1957, p. 1

-2-

season. Frederic March's impersonation of the father is perhaps the most distinguished of his long career. Quintero's direction os of the same high quality. In brief, we believe that the Pulitzer award has seldom gone to so great a play as Long Day's Journey into Night.

Second on my list is Tennessee Williams' Orpheus Descending. My opinion of this work is higher than that of John Mason Brown. In fact, if the author had sustained the mood evoked by the first two acts, particularly the first, I should have thought it a real contender for the prize. Unfortunately, the poetry and what Brooks Atkinson describes as the "lyric intensity" of the characters as first presented, in the last act break down into violent and crude melodrama. This is a pity because the writing is so far superior to that appearing on the contemporary American theatre. Though not one of his best plays, it does give us exciting glimpses of the power of an authentic, if wayward genius.

I put third on my list a play of an entirely different sort, A Visit to a Small Planet, by Gore Vidal. The basic idea is brilliant. A visitor from a highly civilized region in outer space has long made our earthbound civilization his hobby. Since he proves to be a delayed adolescent and a delinquent too, the institution that delights him above everything else is war. He does his best to start a new world war before he is carried off by his keeper. Much of the comment engendered by the situation is wonderful satire and is enormously funny. But, alas, the action deteriorates into a series of vaudeville sketches by the two talented comedians Cyril Ritchard and Eddie Mayehoff. In spite of this disappointment, per haps the drama deserves a bow as the most mature comedy of the season.

Sincerely,

Oscar James Campbell

Oscar James Campbell

Second Drama Jury Report of April 1, 1957, p. 2

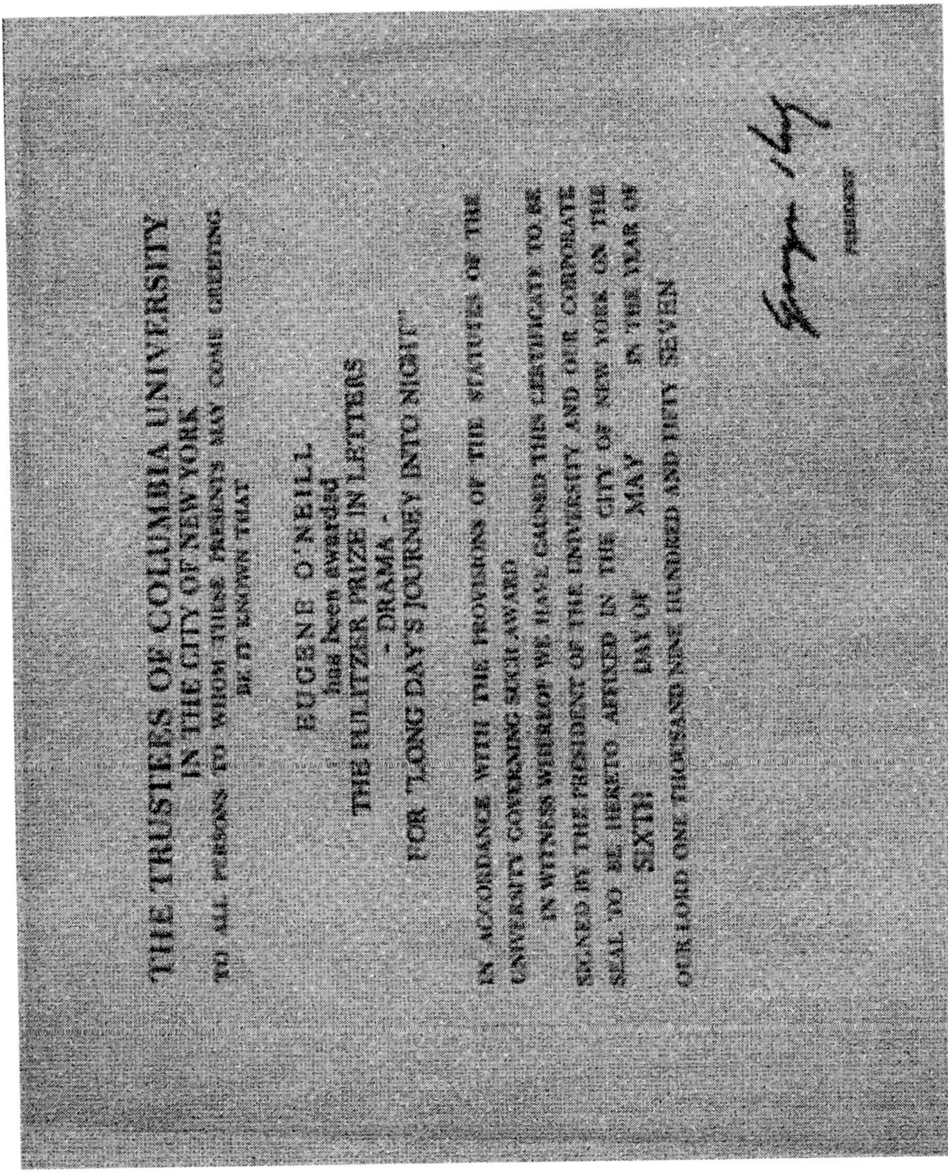
THE TRUSTEES OF COLUMBIA UNIVERSITY
IN THE CITY OF NEW YORK
TO ALL PERSONS TO WHOM THESE PRESENTS MAY COME GREETING
BE IT KNOWN THAT
EUGENE O'NEILL
has been awarded
THE PULITZER PRIZE IN LETTERS
- DRAMA -
FOR "LONG DAY'S JOURNEY INTO NIGHT"

IN ACCORDANCE WITH THE PROVISIONS OF THE STATUTES OF THE UNIVERSITY GOVERNING SUCH AWARD
IN WITNESS WHEREOF WE HAVE CAUSED THIS CERTIFICATE TO BE SIGNED BY THE PRESIDENT OF THE UNIVERSITY AND OUR CORPORATE SEAL TO BE HERETO AFFIXED IN THE CITY OF NEW YORK ON THE SIXTH DAY OF MAY IN THE YEAR OF OUR LORD ONE THOUSAND NINE HUNDRED AND FIFTY SEVEN

PRESIDENT

Eugene O'Neill's fourth Pulitzer Prize Certificate for „Long Day's Journey into Night", signed by Columbia University President Grayson Kirk on May 6, 1957

The Play's Act One

CHARACTERS

JAMES TYRONE
MARY CAVAN TYRONE, *his wife*
JAMES TYRONE, JR., *their elder son*
EDMUND TYRONE, *their younger son*
CATHLEEN, *second girl*

SCENES

ACT 1

Living room of the Tyrones' summer home 8:30 A.M. of a day in August, 1912

ACT 2

SCENE 1: The same, around 12:45
SCENE 2: The same, about a half hour later

ACT 3

The same, around 6:30 that evening

ACT 4

The same, around midnight

Long Day's Journey into Night

ACT ONE

SCENE—*Living room of James Tyrone's summer home on a morning in August, 1912.*

At rear are two double doorways with portieres. The one at right leads into a front parlor with the formally arranged, set appearance of a room rarely occupied. The other opens on a dark, windowless back parlor, never used except as a passage from living room to dining room. Against the wall between the doorways is a small bookcase, with a picture of Shakespeare above it, containing novels by Balzac, Zola, Stendhal, philosophical and sociological works by Schopenhauer, Nietzsche, Marx, Engels, Kropotkin, Max Stirner, plays by Ibsen, Shaw, Strindberg, poetry by Swinburne, Rossetti, Wilde, Ernest Dowson, Kipling, etc.

In the right wall, rear, is a screen door leading out on the porch which extends halfway around the house. Farther forward, a series of three windows looks over the front lawn to the harbor and the avenue that runs along the water front. A small wicker table and an ordinary oak desk are against the wall, flanking the windows.

In the left wall, a similar series of windows looks out on the grounds in back of the house. Beneath them is a wicker couch with cushions, its head toward rear. Farther back is a large, glassed-in bookcase with sets of Dumas, Victor Hugo, Charles Lever, three sets of Shakespeare, The World's Best Literature in fifty large volumes, Hume's History of England, Thiers' History of the Consulate and Empire, Smollett's History of England, Gibbon's Roman Empire and miscellaneous volumes of old plays, poetry, and several histories of Ireland. The astonishing thing about these sets is that all the volumes have the look of having been read and reread.

The hardwood floor is nearly covered by a rug, inoffensive in design and color. At center is a round table with a green shaded reading lamp, the cord plugged in one of the four sockets in the chandelier above. Around the table within reading-light range are four chairs, three of them wicker armchairs, the fourth (at right front of table) a varnished oak rocker with leather bottom.

It is around 8.30. Sunshine comes through the windows at right.

As the curtain rises, the family have just finished breakfast.

Mary Tyrone and her husband enter together from the back parlor, coming from the dining room.

Mary is fifty-four, about medium height. She still has a young, graceful figure, a trifle plump, but showing little evidence of middle-aged waist and hips, although she is not tightly corseted. Her face is distinctly Irish in type. It must once have been extremely pretty, and is still striking. It does not match her healthy figure but is thin and pale with the bone structure prominent. Her nose is long and straight, her mouth wide with full, sensitive lips. She uses no rouge or any sort of make-up. Her high forehead is framed by thick, pure white hair. Accentuated by her pallor and white hair, her dark brown eyes appear black. They are unusually large and beautiful, with black brows and long curling lashes.

What strikes one immediately is her extreme nervousness. Her hands are never still. They were once beautiful hands, with long, tapering fingers, but rheumatism has knotted the joints and warped the fingers, so that now they have an ugly crippled look. One avoids looking at them, the more so because one is conscious she is sensitive about their appearance and humiliated by her inability to control the nervousness which draws attention to them.

She is dressed simply but with a sure sense of what becomes her. Her hair is arranged with fastidious care. Her voice is soft and attractive. When she is merry, there is a touch of Irish lilt in it.

Her most appealing quality is the simple, unaffected charm of a shy convent-girl youthfulness she has never lost—an innate unworldly innocence.

James Tyrone is sixty-five but looks ten years younger. About five feet eight, broad-shouldered and deep-chested, he seems taller and slenderer because of his bearing, which has a soldierly quality of head up, chest out, stomach in, shoulders squared. His face has begun to break down but he is still remarkably good looking—a big, finely shaped head, a handsome profile, deep-set light-brown eyes. His grey hair is thin with a bald spot like a monk's tonsure.

The stamp of his profession is unmistakably on him. Not that he indulges in any of the deliberate temperamental posturings of the stage star. He is by nature and preference a simple, unpretentious man, whose inclinations are still close to his humble beginnings and his Irish farmer forebears. But the actor shows in all his unconscious habits of speech, movement and gesture. These have the quality of belonging to a studied technique. His voice is remarkably fine, resonant and flexible, and he takes great pride in it.

His clothes, assuredly, do not costume any romantic part. He wears a threadbare, ready-made, grey sack suit and shineless black shoes, a collar-less shirt with a thick white handkerchief knotted loosely around his throat. There is nothing picturesquely careless about this get-up. It is commonplace shabby. He believes in wearing his clothes to the limit of usefulness, is dressed now for gardening, and doesn't give a damn how he looks.

He has never been really sick a day in his life. He has no nerves. There is a lot of stolid, earthy peasant in him, mixed with streaks of sentimental melancholy and rare flashes of intuitive sensibility.

Tyrone's arm is around his wife's waist as they appear from the back parlor. Entering the living room he gives her a playful hug.

TYRONE—You're a fine armful now, Mary, with those twenty pounds you've gained.

MARY—(*smiles affectionately*) I've gotten too fat, you mean, dear. I really ought to reduce.

TYRONE—None of that, my lady! You're just right. We'll have no talk of reducing. Is that why you ate so little breakfast?

MARY—So little? I thought I ate a lot.

TYRONE—You didn't. Not as much as I'd like to see, anyway.

MARY—(*teasingly*) Oh you! You expect everyone to eat the enormous breakfast you do. No one else in the world could without dying of indigestion. (*She comes forward to stand by the right of table.*)

TYRONE—(*following her*) I hope I'm not as big a glutton as that sounds. (*with hearty satisfaction*) But thank God, I've kept my appetite and I've the digestion of a young man of twenty, if I am sixty-five.

MARY—You surely have, James. No one could deny that. (*She laughs and sits in the wicker armchair at right rear of table. He comes around in back of her and selects a cigar from a box on the table and cuts off the end with a little clipper. From the dining room Jamie's and Edmund's voices are heard. Mary turns her head that way.*) Why did the boys stay in the dining room, I wonder? Cathleen must be waiting to clear the table.

TYRONE—(*jokingly but with an undercurrent of resentment*) It's a secret confab they don't want me to hear, I suppose. I'll bet they're cooking up some new scheme to touch the Old Man. (*She is silent on this, keeping her head turned toward their voices. Her hands appear on the table top, moving restlessly. He lights his cigar and sits down in the rocker at right of table, which is his chair, and puffs contentedly.*) There's nothing like the first after-breakfast cigar, if it's a good one, and this new lot have the right mellow flavor. They're a great bargain, too. I got them dead cheap. It was McGuire put me on to them.

MARY—(*a trifle acidly*) I hope he didn't put you on to any new piece of property at the same time. His real estate bargains don't work out so well.

TYRONE—(*defensively*) I wouldn't say that, Mary. After all, he was the one who advised me to buy that place on Chestnut Street and I made a quick turnover on it for a fine profit.

MARY—(*smiles now with teasing affection*) I know. The famous one stroke of good luck. I'm sure McGuire never dreamed— (*Then she pats his hand.*) Never mind, James. I know it's a waste of breath trying to convince you you're not a cunning real estate speculator.

TYRONE—(*huffily*) I've no such idea. But land is land, and it's safer than the stocks and bonds of Wall Street swindlers. (*then placatingly*) But let's not argue about business this early in the morning. (*A pause. The boys' voices are again heard and one of them has a fit of coughing. Mary listens worriedly. Her fingers play nervously on the table top.*)

MARY—James, it's Edmund you ought to scold for not eating enough. He hardly touched anything except coffee. He needs to eat to keep up his strength. I keep telling him that but he says he simply has no appetite. Of course, there's nothing takes away your appetite like a bad summer cold.

TYRONE—Yes, it's only natural. So don't let yourself get worried—

MARY—(*quickly*) Oh, I'm not. I know he'll be all right in a few days if he takes care of himself. (*as if she wanted to dismiss the subject but can't*) But it does seem a shame he should have to be sick right now.

TYRONE—Yes, it is bad luck. (*He gives her a quick, worried look.*) But you mustn't let it upset you, Mary. Remember, you've got to take care of yourself, too.

MARY—(*quickly*) I'm not upset. There's nothing to be upset about. What makes you think I'm upset?

TYRONE—Why, nothing, except you've seemed a bit high-strung the past few days.

MARY—(*forcing a smile*) I have? Nonsense, dear. It's your imagination. (*with sudden tenseness*) You really must not watch me all the time, James. I mean, it makes me self-conscious.

TYRONE—(*putting a hand over one of her nervously playing ones*) Now, now, Mary. That's your imagination. If I've watched you it was to admire how fat and beautiful you looked. (*His voice is suddenly moved by deep feeling.*) I can't tell you the deep happiness it gives me, darling, to see you as you've been since you came back to us, your dear old self again. (*He leans over and kisses her cheek impulsively—then turning back adds with a constrained air*) So keep up the good work, Mary.

MARY—(*has turned her head away*) I will, dear. (*She gets up restlessly and goes to the windows at right.*) Thank heavens, the fog is gone. (*She turns back.*) I do feel out of sorts this morning. I wasn't able to get much sleep with that awful foghorn going all night long.

TYRONE—Yes, it's like having a sick whale in the back yard. It kept me awake, too.

MARY—(*affectionately amused*) Did it? You had a strange way of showing your restlessness. You were snoring so hard I couldn't tell which was the foghorn! (*She comes to him, laughing, and pats his cheek playfully.*) Ten foghorns couldn't disturb you. You haven't a nerve in you. You've never had.

TYRONE—(*his vanity piqued—testily*) Nonsense. You always exaggerate about my snoring.

MARY—I couldn't. If you could only hear yourself once—(*A burst of laughter comes from the dining room. She turns her head, smiling.*) What's the joke, I wonder?

TYRONE—(*grumpily*) It's on me. I'll bet that much. It's always on the Old Man.

MARY—(*teasingly*) Yes, it's terrible the way we all pick on you, isn't it? You're so abused! (*She laughs—then with a pleased, relieved air*) Well, no matter what the joke is about, it's a relief to hear Edmund laugh. He's been so down in the mouth lately.

TYRONE—(*ignoring this—resentfully*) Some joke of Jamie's, I'll wager. He's forever making sneering fun of somebody, that one.

MARY—Now don't start in on poor Jamie, dear. (*without conviction*) He'll turn out all right in the end, you wait and see.

TYRONE—He'd better start soon, then. He's nearly thirty-four.

MARY—(*ignoring this*) Good heavens, are they going to stay in the dining room all day? (*She goes to the back parlor doorway and calls*) Jamie! Edmund! Come in the living room and give Cathleen a chance to clear the table. (*Edmund calls back,* "We're coming, Mama." *She goes back to the table.*)

TYRONE—(*grumbling*) You'd find excuses for him no matter what he did.

MARY—(*sitting down beside him, pats his hand*) Shush. (*Their sons James, Jr., and Edmund enter together from the back parlor. They are both grinning, still chuckling over what had caused their laughter, and as they come forward they glance at their father and their grins grow broader.*)

(*Jamie, the elder, is thirty-three. He has his father's broad-shouldered, deep-chested physique, is an inch taller and weighs less, but appears shorter and stouter because he lacks Tyrone's bearing and graceful carriage. He also lacks his father's vitality. The signs of premature disintegration are on him. His face is still good looking, despite marks of dissipation, but it has never been handsome like Tyrone's, although Jamie resembles him rather than his mother. He has fine brown eyes, their color midway between his father's lighter and his mother's darker ones. His hair is thinning and already there is indication of a bald spot like Tyrone's. His nose is unlike that of any other member of the family, pronouncedly aquiline. Combined with his habitual expression of cynicism it gives his countenance a Mephistophelian cast. But on the rare occasions when he smiles without sneering, his personality possesses the remnant of a humorous, romantic, irresponsible Irish charm—that of the beguiling ne'er-do-well, with a strain of the sentimentally poetic, attractive to women and popular with men.*

(*He is dressed in an old sack suit, not as shabby as Tyrone's, and wears a collar and tie. His fair skin is sunburned a reddish, freckled tan.*

(Edmund is ten years younger than his brother, a couple of inches taller, thin and wiry. Where Jamie takes after his father, with little resemblance to his mother, Edmund looks like both his parents, but is more like his mother. Her big, dark eyes are the dominant feature in his long, narrow Irish face. His mouth has the same quality of hypersensitiveness hers possesses. His high forehead is hers accentuated, with dark brown hair, sunbleached to red at the ends, brushed straight back from it. But his nose is his father's and his face in profile recalls Tyrone's. Edmund's hands are noticeably like his mother's, with the same exceptionally long fingers. They even have to a minor degree the same nervousness. It is in the quality of extreme nervous sensibility that the likeness of Edmund to his mother is most marked.

(He is plainly in bad health. Much thinner than he should be, his eyes appear feverish and his cheeks are sunken. His skin, in spite of being sunburned a deep brown, has a parched sallowness. He wears a shirt, collar and tie, no coat, old flannel trousers, brown sneakers.)

MARY—(*turns smilingly to them, in a merry tone that is a bit forced*) I've been teasing your father about his snoring. (*to Tyrone*) I'll leave it to the boys, James. They must have heard you. No, not you, Jamie. I could hear you down the hall almost as bad as your father. You're like him. As soon as your head touches the pillow you're off and ten foghorns couldn't wake you. (*She stops abruptly, catching Jamie's eyes regarding her with an uneasy, probing look. Her smile vanishes and her manner becomes self-conscious.*) Why are you staring, Jamie? (*Her hands flutter up to her hair.*) Is my hair coming down? It's hard for me to do it up properly now. My eyes are getting so bad and I never can find my glasses.

JAMIE—(*looks away guiltily*) Your hair's all right, Mama. I was only thinking how well you look.

TYRONE—(*heartily*) Just what I've been telling her, Jamie. She's so fat and sassy, there'll soon be no holding her.

EDMUND—Yes, you certainly look grand, Mama. (*She is reassured and smiles at him lovingly. He winks with a kidding grin.*) I'll back you up about Papa's snoring. Gosh, what a racket!

JAMIE—I heard him, too. (*He quotes, putting on a ham-actor manner*) "The Moor, I know his trumpet." (*His mother and brother laugh.*)

TYRONE—(*scathingly*) If it takes my snoring to make you remember Shakespeare instead of the dope sheet on the ponies, I hope I'll keep on with it.

MARY—Now, James! You mustn't be so touchy. (*Jamie shrugs his shoulders and sits down in the chair on her right.*)

EDMUND—(*irritably*) Yes, for Pete's sake, Papa! The first thing after breakfast! Give it a rest, can't you? (*He slumps down in the chair at left of table next to his brother. His father ignores him.*)

MARY—(*reprovingly*) Your father wasn't finding fault with you. You don't have to always take Jamie's part. You'd think you were the one ten years older.

JAMIE—(*boredly*) What's all the fuss about? Let's forget it.

TYRONE—(*contemptuously*) Yes, forget! Forget everything and face nothing! It's a convenient philosophy if you've no ambition in life except to—

MARY—James, do be quiet. (*She puts an arm around his shoulder—coaxingly*) You must have gotten out of the wrong side of the bed this morning. (*to the boys, changing the subject*) What were you two grinning about like Cheshire cats when you came in? What was the joke?

TYRONE—(*with a painful effort to be a good sport*) Yes, let us in on it, lads. I told your mother I knew damned well it would be one on me, but never mind that, I'm used to it.

JAMIE—(*dryly*) Don't look at me. This is the Kid's story.

EDMUND—(*grins*) I meant to tell you last night, Papa, and forgot it. Yesterday when I went for a walk I dropped in at the Inn—

MARY—(*worriedly*) You shouldn't drink now, Edmund.

EDMUND—(*ignoring this*) And who do you think I met there, with a beautiful bun on, but Shaughnessy, the tenant on that farm of yours.

MARY—(*smiling*) That dreadful man! But he is funny.

TYRONE—(*scowling*) He's not so funny when you're his landlord. He's a wily Shanty Mick, that one. He could hide behind a corkscrew. What's he complaining about now, Edmund—for I'm damned sure he's complaining. I suppose he wants his rent lowered. I let him have the place for almost nothing, just to keep someone on it, and he never pays that till I threaten to evict him.

EDMUND—No, he didn't beef about anything. He was so pleased with life he even bought a drink, and that's practically unheard of. He was delighted because he'd had a fight with your friend, Harker, the Standard Oil millionaire, and won a glorious victory.

MARY—(*with amused dismay*) Oh, Lord! James, you'll really have to do something—

TYRONE—Bad luck to Shaughnessy, anyway!

JAMIE—(*maliciously*) I'll bet the next time you see Harker at the Club and give him the old respectful bow, he won't see you.

EDMUND—Yes. Harker will think you're no gentleman for harboring a tenant who isn't humble in the presence of a king of America.

TYRONE—Never mind the Socialist gabble. I don't care to listen—

MARY—(*tactfully*) Go on with your story, Edmund.

EDMUND—(*grins at his father provocatively*) Well, you remember, Papa, the ice pond on Harker's estate is right next to the farm, and you remember Shaughnessy keeps pigs. Well, it seems there's a break in the fence and the pigs have been bathing in the millionaire's ice pond, and Harker's foreman told him he was sure Shaughnessy had broken the fence on purpose to give his pigs a free wallow.

MARY—(*shocked and amused*) Good heavens!

TYRONE—(*sourly, but with a trace of admiration*) I'm sure he did, too, the dirty scallywag. It's like him.

EDMUND—So Harker came in person to rebuke Shaughnessy. (*He chuckles.*) A very bonehead play! If I needed any further proof that our ruling plutocrats, especially the ones who inherited their boodle, are not mental giants, that would clinch it.

TYRONE—(*with appreciation, before he thinks*) Yes, he'd be no match for Shaughnessy. (*Then he growls*) Keep your damned anarchist remarks to yourself. I won't have them in my house. (*But he is full of eager anticipation.*) What happened?

EDMUND—Harker had as much chance as I would with Jack Johnson. Shaughnessy got a few drinks under his belt and was waiting at the gate to welcome him. He told me he never gave Harker a chance to open his mouth. He began by shouting that he was no slave Standard Oil could trample on. He was a King of Ireland, if he had his rights, and scum was scum to him, no matter how much money it had stolen from the poor.

MARY—Oh, Lord! (*But she can't help laughing.*)

EDMUND—Then he accused Harker of making his foreman break down the fence to entice the pigs into the ice pond in order to destroy them. The poor pigs, Shaughnessy yelled, had caught their death of cold. Many of them were dying of pneumonia, and several others had been taken down with cholera from drinking the poisoned water. He told Harker he was hiring a lawyer to sue him for damages. And he wound up by saying that he had to put up with poison ivy, ticks, potato bugs, snakes and skunks on his farm, but he was an honest man who drew the line somewhere, and he'd be damned if he'd stand for a Standard Oil thief trespassing. So would Harker kindly remove his dirty feet from the premises before he sicked the dog on him. And Harker did! (*He and Jamie laugh.*)

MARY—(*shocked but giggling*) Heavens, what a terrible tongue that man has!

TYRONE—(*admiringly before he thinks*) The damned old scoundrel! By God, you can't beat him! (*He laughs—then stops abruptly and scowls.*) The dirty blackguard! He'll get me in serious trouble yet. I hope you told him I'd be mad as hell—

EDMUND—I told him you'd be tickled to death over the great Irish victory, and so you are. Stop faking, Papa.

TYRONE—Well, I'm not tickled to death.

MARY—(*teasingly*) You are, too, James. You're simply delighted!

TYRONE—No, Mary, a joke is a joke, but—

EDMUND—I told Shaughnessy he should have reminded Harker that a Standard Oil millionaire ought to welcome the flavor of hog in his ice water as an appropriate touch.

TYRONE—The devil you did! (*frowning*) Keep your damned Socialist anarchist sentiments out of my affairs!

EDMUND—Shaughnessy almost wept because he hadn't thought of that one, but he said he'd include it in a letter he's writing to Harker, along with a few other insults he'd overlooked. (*He and Jamie laugh.*)

TYRONE—What are you laughing at? There's nothing funny— A fine son you are to help that blackguard get me into a lawsuit!

MARY—Now, James, don't lose your temper.

TYRONE—(*turns on Jamie*) And you're worse than he is, encouraging him. I suppose you're regretting you weren't there to prompt Shaughnessy with a few nastier insults. You've a fine talent for that, if for nothing else.

MARY—James! There's no reason to scold Jamie. (*Jamie is about to make some sneering remark to his father, but he shrugs his shoulders.*)

EDMUND—(*with sudden nervous exasperation*) Oh, for God's sake, Papa! If you're starting that stuff again, I'll beat it. (*He jumps up.*) I left my book upstairs, anyway. (*He goes to the front parlor, saying disgustedly*) God, Papa, I should think you'd get sick of hearing yourself— (*He disappears. Tyrone looks after him angrily.*)

MARY—You mustn't mind Edmund, James. Remember he isn't well. (*Edmund can be heard coughing as he goes upstairs. She adds nervously*) A summer cold makes anyone irritable.

JAMIE—(*genuinely concerned*) It's not just a cold he's got. The Kid is damned sick. (*His father gives him a sharp warning look but he doesn't see it.*)

MARY—(*turns on him resentfully*) Why do you say that? It *is* just a cold! Anyone can tell that! You always imagine things!

TYRONE—(*with another warning glance at Jamie—easily*) All Jamie meant was Edmund might have a touch of something else, too, which makes his cold worse.

JAMIE—Sure, Mama. That's all I meant.

TYRONE—Doctor Hardy thinks it might be a bit of malarial fever he caught when he was in the tropics. If it is, quinine will soon cure it.

MARY—(*A look of contemptuous hostility flashes across her face.*) Doctor Hardy! I wouldn't believe a thing he said, if he swore on a stack of Bibles! I know what doctors are. They're all alike. Anything, they don't care what, to keep you coming to them. (*She stops short, overcome by a fit of acute self-consciousness as she catches their eyes fixed on her. Her hands jerk nervously to her hair. She forces a smile.*) What is it? What are you looking at? Is my hair—?

TYRONE—(*puts his arm around her—with guilty heartiness, giving her a playful hug*) There's nothing wrong with your hair. The healthier and fatter you get, the vainer you become. You'll soon spend half the day primping before the mirror.

MARY—(*half reassured*) I really should have new glasses. My eyes are so bad now.

TYRONE—(*with Irish blarney*) Your eyes are beautiful, and well you know it. (*He gives her a kiss. Her face lights up with a charming, shy embarrassment. Suddenly and startlingly one sees in her face the girl she had once been, not a ghost of the dead, but still a living part of her.*)

MARY—You mustn't be so silly, James. Right in front of Jamie!

TYRONE—Oh, he's on to you, too. He knows this fuss about eyes and hair is only fishing for compliments. Eh, Jamie?

JAMIE—(*His face has cleared, too, and there is an old boyish charm in his loving smile at his mother.*) Yes. You can't kid us, Mama.

MARY—(*laughs and an Irish lilt comes into her voice*) Go along with both of you! (*Then she speaks with a girlish gravity.*) But I did truly have beautiful hair once, didn't I, James?

TYRONE—The most beautiful in the world!

MARY—It was a rare shade of reddish brown and so long it came down below my knees. You ought to remember it, too, Jamie. It wasn't until after Edmund was born that I had a single grey hair. Then it began to turn white. (*The girlishness fades from her face.*)

TYRONE—(*quickly*) And that made it prettier than ever.

MARY—(*again embarrassed and pleased*) Will you listen to your father, Jamie—after thirty-five years of marriage! He isn't a great actor for nothing, is he? What's come over you, James? Are you pouring coals of fire on my head for teasing you about snoring? Well then, I take it all back. It must have been only the foghorn I heard. (*She laughs, and they laugh with her. Then she changes to a brisk businesslike air.*) But I can't stay with you any longer, even to hear compliments. I must see the cook about dinner and the day's marketing. (*She gets up and sighs with humorous exaggeration.*) Bridget is so lazy. And so sly. She begins telling me about her relatives so I can't get a word in edgeways and scold her. Well, I might as well get it over. (*She goes to the back-parlor doorway, then turns, her face worried again.*) You mustn't make Edmund work on the grounds with you, James, remember. (*again with the strange obstinate set to her face*) Not that he isn't strong enough, but he'd perspire and he might catch more cold. (*She disappears through the back parlor. Tyrone turns on Jamie condemningly.*)

TYRONE—You're a fine lunkhead! Haven't you any sense? The one thing to avoid is saying anything that would get her more upset over Edmund.

JAMIE—(*shrugging his shoulders*) All right. Have it your way. I think it's the wrong idea to let Mama go on kidding herself. It will only make the shock worse when she has to face it. Anyway, you can see she's deliberately fooling herself with that summer cold talk. She knows better.

TYRONE—Knows? Nobody knows yet.

JAMIE—Well, I do. I was with Edmund when he went to Doc Hardy on Monday. I heard him pull that touch of malaria stuff. He was stalling. That isn't what he thinks any more. You know it as well as I do. You talked to him when you went uptown yesterday, didn't you?

TYRONE—He couldn't say anything for sure yet. He's to phone me today before Edmund goes to him.

JAMIE—(*slowly*) He thinks it's consumption, doesn't he, Papa?

TYRONE—(*reluctantly*) He said it might be.

JAMIE—(*moved, his love for his brother coming out*) Poor kid! God damn it! (*He turns on his father accusingly.*) It might never have happened if you'd sent him to a real doctor when he first got sick.

TYRONE—What's the matter with Hardy? He's always been our doctor up here.

JAMIE—Everything's the matter with him! Even in this hick burg he's rated third class! He's a cheap old quack!

TYRONE—That's right! Run him down! Run down everybody! Everyone is a fake to you!

JAMIE—(*contemptuously*) Hardy only charges a dollar. That's what makes you think he's a fine doctor!

TYRONE—(*stung*) That's enough! You're not drunk now! There's no excuse— (*He controls himself—a bit defensively*) If you mean I can't afford one of the fine society doctors who prey on the rich summer people—

JAMIE—Can't afford? You're one of the biggest property owners around here.

TYRONE—That doesn't mean I'm rich. It's all mortgaged—

JAMIE—Because you always buy more instead of paying off mortgages. If Edmund was a lousy acre of land you wanted, the sky would be the limit!

TYRONE—That's a lie! And your sneers against Doctor Hardy are lies! He doesn't put on frills, or have an office in a fashionable location, or drive around in an expensive automobile. That's what you pay for with those other five-dollars-to-look-at-your-tongue fellows, not their skill.

JAMIE—(*with a scornful shrug of his shoulders*) Oh, all right. I'm a fool to argue. You can't change the leopard's spots.

TYRONE—(*with rising anger*) No, you can't. You've taught me that lesson only too well. I've lost all hope you will ever change yours. You dare tell me what I can afford? You've never known the value of a dollar and never will! You've never saved a dollar in your life! At the end of each season you're penniless! You've thrown your salary away every week on whores and whiskey!

JAMIE—My salary! Christ!

TYRONE—It's more than you're worth, and you couldn't get that if it wasn't for me. If you weren't my son, there isn't a manager in the business who would give you a part, your reputation stinks so. As it is, I have to humble my pride and beg for you, saying you've turned over a new leaf, although I know it's a lie!

JAMIE—I never wanted to be an actor. You forced me on the stage.

TYRONE—That's a lie! You made no effort to find anything else to do. You left it to me to get you a job and I have no influence except in the theater. Forced you! You never wanted to do anything except loaf in barrooms! You'd have been content to sit back like a lazy lunk and sponge on me for the rest of your life! After all the money I'd wasted on your education, and all you did was get fired in disgrace from every college you went to!

JAMIE—Oh, for God's sake, don't drag up that ancient history!

TYRONE—It's not ancient history that you have to come home every summer to live on me.

JAMIE—I earn my board and lodging working on the grounds. It saves you hiring a man.

TYRONE—Bah! You have to be driven to do even that much! (*His anger ebbs into a weary complaint.*) I wouldn't give a damn if you ever displayed the slightest sign of gratitude. The only thanks is to have you sneer at me for a dirty miser, sneer at my profession, sneer at every damned thing in the world—except yourself.

JAMIE—(*wryly*) That's not true, Papa. You can't hear me talking to myself, that's all.

TYRONE—(*stares at him puzzledly, then quotes mechanically*) "Ingratitude, the vilest weed that grows"!

JAMIE—I could see that line coming! God, how many thousand times—! (*He stops, bored with their quarrel, and shrugs his shoulders.*) All right, Papa. I'm a bum. Anything you like, so long as it stops the argument.

TYRONE—(*with indignant appeal now*) If you'd get ambition in your head instead of folly! You're young yet. You could still make your mark. You had the talent to become a fine actor! You have it still. You're my son—!

JAMIE—(*boredly*) Let's forget me. I'm not interested in the subject. Neither are you. (*Tyrone gives up. Jamie goes on casually.*) What started us on this? Oh, Doc Hardy. When is he going to call you up about Edmund?

TYRONE—Around lunch time. (*He pauses—then defensively*) I couldn't have sent Edmund to a better doctor. Hardy's treated him whenever he was sick up here, since he was knee high. He knows his constitution as no other doctor could. It's not a question of my being miserly, as you'd like to make out. (*bitterly*) And what could the finest specialist in America do for Edmund, after he's deliberately ruined his health by the mad life he's led ever since he was fired from college? Even before that when he was in prep school, he began dissipating and playing the Broadway sport to imitate you, when he's never had your constitution to stand it. You're a healthy hulk like me—or you were at his age—but he's always been a bundle of nerves like his mother. I've warned him for years his body couldn't stand it, but he wouldn't heed me, and now it's too late.

JAMIE—(*sharply*) What do you mean, too late? You talk as if you thought—

TYRONE—(*guiltily explosive*) Don't be a damned fool! I meant nothing but what's plain to anyone! His health has broken down and he may be an invalid for a long time.

JAMIE—(*stares at his father, ignoring his explanation*) I know it's an Irish peasant idea consumption is fatal. It probably is when you live in a hovel on a bog, but over here, with modern treatment—

TYRONE—Don't I know that! What are you gabbing about, anyway? And keep your dirty tongue off Ireland, with your sneers about peasants and bogs and hovels! (*accusingly*) The less you say about Edmund's sickness, the better for your conscience! You're more responsible than anyone!

JAMIE—(*stung*) That's a lie! I won't stand for that, Papa!

TYRONE—It's the truth! You've been the worst influence for him. He grew up admiring you as a hero! A fine example you set him! If you ever gave him advice except in the ways of rottenness, I've never heard of it! You made him old before his time, pumping him full of what you consider worldly wisdom, when he was too young to see that your mind was so poisoned by your own failure in life, you wanted to believe every man was a knave with his soul for sale, and every woman who wasn't a whore was a fool!

JAMIE—(*with a defensive air of weary indifference again*) All right. I did put Edmund wise to things, but not until I saw he'd started to raise hell, and knew he'd laugh at me if I tried the good advice, older brother stuff. All I did was make a pal of him and be absolutely frank so he'd learn from my mistakes that— (*He shrugs his shoulders—cynically*) Well, that if you can't be good you can at least be careful. (*His father snorts contemptuously. Suddenly Jamie becomes really moved.*) That's a rotten accusation, Papa. You know how much the Kid means to me, and how close we've always been—not like the usual brothers! I'd do anything for him.

TYRONE—(*impressed—mollifyingly*) I know you may have thought it was for the best, Jamie. I didn't say you did it deliberately to harm him.

JAMIE—Besides it's damned rot! I'd like to see anyone influence Edmund more than he wants to be. His quietness fools people into thinking they can do what they like with him. But he's stubborn as hell inside and what he does is what he wants to do, and to hell with anyone else! What had I to do with all the crazy stunts he's pulled in the last few years—working his way all over the map as a sailor and all that stuff. I thought that was a damned fool idea, and I told him so. You can't imagine me getting fun out of being on the beach in South America, or living in filthy dives, drinking rotgut, can you? No, thanks! I'll stick to Broadway, and a room with a bath, and bars that serve bonded Bourbon.

TYRONE—You and Broadway! It's made you what you are! (*with a touch of pride*) Whatever Edmund's done, he's had the guts to go off on his own, where he couldn't come whining to me the minute he was broke.

JAMIE—(*stung into sneering jealousy*) He's always come home broke finally, hasn't he? And what did his going away get him? Look at him now! (*He is suddenly shamefaced.*) Christ! That's a lousy thing to say. I don't mean that.

TYRONE—(*decides to ignore this*) He's been doing well on the paper. I was hoping he'd found the work he wants to do at last.

JAMIE—(*sneering jealously again*) A hick town rag! Whatever bull they hand you, they tell me he's a pretty bum reporter. If he weren't your son— (*ashamed again*) No, that's not true! They're glad to have him, but it's the special stuff that gets him by. Some of the poems and parodies he's written are damned good. (*grudgingly again*) Not that they'd ever get him anywhere on the big time. (*hastily*) But he's certainly made a damned good start.

TYRONE—Yes. He's made a start. You used to talk about wanting to become a newspaper man but you were never willing to start at the bottom. You expected—

JAMIE—Oh, for Christ's sake, Papa! Can't you lay off me!

TYRONE—(*stares at him—then looks away—after a pause*) It's damnable luck Edmund should be sick right now. It couldn't have come at a worse time for him. (*He adds, unable to conceal an almost furtive uneasiness*) Or for your mother. It's damnable she should have this to upset her, just when she needs peace and freedom from worry. She's been so well in the two months since she came home. (*His voice grows husky and trembles a little.*) It's been heaven to me. This home has been a home again. But I needn't tell you, Jamie. (*His son looks at him, for the first time with an understanding sympathy. It is as if suddenly a deep bond of common feeling existed between them in which their antagonisms could be forgotten.*)

JAMIE—(*almost gently*) I've felt the same way, Papa.

TYRONE—Yes, this time you can see how strong and sure of herself she is. She's a different woman entirely from the other times. She has control of her nerves—or she had until Edmund got sick. Now you can feel her growing tense and frightened underneath. I wish to God we could keep the truth from her, but we can't if he has to be sent to a sanatorium. What makes it worse is her father died of consumption. She worshiped him and she's never forgotten. Yes, it will be hard for her. But she can do it! She has the will power now! We must help her, Jamie, in every way we can!

JAMIE—(*moved*) Of course, Papa. (*hesitantly*) Outside of nerves, she seems perfectly all right this morning.

TYRONE—(*with hearty confidence now*) Never better. She's full of fun and mischief. (*Suddenly he frowns at Jamie suspiciously.*) Why do you say, seems? Why shouldn't she be all right? What the hell do you mean?

JAMIE—Don't start jumping down my throat! God, Papa, this ought to be one thing we can talk over frankly without a battle.

TYRONE—I'm sorry, Jamie. (*tensely*) But go on and tell me—

JAMIE—There's nothing to tell. I was all wrong. It's just that last night— Well, you know how it is, I can't forget the past. I can't help being suspicious. Any more than you can. (*bitterly*) That's the hell of it. And it makes it hell for Mama! She watches us watching her—

TYRONE—(*sadly*) I know. (*tensely*) Well, what was it? Can't you speak out?

JAMIE—Nothing, I tell you. Just my damned foolishness. Around three o'clock this morning, I woke up and heard her moving around in the spare room. Then she went to the bathroom. I pretended to be asleep. She stopped in the hall to listen, as if she wanted to make sure I was.

TYRONE—(*with forced scorn*) For God's sake, is that all? She told me herself the foghorn kept her awake all night, and every night since Edmund's been sick she's been up and down, going to his room to see how he was.

JAMIE—(*eagerly*) Yes, that's right, she did stop to listen outside his room. (*hesitantly again*) It was her being in the spare room that scared me. I couldn't help remembering that when she starts sleeping alone in there, it has always been a sign—

TYRONE—It isn't this time! It's easily explained. Where else could she go last night to get away from my snoring? (*He gives way to a burst of resentful anger.*) By God, how you can live with a mind that sees nothing but the worst motives behind everything is beyond me!

JAMIE—(*stung*) Don't pull that! I've just said I was all wrong. Don't you suppose I'm as glad of that as you are!

TYRONE—(*mollifyingly*) I'm sure you are, Jamie. (*A pause. His expression becomes somber. He speaks slowly with a superstitious dread.*) It would be like a curse she can't escape if worry over Edmund— It was in her long sickness after bringing him into the world that she first—

JAMIE—She didn't have anything to do with it!

TYRONE—I'm not blaming her.

JAMIE—(*bitingly*) Then who are you blaming? Edmund, for being born?

TYRONE—You damned fool! No one was to blame.

JAMIE—The bastard of a doctor was! From what Mama's said, he was another cheap quack like Hardy! You wouldn't pay for a first-rate—

TYRONE—That's a lie! (*furiously*) So I'm to blame! That's what you're driving at, is it? You evil-minded loafer!

JAMIE—(*warningly as he hears his mother in the dining room*) Ssh! (*Tyrone gets hastily to his feet and goes to look out the windows at right. Jamie speaks with a complete change of tone.*) Well, if we're going to cut the front hedge today, we'd better go to work. (*Mary comes in from the back parlor. She gives a quick, suspicious glance from one to the other, her manner nervously self-conscious.*)

TYRONE—(*turns from the window—with an actor's heartiness*) Yes, it's too fine a morning to waste indoors arguing. Take a look out the window, Mary. There's no fog in the harbor. I'm sure the spell of it we've had is over now.

MARY—(*going to him*) I hope so, dear. (*to Jamie, forcing a smile*) Did I actually hear you suggesting work on the front hedge, Jamie? Wonders will never cease! You must want pocket money badly.

JAMIE—(*kiddingly*) When don't I? (*He winks at her, with a derisive glance at his father.*) I expect a salary of at least one large iron man at the end of the week—to carouse on!

MARY—(*does not respond to his humor—her hands fluttering over the front of her dress*) What were you two arguing about?

JAMIE—(*shrugs his shoulders*) The same old stuff.

MARY—I heard you say something about a doctor, and your father accusing you of being evil-minded.

JAMIE—(*quickly*) Oh, that. I was saying again Doc Hardy isn't my idea of the world's greatest physician.

MARY—(*knows he is lying—vaguely*) Oh. No, I wouldn't say he was, either. (*changing the subject—forcing a smile*) That Bridget! I thought I'd never get away. She told me all about her second cousin on the police force in St. Louis. (*then with nervous irritation*) Well, if you're going to work on the hedge why don't you go? (*hastily*) I mean, take advantage of the sunshine before the fog comes back. (*strangely, as if talking aloud to herself*) Because I know it will. (*Suddenly she is self-consciously aware that they are both staring fixedly at her—flurriedly, raising her hands*) Or I should say, the rheumatism in my hands knows. It's a better weather prophet than you are, James. (*She stares at her hands with fascinated repulsion.*) Ugh! How ugly they are! Who'd ever believe they were once beautiful? (*They stare at her with a growing dread.*)

TYRONE—(*takes her hands and gently pushes them down*) Now, now, Mary. None of that foolishness. They're the sweetest hands in the world. (*She smiles, her face lighting up, and kisses him gratefully. He turns to his son.*) Come on Jamie.

Your mother's right to scold us. The way to start work is to start work. The hot sun will sweat some of that booze fat off your middle. (*He opens the screen door and goes out on the porch and disappears down a flight of steps leading to the ground. Jamie rises from his chair and, taking off his coat, goes to the door. At the door he turns back but avoids looking at her, and she does not look at him.*)

JAMIE—(*with an awkward, uneasy tenderness*) We're all so proud of you, Mama, so darned happy. (*She stiffens and stares at him with a frightened defiance. He flounders on.*) But you've still got to be careful. You mustn't worry so much about Edmund. He'll be all right.

MARY—(*with a stubborn, bitterly resentful look*) Of course, he'll be all right. And I don't know what you mean, warning me to be careful.

JAMIE—(*rebuffed and hurt, shrugs his shoulders*) All right, Mama. I'm sorry I spoke. (*He goes out on the porch. She waits rigidly until he disappears down the steps. Then she sinks down in the chair he had occupied, her face betraying a frightened, furtive desperation, her hands roving over the table top, aimlessly moving objects around. She hears Edmund descending the stairs in the front hall. As he nears the bottom he has a fit of coughing. She springs to her feet, as if she wanted to run away from the sound, and goes quickly to the windows at right. She is looking out, apparently calm, as he enters from the front parlor, a book in one hand. She turns to him, her lips set in a welcoming, motherly smile.*)

MARY—Here you are. I was just going upstairs to look for you.

EDMUND—I waited until they went out. I don't want to mix up in any arguments. I feel too rotten.

MARY—(*almost resentfully*) Oh, I'm sure you don't feel half as badly as you make out. You're such a baby. You like to get us worried so we'll make a fuss over you. (*hastily*) I'm only teasing, dear. I know how miserably uncomfortable you must be. But you feel better today, don't you? (*worriedly, taking his arm*) All the same, you've grown much too thin. You need to rest all you can. Sit down and I'll make you comfortable. (*He sits down in the rocking chair and she puts a pillow behind his back.*) There. How's that?

EDMUND—Grand. Thanks, Mama.

MARY—(*kisses him—tenderly*) All you need is your mother to nurse you. Big as you are, you're still the baby of the family to me, you know.

EDMUND—(*takes her hand—with deep seriousness*) Never mind me. You take care of yourself. That's all that counts.

MARY—(*evading his eyes*) But I am, dear. (*forcing a laugh*) Heavens, don't you see how fat I've grown! I'll have to have all my dresses let out. (*She turns away and goes to the windows at right. She attempts a light, amused tone.*) They've started clipping the hedge. Poor Jamie! How he hates working in front where everyone passing can see him. There go the Chatfields in their new Mercedes. It's a beautiful car, isn't it? Not like our secondhand Packard. Poor Jamie! He bent almost under the hedge so they wouldn't notice him. They bowed to your father and he bowed back as if he were taking a curtain call. In that filthy old suit I've tried to make him throw away. (*Her voice has grown bitter.*) Really, he ought to have more pride than to make such a show of himself.

EDMUND—He's right not to give a damn what anyone thinks. Jamie's a fool to care about the Chatfields. For Pete's sake, who ever heard of them outside this hick burg?

MARY—(*with satisfaction*) No one. You're quite right, Edmund. Big frogs in a small puddle. It is stupid of Jamie. (*She pauses, looking out the window—then with an undercurrent of lonely yearning*) Still, the Chatfields and people like them stand for something. I mean they have decent, presentable homes they don't have to be ashamed of. They have friends who entertain them and whom they entertain. They're not cut off from everyone. (*She turns back from the window.*) Not that I want anything to do with them. I've always hated this town and everyone in it. You know that. I never wanted to live here in the first place, but your father liked it and insisted on building this house, and I've had to come here every summer.

EDMUND—Well, it's better than spending the summer in a New York hotel, isn't it? And this town's not so bad. I like it well enough. I suppose because it's the only home we've had.

MARY—I've never felt it was my home. It was wrong from the start. Everything was done in the cheapest way. Your father would never spend the money to make it right. It's just as well we haven't any friends here. I'd be ashamed to have them step in the door. But he's never wanted family friends. He hates calling on people, or receiving them. All he likes is to hobnob with men at the Club or in a barroom. Jamie and you are the same way, but you're not to blame. You've never had a chance to meet decent people here. I know you both would have been so different if you'd been able to associate with nice girls instead of— You'd never have disgraced yourselves as you have, so that now no respectable parents will let their daughters be seen with you.

EDMUND—(*irritably*) Oh, Mama, forget it! Who cares? Jamie and I would be bored stiff. And about the Old Man, what's the use of talking? You can't change him.

MARY—(*mechanically rebuking*) Don't call your father the Old Man. You should have more respect. (*then dully*) I know it's useless to talk. But sometimes I feel so lonely. (*Her lips quiver and she keeps her head turned away.*)

EDMUND—Anyway, you've got to be fair, Mama. It may have been all his fault in the beginning, but you know that later on, even if he'd wanted to, we couldn't have had people here— (*He flounders guiltily.*) I mean, you wouldn't have wanted them.

MARY—(*wincing—her lips quivering pitifully*) Don't. I can't bear having you remind me.

EDMUND—Don't take it that way! Please, Mama! I'm trying to help. Because it's bad for you to forget. The right way is to remember. So you'll always be on your guard. You know what's happened before. (*miserably*) God, Mama, you know I hate to remind you. I'm doing it because it's been so wonderful having you home the way you've been, and it would be terrible—

MARY—(*strickenly*) Please, dear. I know you mean it for the best, but— (*A defensive uneasiness comes into her voice again.*) I don't understand why you should suddenly say such things. What put it in your mind this morning?

EDMUND—(*evasively*) Nothing. Just because I feel rotten and blue, I suppose.

MARY—Tell me the truth. Why are you so suspicious all of a sudden?

EDMUND—I'm not!

MARY—Oh, yes you are. I can feel it. Your father and Jamie, too—particularly Jamie.

EDMUND—Now don't start imagining things, Mama.

MARY—(*her hands fluttering*) It makes it so much harder, living in this atmosphere of constant suspicion, knowing everyone is spying on me, and none of you believe in me, or trust me.

EDMUND—That's crazy, Mama. We do trust you.

MARY—If there was only some place I could go to get away for a day, or even an afternoon, some woman friend I could talk to—not about anything serious, simply laugh and gossip and forget for a while—someone besides the servants—that stupid Cathleen!

EDMUND—(*gets up worriedly and puts his arm around her*) Stop it, Mama. You're getting yourself worked up over nothing.

MARY—Your father goes out. He meets his friends in barrooms or at the Club. You and Jamie have the boys you know. You go out. But I am alone. I've always been alone.

EDMUND—(*soothingly*) Come now! You know that's a fib. One of us always stays around to keep you company, or goes with you in the automobile when you take a drive.

MARY—(*bitterly*) Because you're afraid to trust me alone! (*She turns on him—sharply*) I insist you tell me why you act so differently this morning—why you felt you had to remind me—

EDMUND—(*hesitates—then blurts out guiltily*) It's stupid. It's just that I wasn't asleep when you came in my room last night. You didn't go back to your and Papa's room. You went in the spare room for the rest of the night.

MARY—Because your father's snoring was driving me crazy! For heaven's sake, haven't I often used the spare room as my bedroom? (*bitterly*) But I see what you thought. That was when—

EDMUND—(*too vehemently*) I didn't think anything!

MARY—So you pretended to be asleep in order to spy on me!

EDMUND—No! I did it because I knew if you found out I was feverish and couldn't sleep, it would upset you.

MARY—Jamie was pretending to be asleep, too, I'm sure, and I suppose your father—

EDMUND—Stop it, Mama!

MARY—Oh, I can't bear it, Edmund, when even you—! (*Her hands flutter up to pat her hair in their aimless, distracted way. Suddenly a strange undercurrent of revengefulness comes into her voice.*) It would serve all of you right if it was true!

EDMUND—Mama! Don't say that! That's the way you talk when—

MARY—Stop suspecting me! Please, dear! You hurt me! I couldn't sleep because I was thinking about you. That's the real reason! I've been so worried ever since you've been sick. (*She puts her arms around him and hugs him with a frightened, protective tenderness.*)

EDMUND—(*soothingly*) That's foolishness. You know it's only a bad cold.

MARY—Yes, of course, I know that!

EDMUND—But listen, Mama. I want you to promise me that even if it should turn out to be something worse, you'll know I'll soon be all right again, anyway, and you won't worry yourself sick, and you'll keep on taking care of yourself—

MARY—(*frightenedly*) I won't listen when you're so silly! There's absolutely no reason to talk as if you expected something dreadful! Of course, I promise you. I give you my sacred word of honor! (*then with a sad bitterness*) But I suppose you're remembering I've promised before on my word of honor.

EDMUND—No!

MARY—(*her bitterness receding into a resigned helplessness*) I'm not blaming you, dear. How can you help it? How can any one of us forget? (*strangely*) That's what makes it so hard—for all of us. We can't forget.

EDMUND—(*grabs her shoulder*) Mama! Stop it!

MARY—(*forcing a smile*) All right, dear. I didn't mean to be so gloomy. Don't mind me. Here. Let me feel your head. Why, it's nice and cool. You certainly haven't any fever now.

EDMUND—Forget! It's you—

MARY—But I'm quite all right, dear. (*with a quick, strange,*

Fischer, Heinz-Dietrich: Pulitzer Prize Winners in the Performing Arts - Communications and Biographies about Dramatists and Composers 1918-2000, Vienna - Zurich 2022

Fischer, Heinz-D./Dickhut, Ingrid: Broadway-Theater in der Kritik - Pulitzerpreis-Stücke 1917-2009 im Urteil von Fachjuroren, Berlin 2009

Fischer, Heinz-D./Fischer, Erika J.: Pulitzer Drama/Comedy Awards 1917-1996, Munich 1998

Fischer, Heinz-D./Fischer, Erika J.: Der Pulitzer-Preis - Konkurrenten, Kämpfe, Kontroversen, Berlin 2007

Floyd, Virginia: Eugene O'Neill at Work - Newly Released Ideas for Plays, New York 1981

Frenz, Horst/Tuck, Susan: Eugene O'Neill's Critics - Voices from abroad, Cerbondale, Ill., 1984

Gallup, Donald C.: (O'Neill) Work Diary 1924-1943, New Haven, Ct., 1981

Gelb, Arthur/Gelb, Barbara: O'Neill, New York 1962

Hohenberg, John: The Pulitzer Diaries - Inside America's Greatest Prize, Syracuse, NY, 1997

Hohenberg, John: The Pulitzer Prizes - A History of the Awards in Books, Drama, Music and Journalism, New York - London 1974

Kimura, Toshio: Eugene O'Neill, Osaka 1953

Koischwitz, Otto: O'Neill, Berlin 1938

Link, Franz: Eugen O'Neill und die Wiedergeburt der Tragödie aus dem Unbewussten, Frankfurt 1967

Manheim, Michael: Eugene O'Neill's New Language of Kinship, Syracuse, N.Y., 1982

Marzal, Manuel: Eugene O'Neill y su teatro, Havana 1943

Martine, James J.: Critical Essays on Eugene O'Neill, Boston 1984

Olsson, Tom: O'Neill och Dramaten, Stockholm 1977

Sheaffer, Louis: O'Neill - Son and Artist, Boston 1973

Sheaffer, Louis: O'Neill - Son and Playwright, Boston 1968

Skinner Richard D.. Eugene O Neill A Poet'S Guests, New York 1935

Stroupe, John H.: Critical Approaches to O'Neill, New York 1988

Tiusanen, Timo: O'Neill's Scenic Images, Princeton N.J., 1968

Toohey, John L.: A History of the Pulitzer Prize Plays, New York 1967

Winther, Sophus K.: Eugene O'Neill - A Critical Study, New York 1934

Zeraffa, Michael: Eugene O'Neil1 - Dramaturge, Paris 1956

220

Heinz-Dietrich Fischer

Both Pulitzer and Nobel Prize Laureates for Literature

Jury Communications about Winners and Works from Sinclair Lewis to Bob Dylan

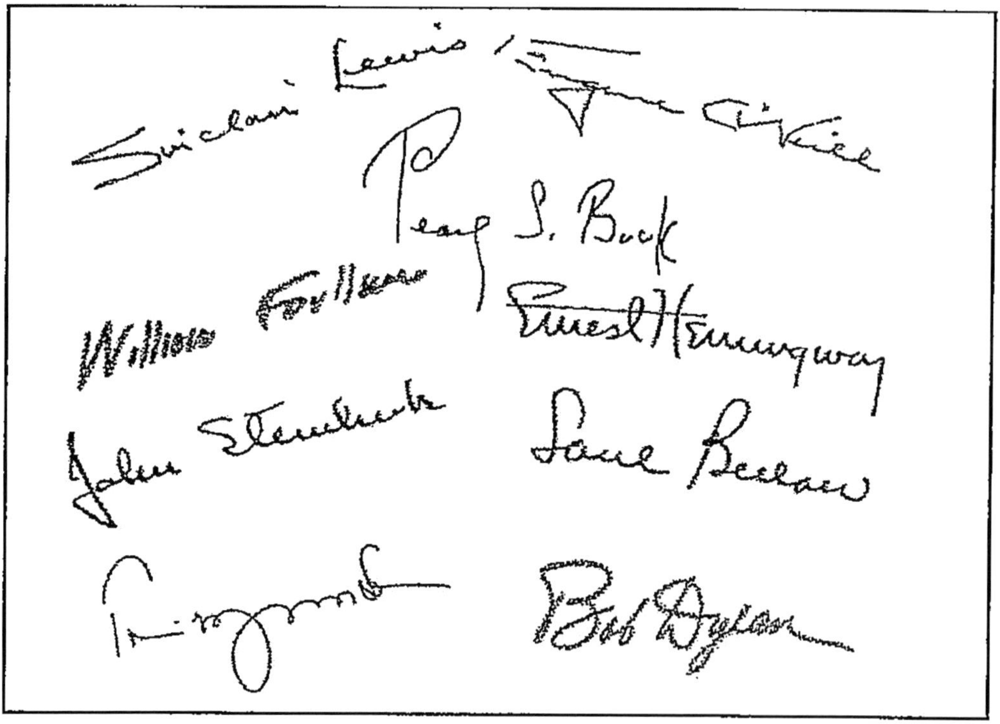

Pulitzer Prize Panorama No. 24

LIT